W9-DIR-677

THE ECONOMIC
TRANSFORMATION OF AMERICA
SINCE 1865

THE ECONOMIC TRANSFORMATION OF AMERICA SINCE 1865

ROBERT HEILBRONER
New School for Social Research

AARON SINGER

HARCOURT BRACE COLLEGE PUBLISHERS

*Fort Worth   Philadelphia   San Diego   New York   Orlando   Austin   San Antonio
Toronto   Montreal   London   Sydney   Tokyo*

SCCCC - LIBRARY
WITHDRAWN
St. Peters, MO 63376

PUBLISHER *Ted Buchholz*

SENIOR ACQUISITIONS EDITOR *Drake Bush*

DEVELOPMENTAL EDITOR *Kristie Kelly*

PROJECT EDITORS *Nicole Boyle, Jeff Beckham*

PRODUCTION MANAGER *Debra A. Jenkin*

ART DIRECTOR *Nick Welch*

Copyright © 1994 by Harcourt Brace & Company

All rights reserved. No part of this publication may be reproduced or transmitted in any form or by any means, electronic or mechanical, including photocopy, recording, or any information storage and retrieval system, without permission in writing from the publisher.

Requests for permission to make copies of any part of the work should be mailed to: Permissions Department, Harcourt Brace & Company, 8th Floor, Orlando, Florida 32887

Address for Editorial Correspondence: Harcourt Brace College Publishers, 301 Commerce Street, Suite 3700, Fort Worth, TX 76102.

Address for Orders: Harcourt Brace & Company, 6277 Sea Harbor Drive, Orlando, FL 32887. 1-800-782-4479, or 1-800-433-0001 (in Florida).

Credits and permissions acknowledgments are on page 259.

Printed in the United States of America

ISBN 0-15-501242-8

Library of Congress Catalog Card Number 93-78560

3 4 5 6 7 8 9 0 1 2 016 9 8 7 6 5 4 3 2 1

TO SHIRLEY AND AUDREY, AGAIN.

Contents

THE ECONOMIC
TRANSFORMATION OF AMERICA
SINCE 1865

A London market in the seventeenth century

Chapter 1

ECONOMIC TRANSFORMATION AS A THEME OF HISTORY

We are about to begin the study of American history from an unaccustomed perspective—the perspective of the economic transformation of American life. And we are going to open our examination of this perspective by asking an unaccustomed question: *What is history?*

WHAT IS HISTORY?

This may seem a roundabout and pointless way to broach our subject. Why not proceed directly to the matter at hand? What is to be gained by asking so simple a question? Is history not the record of what has happened, the chronicle of what we know about the past?

The question is not so simple, however. For *which* among many pasts is our history? Is it the past that we learn when we memorize lists of presidents? Is it the past memorialized by the dates of wars? Is it the past reflected in the archives of newspapers? Or is it all these pasts together, some immense volume in which we find presidents, wars, the news, and all else?

The inquiry brings us to a disconcerting recognition. There is no such immense volume. Indeed, none is possible. A history that included all the threads of our past would require us to know everything that had ever happened. That is more than we can know about our own lives, much less the lives of others. History in this all-encompassing sense can never be written.

We are left, then, with the need to write history from some perspective, highlighting one theme or another from our "total" history. There are innumerable such possibilities. We can write histories of American politics, art, social life, crime—each with its own cast of characters and plot. Needless to say, the same event may enter into more than one such history, and different histories may feature quite different events. The assassinations of Lincoln and Kennedy, for example, certainly bulk large in the history of politics, but they would figure as well in a history of American crime—although in that context they would be reduced to the insignificant status of mere homicides. The development of jazz figures large in American social history but not in American diplomatic history. *Thus the choice of a theme is a decisive determinant of what we will find in "history."*

These brief reflections help us when we now turn to the theme of this book. For the choice of economic transformation causes us to view events from a perspective different from that of the usual American history. Its cast of characters features business leaders, working men and women, and inventors rather than the usual presidents, generals, or patriots. Its plot ignores the great epic of American democratic development and dwells instead on the less familiar currents of economic expansion and conflict. Technical processes, such as steelmaking, play a role as central as those usually accorded to political processes such as lawmaking. Enormous events like the Civil War appear only in the background; whereas matters that we ordinarily overlook, such as J. P. Morgan's purchase of the Carnegie Steel Company, suddenly loom very large.

Why study the past from such an unusual angle? The answer is that our perspective has an extraordinary power of illumination. Not all themes of history shed equal light on other themes. It is the property of the theme of economic transformation that it touches on so many others. In fact, it is not too much to say that without a comprehension of the American economic transformation, many other histories of American life remain unintelligible. Certainly the great drama of our democratic evolution loses most of its meaning unless we project it against the changeful backdrop of economic events. So, too, the histories of social change, of science or literature, or even fashion—in short, most of the innumerable histories that can be written about America—require for their full understanding a grasp of the profound economic transformation through which America has passed.

THE INTERTWINED STRANDS OF HISTORY

Material Life

And so we arrive at our beginning and can put forth the question we have been waiting for: What do we mean by the economic transformation of America?

In one sense we know immediately what we mean. America in the beginning was a vast, untamed wilderness; today it is a complex industrial civilization. Where there were once virgin forests there are today interstate highways. Where rivers met in solitude there are great cities. Where the voice of the continent was the murmur of nature it is now the chatter of trade and commerce. The economic transformation of America is the narrative of that all-embracing change, a change we are all generally familiar with, however imprecisely we can describe its historic course.

Peasants plowing with wooden plow and sowing by hand

But we need something more sharply focused if we are to study the transformation in a systematic rather than an impressionistic way. Here it is useful to view the great transformation in terms proposed by the great modern French historian Fernand Braudel.[1] Braudel sees in history three intertwined but distinguishable strands.

One of these he calls *material life*. By material life Braudel means the routines of daily work, the everyday round of the tasks by which we sustain ourselves. Thus material life covers the means by which we travel to work, the efforts we perform there, the products we make and use. We would not be far wrong if we thought of material life as the technology at hand and the goods we enjoy. Needless to say, both change dramatically over time: compare the material life of the peasant walking to his task, swinging his scythe, eating his coarse bread, with that of today's worker, driving to his office, using his computer, shopping on the way home.

Part of the economic transformation therefore consists of the evolving technology with which we undertake our worldly tasks. Braudel has a phrase that highlights vividly its importance: material life, he says, sets "the limits of the possible." We cannot understand the overarching narrative of our economic transformation without understanding how those limits have changed.

Economic Life

A second strand of our economic transformation touches on a level that Braudel calls *economic life*. Braudel does not mean the whole range of activities that we think of as "economic," but a level of activity just above the routines and techniques of workaday activity itself. Mainly it encompasses market activity—the jostling of buyers and sellers on the market square, the complex acts of offer and bid, purchase and sale, that make possible the essential social relationship of exchange.

Perhaps we would not ordinarily think of economic life as constituting an aspect of economic experience of equal importance with material life. But we would be wrong. As Braudel points out, it is in the marketplace that the peasant first transcends the narrow world of family and friends and fellow workers to enter into relationships with utter strangers, thereby becoming aware, however dimly, of a world beyond that of his or her immediate experience. In the same way, economic life today continues to bind us into a larger (and still often

Modern four-wheel-power tractor

dimly perceived) world when market forces that we ordinarily ignore suddenly take on hurricane force and raise the price of oil fivefold, or blow away the whole market for the goods we produce or the skills we offer.

Thus another strand of our overall theme is the evolution of our involvement with the market, both as buyers of goods and as suppliers of our energies. A vital part of the economic transformation of America is the enlargement of economic life, from the near self-sufficiency of Pilgrim days, when market influences were reduced to a minimum, to contemporary life when its forces affect our destinies as decisively as the material foundation on which we stand.

Capitalism

Third, Braudel refers to *capitalism* itself. Capitalism is not an easy term to define. It embraces material and economic life, but it is also something more than the concrete processes of production and the realities of consumption, something larger than the skein of market relationships. Capitalism is a historic structure—a framework of forces, an ongoing process of historic change—that arches over both material and economic life, imbuing them with its particular dynamism, its unique influence.

And what is that dynamism, that influence? There is no single, and certainly no simple way of describing how capitalism molds and shapes and impels material and economic change. But we can gain some understanding of the nature of capitalism as the third, and most all-inclusive aspect of our economic transformation, if we pay heed to three elements that it introduces into material and economic life: capital, the market mechanism, and the division of economic and political activity.

1. *Capitalism is oriented to the continual accumulation of material wealth—as capital.*

Capitalism is not unique in its quest for wealth. All social systems above the level of the most primitive cultures accumulate wealth. Indeed, one might say that one of the hallmarks of the first formation of "states"—whether they be kingdoms, empires, or what Karl Marx called "Asiatic despotisms"—is that they seek to amass wealth. Moreover, the wealth amassed by these early imperial states can be dazzlingly great. The Great Wall of China, the immense pyramids of Egypt, the temple complexes of India or of the Inca and Aztec civilizations all testify to the ability of societies with low levels of material life to accumulate vast surpluses from sheer human labor. What is quintessentially different about capitalism is that its wealth takes on a form unlike that of any of these societies—the form of productive *capital.*

Precapitalist societies all used their accumulations of wealth for consumption purposes. The consumption was partly private—the luxuries made available to the ruling strata—and partly public—the great works whose splendors were shared by the populace, even though they were mainly intended to glorify the name of some ruler. Thus many centuries of Asian and European history present us with endless variations on a common theme—a vast, usually impoverished peasantry on the bottom, a ruling personage, with his entourage, on top celebrating his power with lavish consumption and magnificent works to immortalize his name.

Capitalism also has a ruling stratum that enjoys the wealth the system produces, and capitalism also builds mighty public works. But under capitalism the accumulation of society's wealth is put to a use that cannot be found in prior societies. *Wealth is used to build machines and equipment whose sole purpose is to create still more wealth.* The primary purpose of capitalist accumulation is not consumption for the upper classes or public monuments, but the creation of *capital*—wealth-in-general, produced for the sake of producing still more wealth. The nature of this wealth often takes the form of things that would never even be considered as wealth in a precapitalist society—steel ingots, or vats of chemicals, or parts of machines. The form does not matter, as long as the products can be sold and proceeds invested to create still more saleable wealth, more "capital." As a consequence of this search for capital—wealth in any saleable form—capitalism takes on a property not to be found in prior societies. It becomes *expansive*—not so much in geographic extent (although capitalism does indeed move from its original locales into peripheral areas), as in the value and volume of its output. "Taken at face value, the quantity of manufacturing production in the world increased by about 1,730 times [from 1785 to 1971]," writes economic historian W.

An urban U.S. business—one seller with many items

W. Rostow.[2] This expansive, explosive character of capitalism is the source of its extraordinary historic impact, both for good and bad. It is a force that will dominate the economic transformation of America.

2. *Under capitalism, the production and distribution of wealth is entrusted to the market mechanism.*

All societies require some means of assuring the performance of the tasks necessary for their survival, as well as those that create new wealth. Prior to the advent of capitalism, societies depended mainly on the hand of tradition for the first task and on that of command for the second. Thus the basic perpetuation of society was established because son followed father, and daughter followed mother into the traditional routines of planting, reaping, weaving, and maintaining the household; while the Great Wall and pyramids and cathedrals were built because rulers *ordered* them to be built, sometimes paying gangs of workmen to perform their bidding, sometimes literally dragooning armies of laborers to toil on their immense projects.

What was absent in the organization of social effort was the market. Of course, from earliest times, markets played some role in bringing

A Guatemalan village market—many sellers with few items

production into being. All through history a trickle of production finds its way from the fields to the village square where it is sold by the peasant's wife squatting over her tiny stock of fruit or her heap of rye or wheat. And beyond the village square we find more ambitious market ventures—as far back as neolithic times, when there was trade among distant tribes, bronze axe heads being exchanged for we do not know what, perhaps with the use of cowrie shells as money.[3]

But market squares, or even adventurous trading expeditions, are not market *systems*. A market system describes a society in which the village square expands to include the entire city and countryside, and in which relations of purchase and sale extend like many-spoked wheels from a thousand sources of production to ten thousand places of distribution. *A market system comes into being when a society entrusts its own basic replenishment to the forces of the marketplace*—when decisions formerly guided by tradition and command are handed over to the push and pull of market forces, to negotiations between buyers and sellers whose aim is simply to make money, not to abide by age-old routines or to follow anyone's orders.

How can such a system work? How can society rest its very continuance on such a self-regarding, uncoordinated process? That question takes us into the field of economics, beyond the bounds of this book. But the essential elements of the answer are not difficult to give. As we have said, the market system depends on a powerful driving force, the drive to make money. At its most basic level this is the drive to survive by finding work. At its most elevated level it is the drive to succeed in the manner recognized and admired in a commercial society, by running a profitable enterprise. Economists call this essential motive "maximizing"—a technical way of describing a kind of behavior generally familiar to all of us.

The market requires a maximizing drive, but it would not be a *system* without another element, competition. It is the competition among workers vying for work, as well as among capitalists seeking to establish or to steal away shares of the market, that guides the economic energy generated by the maximizing motive. Competition forces both workers and capitalists to direct their energies toward those tasks that society wants done, and to perform their services at prices that society will pay. Both can, of course, ignore the pressures and signals of the marketplace—but at the risk of unemployment or bankruptcy.

The market system is therefore a combination of maximizing drive generated throughout society, and the disciplining pressures exerted by the pressure of other, rivalling, maximizing drives. It is this combination that gives to capitalism its historic dynamism—its restless search for economic opportunities, the constant organization and reorganization of its efforts to match production to demand.

It is important to stress that this combination does not only yield economic triumphs, such as its vast increase in output, it is also the source of another attribute of capitalism—a built-in insecurity, a self-endangering changefulness. The market system can bring disruptions as well as successes. Supply may not match demand. Markets may "disappear." The expansive drive may falter. Tensions between workers and employers may block the accumulation process, or a failure to distribute rewards properly may undermine the creation and growth of the purchasing power required to justify continued business growth.

Thus the market system is as much the cause of instability as it is the source of growth. Capitalism is intrinsically as vulnerable as it is powerful. As we shall see in the economic transformation of America, the process of development is a two-sided affair, failure accompanying success, success emerging from failure.

3. *Capitalism creates a new division between economic and political activity.*

Here we must again look back for a moment to precapitalist societies to understand the change that capitalism brings. Under feudalism, or in the imperial societies of antiquity, there was no clear distinction between "political" and "economic" activity. The serf performing his field tasks, the lord filling his granaries, the tax official attending to the payment of imposts, were at one and the same time ensuring the continuation of the pattern of command and obedience that is the core of political authority, and of the material provisioning that lies at the heart of the economic process. In precapitalist society, political and economic activity were indissolubly one.

In this seamless web the merchant always fitted poorly. The inherent changefulness of market dealings, and the possibility of winning wealth without deferring to imperial pleasure, placed the merchant outside the structure of unified economic and political rule. That is why the fall of the Roman Empire bulks so large in economic history.

For the collapse of its central structure created a new fragmentation and compartmentalization of power, as a thousand contesting dukes and lords and barons filled the space once occupied by imperial Rome. In this unprecedented fragmentation of power, mercantile influence could establish itself on a wholly new footing.

This did not happen at once. In the disorganization that followed the collapse of the empire, trade dried up and the merchant nearly disappeared from view. But beginning about the tenth century economic life began to quicken. More important, in the absence of a unified imperial system, the function of the merchant became increasingly indispensable. It was only through trade, not through the direct exercise of imperial power, that goods could now be brought across the face of Europe to isolated castles. It was only through merchants, not tax officials, that feudal lords could raise cash for wars or special luxuries. As the strategic role of the merchant increased, so did his power. By the twelfth and thirteenth centuries, merchants had secured the *independence* of many towns from lordly rule, an assertion of power unimaginable in the empires of the past.

What we then begin to see across the face of the continent is the emergence of two distinct spheres of authority and power. One of them, the political sphere, retains from the imperial past the functions of statecraft—the waging of war, the conclusion of alliances, the promulgation of law, and the responsibility of internal order. The other, the economic sphere, takes into its charge the production and distribution of material goods—no longer under the command of a central imperial power but more and more under the sway of market forces, commanded by merchants competing in search of a profit.

This separation of an economic realm from the political state does not achieve its final clarity until well into the nineteenth century. In the seventeenth century, when our own narrative really begins, there is nothing like the public and private "sectors" of a later age. On the contrary, economic and political life are still intimately entwined, both at the summit of European society where great merchants are directly supported by royal prerogatives, and at the lower levels of the market system where elaborate rules and regulations usually surround the way in which economic life is carried on.

Nonetheless, a cleavage had been introduced. Economic power had been separated from political power in a manner that will become a central feature of capitalism. Indeed we can now see that the division of unitary imperial power into two spheres is an essential element of the capitalist structure—an element that brings with it new conceptions of economic freedom, and new sources of political conflict.

The Dynamic of Capitalism

Our brief survey of capitalism helps us understand and define more sharply the focus of our studies. For it must now be clear that the theme of the economic transformation of America is in fact the theme of the development of American capitalism. To follow the development of capitalism means, of course, that we watch the unfolding of material life as it constantly expands the limits of the possible, and it obviously requires that we observe the expansion of economic life as market transactions knit us ever more tightly together.

But over and beyond these subthemes, America's economic transformation will direct our attention to the contours, the rhythms, the achievements and failures of the larger structure that we call capitalism. It is the explosive drive and tensions of the accumulation process, the successes and failures of the market mechanism, and the changing relationships between the exercise of political and economic power that will become the great threads of our narrative; and we now see that these threads constitute nothing less than the historic evolution of capitalism itself.

The task now is to take up our main theme, but the question is where to begin. In our study of the development of American capitalism to 1865, we stressed the role economic growth. Such a study would set the stage for the great drama to follow, the Industrialization of the United States. That is where this work begins.

Notes

[1] *Civilization & Capitalism, 15th–18th Century* (3 vols., 1979–84), I: 27–29.
[2] *The World Economy* (1979), p. 48.
[3] *Cambridge Economic History of Europe* (1952), 2:4.

The Cincinnati Chamber of Commerce, 1902

Chapter 2

THE AGE OF THE BUSINESSMAN

THE BUSINESS THRUST

We are about to examine a "chapter" in our history of economic growth that will change the character of life far more dramatically and decisively than anything Americans had witnessed up to that point. In a dazzling period of sixty years following the Civil War, the face of the country will literally be made over. Railroads will cross and recross the continent; enormous cities will arise out of prairie wilderness; gigantic mechanical monsters will devour mountains in search of ore; astonishing inventions will enable individuals to talk to one another over wires; carriages will carry people about their business without horses. Between 1790 and 1860 the U.S. Patent Office granted a total of 31,000 patents; over the period 1860 to 1930 it awarded 1.5 million.

In the background of these alterations a tremendous structure of steel will come to undergird the economy, and a torrent of power will come to drive it: the 16,000 tons of steel produced in 1865 will multiply to fifty-six million tons; the sixteen million horsepower of energy used in the nation after the Civil War will become 1.6 billion horsepower by 1929. Perhaps we can sum up the change by saying that the omnipresence of machines will become more and more noticeable in the period from 1865 to 1929, when still another "chapter" of economic history will begin. We call this era of intensified machine building and machine use the *industrialization of America,* and in the chapters to come we shall examine the process as it took place. But here we must take a moment to think back on our frame of reference, to help us place the entire drama in clear perspective.

Three Effects of Industrialization

Industrialization changes America in three ways. First, it alters—indeed, it truly revolutionizes—material life. The daily routines of work, the objects of everyday use, are more profoundly affected by the advent of industrial technology than by any previous change in the economic history of mankind.

Second, industrialization changes economic life. The reach and penetration of the market expand. The manner in which men and women are mobilized for the economic tasks will shift from a relationship of indenture and apprenticeship to those of wage work in factories.

Third, the rhythm and pace of capitalist expansion will also undergo a vast change. Growth will move more rapidly. Instability will become more pronounced as production takes place more and more in factories, not on farms. The texture of institutional life will take on a new aspect as huge business enterprises arise, as buccaneers become bureaucrats, and as the government itself is presented with new tasks and challenges.

All these changes await us in the pages to come. We mention them here to trace out in advance the central thread of the narrative whose complicated path we are now about to examine.

The Market Mechanism

There is no better way to begin than to ask: Who planned the industrialization of America? Who determined where the railroads would go? Where the cities would grow and the iron mines be developed? Who planned the changeover from horse-drawn to horseless carriages, or the knitting together of the nation by telephone wires?

The answer is that no one planned it. In contrast with the late Soviet Union, where every steel mill, every technological change, every major new city was first determined by a group of planners and then built according to the blueprints of a central authority, no single individual or group of individuals designed the industrial transformation of America. Instead, the enormous process was largely left to the working-out of the market mechanism.

That mechanism basically consists of two elements, each equally important. The first is the organization of the bulk of the nation's production as profit-seeking enterprise, free to carry on whatever activities are permitted by law. The drive for profit thus becomes the central driving force of the market system.

This search to make profits pushes business enterprises in two directions. It serves as a force for the expansion of business, because a large business almost always makes more money than a small one. And it also serves to put businessmen on the alert for new opportunities for profit-making. In this way the drive for profit propels business into the development of new products, as well as into the expansion of facilities to provide more of existing products.

Therefore we can see that the drive for profits serves as a generalized imperative for action. That imperative is lodged, however, not in the directives and blueprints of a central command agency, but in the acquisitive drives of thousands of business executives or capitalists.*

But the drive for profits is only one part of the market mechanism. If it were the only operating factor, the market would be better characterized as a profiteering system than a profit system. Each enterprise, out to maximize its income, would be able to charge all that the traffic would bear. Monopoly would be the natural result of such a system, with business enterprises charging extremely high prices, and reaping extremely high returns, on every article sold either to households or to other businesses.**

Thus a control system is a necessary part of the market mechanism. It is not a system of inspectors or rigidly enforced directives, such as we found in the Soviet Union or still find in centrally planned systems. It is the institution of competition that provides control—the institution of businesses vying one against another to obtain the favor of their customers. Competition thereby turns potential profiteering and

---

*It is worthwhile learning a bit of terminology here. A capitalist is someone who owns capital and risks it in a business enterprise. An executive, or an entrepreneur (the word much used by economists), is a business decision-maker. One can be a capitalist without being an entrepreneur, as when a capitalist lends his money to or buys stock in an enterprise run by someone else. (We will learn more about stocks in the following chapter.) One can also be an entrepreneur without being a capitalist—for example, a manager of a business who is paid a high salary or a bonus but who does not himself own a substantial portion of the enterprise.

**Just as a cautionary note, it should be added that monopolies cannot charge *any* price that they like if they wish to maximize their profits. If a monopoly railroad charged a million dollars per ticket, it would not sell many tickets. What a monopoly can do is to establish the price that gives it the highest profit obtainable. A competitive firm has to charge a price that "meets competition," and its profits are accordingly lower.

monopoly into a struggle in which profits are constantly under pressure from enterprises eager to steal away the business of any firm that fails to trim costs or that prices its goods with a higher profit margin than is necessary for business survival.

Businesses

To learn more about the theory of the market mechanism we study economics, for a large part of that subject is concerned with elucidating the way in which the profit drive on the one hand, and the constraint of competition on the other, bring about the process of material replenishment and growth. But here we want to see the market mechanism in action and the overarching dynamics of capitalism. We want to follow the actual careers of nineteenth-century businessmen who were struggling to make money by expanding their businesses or by pioneering in new fields. We want as well to watch the competitive control system at work, for here lies one of the great sources of change in the period we are studying.

So let us begin by taking a survey of the business system as it existed in the first decade or two after the Civil War. There were about 500,000 business firms in America in 1870, not counting the nation's farms. Most of them were very small, employing one or two persons besides the owner-proprietor. A great many were small retail stores. But we are interested in a particular sector of the business world—the sector of manufacturing, for this is where the industrial growth of the nation will mainly take place.

From the census of 1870 we know something about that sector. Of the nation's total labor force of almost thirteen million, nearly 2.5 million worked in manufacturing. The ten biggest industries were flour-milling, cotton goods, lumber, boots and shoes, men's clothing, iron, leather, woolen goods, liquor, and machinery—in that order. However, the biggest employer, lumber, gave work to only 160,000 employees—far fewer than we would find in most giant companies today.

Businessmen-Inventors

Who ran these small businesses that were to play such an important role in our economic growth? They were a varied lot. A few were inventors, such as Thomas Alva Edison, who not only established the nation's first industrial research center—his so-called invention factory—at Menlo Park, New Jersey, in 1876, but who was actively engaged in creating companies to market his many inventions. As one observer noted, Edison was "the first great scientific inventor who clearly conceived of inventions as subordinate to commerce." Edison would have taken this remark as a compliment. Discussing his role as a scientist, Edison said:

> I do not regard myself as a pure scientist, as so many persons have insisted that I am. I do not search for the laws of nature, and have made no great discoveries of such laws. I do not study science as Newton and Faraday and Henry studied it, simply for the purpose of learning truth. I am only a professional inventor. My studies and experiments have been conducted entirely with the object of inventing that which will have commercial utility.[1]

Other businessmen had the prescience to put together other people's innovations to create new industries: Gustavus Swift, for example, who left Massachusetts in the mid-1870s to become a butcher in Chicago, combined the ice-cooled railway car with the ice-cooled warehouse to create the first national meat-packing company in 1885.

Still others were simply men with a talent for organization, finance, and management. James Buchanan Duke made his fortune by welding technology and merchandising. When the company in which he was a partner turned to cigarette manufacturing in 1881, Duke reduced the firm's operating costs by installing the new Bonsack cigarette-rolling machine, a one-ton contraption that fed paper and tobacco in continuous rolls, pasted and cut the tubes, and made 100,000 cigarettes in a single day. By comparison, the fastest worker could roll only 3,000 daily. The resulting output threatened to glut the market. But by 1884, through the use of advertising and the creation of a crushproof sliding cardboard box, Duke had created a national demand for his product. In 1890 he combined the four major cigarette producers in the nation to form the American Tobacco Company.

And Ordinary Businessmen

But most of the nation's businessmen were not inventors, or merchandising pioneers. They were a much more conventional lot, no more remarkable (and no less) than the businessmen who run small factories or stores or wholesale establishments in the United States today. We tend to think of the entrepreneurs whose combined efforts brought so dramatic a change to the economic landscape as Horatio Alger success stories—men who rose from humble beginnings to achieve fame and fortune.* In fact, the business leadership largely came from substantial and conservative backgrounds.

A study by Francis W. Gregory and Irene D. Neu on the social origins of 303 business leaders in textiles, railroads, and steel during the 1870s finds that the overwhelming majority were born in the United States; that of those native-born executives only 3 percent had foreign-born fathers, the rest dating their American ancestry back to colonial times; that some 90 percent were raised in either a middle- or upper-class milieu; that roughly a third were college graduates; and that one-half did not go to work before age nineteen, and that less than one-quarter went to work before age sixteen. Summing up their investigation, Gregory and Neu conclude:

> Was the typical industrial leader of the 1870's, then, a 'new man,' an escapee from the slums of Europe or from the paternal farm? Did he arise from his own efforts from a boyhood of poverty? Was he as inno-cent of education and of formal training as has often been alleged? He seems to have been none of these things. American by birth, of a New England father, English in national origin, Congregational, Presbyterian, or Episcopalian in religion, urban in early environment, he was rather born and bred in an atmosphere in which business and a relatively high social standing were intimately associated with his family life. Only at about eighteen did he take his first regular job, prepared to rise from it, moreover, not by a rigorous apprenticeship begun when he was virtu-ally a child, but by an academic education well above the average.[2]

THE ROBBER BARONS

Thus the average business enterpriser does not seem like a very promising figure to be the agent for the industrial transformation of

---

*Horatio Alger business romances were about poor, hard-working boys who made good. They were not essentially rags-to-riches stories, but morality fables. Few people read these once-popular tales any more. If they did, they would soon discover an underlying pattern. Alger's heroes did not gain respectability and virtue because they displayed sterling qualities of business acumen, loyalty, etc. Invariably recognition came to them because they had the chance one day to stop a runaway carriage in which sat a terrified golden-ringleted girl who turned out to be—you'll never guess—the boss's daughter. After that, things changed dramatically for plucky Dick, Tom, or Harry.

the nation. But what makes the businessman so dramatic a personage in the post–Civil War era is not the average entrepreneur. Rather, it is a handful of business leaders who arose in virtually every line of business to dominate and drive and dazzle their fellow businessmen. By virtue of their personalities, their ambitions, their talents, or their tactics, these business leaders bestrode the economic landscape like Gullivers in the land of Lilliput, endowing the age with many of their personal characteristics. Because their characteristics included some of the predatory habits of feudal lords who exacted tolls and ransoms from those who strayed within their domains, these dramatic figures have been called by their critics the "robber barons," and the period of industrialization in which they played so powerful a role has been dubbed the Age of the Robber Barons. An examination of the career of perhaps the most notorious of them, Jay Gould, will give us some insight into the group as a whole.

Jay Gould

Jay Gould was the "Mephistopheles of Wall Street." He was perhaps the most money-minded man in a money-minded age. One historian writes: "No human instinct of justice or patriotism caused him to deceive himself, or to waver in any perceptible degree from the steadfast pursuit of strategic power and liquid assets."[3]

Gould moved from one wrongdoing to another with striking virtuosity. His career began in 1856, when he became a partner in a tanning factory in Pennsylvania. It was not long before he began investing a large percentage of the *company's* profits in his *personal* banking and real estate ventures. After those embezzlements were discovered, Gould formed a new partnership—but continued his embezzlements. This time one of his partners committed suicide; the other tried unsuccessfully to remove Gould from the tannery. It was not until 1861 that Gould was ousted, but by that time he had already extracted most of the firm's assets.

It was during this period that Gould first turned his attention to the railroad industry. In 1867, Daniel Drew put Gould and Jim Fisk on the board of directors of the Erie Railway. It was quite a trio. Fisk was a man of rapacious appetites and extraordinary unscrupulousness, of whom it was said that he regarded business "as a kind of joke."[4] Drew was famous for having introduced the idea of "watered stock"—

driving thirsty cattle to the market and then bloating them with water just before they were weighed in for sale.*

Cornelius Vanderbilt

Beginning in 1868 the triumvirate of Drew, Gould, and Fisk engaged "Commodore" Cornelius Vanderbilt, a New York shipping magnate who began investing in railroads during the Civil War, in an Olympian struggle for control of the Erie. The threesome began by issuing some $8 million in "watered" stock—corporate securities as bloated as water-filled cattle—despite a judicial restraining order. Thereafter they dispensed $1 million in bribes to obtain passage of a New York law to authorize the stock issue. These manipulations were too much even for Drew and Vanderbilt. Drew recalled the $8 million stock issue, and he and Vanderbilt turned the Erie over to Gould and Fisk, who thereupon issued $23 million in watered stock.

Even in an age of unbridled acquisitiveness, Gould's tactics earned him an unenviable reputation. Yet we should recognize that his chicanery and unscrupulousness represented an exaggeration of, but not a departure from, the behavior of many of his fellow business titans. Bribery, for example, was not uncommon—even Thomas Edison promised certain New Jersey representatives a thousand dollars apiece if legislation favorable to his interests was passed. Stock-watering and disregard for the law were widespread. After obtaining control of the New York Central Railway, Cornelius Vanderbilt arbitrarily increased its capitalization by $23 million, virtually every dollar of which represented inside profits for himself and his associates. When told this was illegal, he supposedly replied: "Law! What do I care about the Law? Hain't I got the power?"[5]

Fraud and deception were thus all too common practices of the day—the federal government, for example, was billed at three times actual cost by the first transcontinental railway construction company,

---

*Drew was also known for the bandanna trick. Feigning confusion and dismay on the floor of the stock exchange, he would mop his forehead with a red bandanna, causing a slip of paper to fall from his pocket. Another speculator would retrieve the note on which were written Drew's instructions to his brokers to buy or sell stocks. Thinking that Drew's plans were now discovered, his adversary would place his stock orders to take advantage of Drew's plans. But of course the whole thing was a ruse that enabled Drew himself to outwit his opponents because he knew what *their* operations would be.

Jay Gould (1836–1892)

whose expenses Congress had agreed to underwrite; and afterward, when the depredations of the company were in danger of being dragged into the open, the company's books were brazenly burned.

Baron or Builder?

Yet like many of the robber barons, Vanderbilt was also an empire-builder. The enterprise that set the motif for America's post–Civil War expansion was the railroad industry. The iron horse symbolized the boundless energy and forward motion of the nation. When the war broke out there were only 30,000 miles of railroad track in the country. Most roads were short, averaging no more than 100 miles, built to connect two or three local market centers; and there were few direct lines between major cities. Passengers travelling from New York to Chicago, for example, had to be transferred from one line to another seventeen times. The trip took two full days.

The main task of the postwar generation of builders was to consolidate these independent lines into unified networks. Vanderbilt was a pioneer in this development. By 1869 he had obtained control of the New York Central Railroad, which ran between Buffalo and Albany, and two other lines that connected the Central with New York City. In 1870 he picked up the Lake Shore and Michigan Southern railroads, thereby extending his system from New York City to Chicago by way of Cleveland and Toledo, Ohio. Passengers could thereafter travel between the two great terminals in less than a day without leaving their seats. When he died in 1877, Vanderbilt left a railroad network of some 4,500 miles. In the nation as a whole, by 1900 there were 200,000 miles, more than in all the countries of Europe combined.

THE CELEBRATION OF WEALTH

We will have a chance to look more deeply into the business behavior of the age and its relation to economic growth, for the era of industrial expansion could hardly have flourished if Gould's or Fisk's tactics were ubiquitous. Nonetheless, the styles and aims of the robber barons have an important bearing on the tenor of the times. For they typify a country that had become enamored of wealth. Business became the great avenue of success, and anything that delayed one's entrance into the world of business, including education, was frowned on. It was often remarked with approval that Cornelius Vanderbilt, who left $100 million at his death, had read but one book in his life, and that one at an advanced age. (It was *Pilgrim's Progress;* we can doubt that he learned very much from it.)

Not only was the accumulation of wealth regarded as the most fitting and admirable of all careers, but its ostentatious expenditure was generally admired. Social commentators of the period delighted in describing parties where cigarettes made of dollar bills were smoked for the pleasure of inhaling wealth; where extravaganzas of decoration were employed, including the conversion of one New York hotel into a fake coal mine; where newly made millionaires vied with each other for social distinction, one giving a party where monkeys were seated

A horseback dinner

between the guests, another a dinner party on horseback, yet another a party where each lady found a gold necklace tucked in her napkin as a favor.*

Moreover, the love of money and success permeated all ranks of society, not just the top. Historian Henry Steele Commager comments, "The self made man, not the heir, was the hero. . . ."[6] Small wonder, then, that panegyrics and encomiums celebrated the "captains of industry," and that a general philosophy of "rugged individualism" reached down through all the ranks of American society. Even among the working classes, Charles A. Beard remarks, "all save the most wretched had aspirations. There was a baton in every toolkit."[7]

*In several books published at the end of the nineteenth century, economist Thorstein Veblen observed that the very wealthy literally lived to spend money for the sake of proving they had money. Veblen called this pompous extravagance "conspicuous consumption," and the penchant to flaunt it, "conspicuous waste." See, especially, Veblen's *The Theory of the Leisure Class* (1899).

Social Darwinism

The worship of success thus provided an important source of the drive for profit that set into motion the industrialization process. We should note as well that the quest for wealth was supported by an important intellectual current of the day—a current we call Social Darwinism because it translated the biological theories of Charles Darwin into a social theory that blessed the business struggle as an indispensable means to "progress."

Darwin's theory of evolution did not make pronouncements about "progress." It was essentially a generalization about the struggle for survival in which some species survived and some perished. But in the hands of the English sociologist Herbert Spencer, Darwin's theory became interpreted as a process that chose the "better," as well as the tougher or stronger, among competing individuals or species. Thus the competitive struggle of business was viewed as a contest in which the survivors were the "fittest"—not merely as businessmen, but as champions of civilization itself. Hence businessmen transformed their sense of material superiority into a sense of moral and intellectual superiority. As John D. Rockefeller once stated, "I believe it is my duty to make money and still more money and to use the money I make for the good of my fellow man according to the dictates of my conscience."

Little wonder that such a theory won the approval of successful businessmen and that Darwinian phrases and ideas threaded their way easily into the fabric of business speeches and writings. Andrew Carnegie, for example, lionized Spencer and wrote to him as "Master." In a famous article published in the *North American Review* of 1889, Carnegie wrote:

> While the law [of competition] may be sometimes hard for the individual, it is best for the race, because it insures the survival of the fittest in every department. We accept and welcome, therefore, as conditions to which we must accommodate ourselves, great inequality of environment, the concentration of business . . . in the hands of a few, and the law of competition between these, as being not only beneficial, but essential for the future of the race.[8]

A few years later John D. Rockefeller, Jr., defined Spencerian "competition" to a Sunday school class:

The growth of large business is merely a survival of the fittest. . . . The American Beauty Rose can be produced only by sacrificing the early buds which grow up around it. This is not an evil tendency in business. It is merely the working out of a law of nature and a law of God.[9]

Hence Social Darwinism became a means of excusing as well as explaining the competitive process from which some emerged with power and some were ground into poverty. As one millionaire member of the United States Senate said of himself: "I do not know very much about books; I have not read very much; but I have travelled a good deal and observed men and things and I have made up my mind after all my experiences that the members of the Senate are the survivors of the fittest."[10] We understand his sentiment better when we learn that in 1900 the Senate contained twenty-five millionaires among its ninety members.

Thus Social Darwinism joined with the general adulation of wealth to create an atmosphere in which aggressive business expansion was given the unstinting and uncritical approval of virtually all sections of society. Even the churches were strong supporters of the business ethic, equating worldly success and spiritual superiority in a manner that would have made Cotton Mather blush. An estimated thirteen million people heard the Reverend Russell Conwell deliver his "Acres of Diamonds" sermon: riches were to be had almost for the asking by a little hard work, he claimed, and riches were "holy" because money could be used for good purposes. Conwell certainly had *his* acre of diamonds: his publications earned him over $8 million.* We shall see in later chapters how these prevailing attitudes played an important role in determining the character of the industrialization process.

From Baron to Bureaucrat

We have looked into the careers of the robber barons to get some feelings for the roistering atmosphere of the post–Civil War period. Yet it must be apparent that industrialization would never have found its realization under a business elite composed only of Goulds and Fisks. Therefore we must acquaint ourselves with another type of business

---

*Most of Conwell's wealth was channeled into social and educational causes, including the founding of Temple University.

tycoon, typified by a man very different from Jay Gould in his view of the aims of the business enterprise. Gould is a caricature of the worst of the robber baron age; Andrew Carnegie represents the best of it.

Andrew Carnegie

Born in the attic of a cottage in Dunfermline, Scotland—a center of the Scottish weaving industry—in 1835, Carnegie was the son of a hand-loom weaver who had been thrown out of work by the coming of the Industrial Revolution. When Carnegie was thirteen the family emigrated to Allegheny, Pennsylvania. There he worked as a bobbin boy in the textile mills at $1.20 a week; then as a machine wiper deep in a

Andrew Carnegie (1835–1919)

factory cellar at $3 a week—to the end of his days the merest whiff of machine oil could make him deathly ill.

In America Carnegie found the thing that was so noticeably absent in Scotland—opportunity. When the telegraph came to nearby Pittsburgh in 1849, he got a job as a messenger boy. Like the hero in a Horatio Alger story, he came to the office early and left it late in order to watch the operators at work; then at night he studied Morse code until he became a skilled telegrapher himself. In fact he was soon one of the very few operators in the country who could take messages direct from the buzzes of the machine rather than from its printed dots and dashes: people used to drop into the telegraph office to watch him take a message "hot from the wire."

Also as in every Horatio Alger story, luck and patronage played an important role. One citizen who saw Carnegie at work was Thomas Scott, then the local superintendent of the Pennsylvania Railroad, later to become a great railway baron in his own right. In 1853 Scott took Carnegie on as his assistant, and after the young man had gained his trust offered him a chance to buy a $600 interest, ten shares, in a company called Adams Express. Carnegie did not have $60, much less $600, but Scott lent the funds to this young man of "great expectations." Adams Express prospered mightily and soon paid its first dividend. It was a turning point for Carnegie. As he later wrote: "I shall remember that check as long as I live. It gave me the first penny of revenue from capital—something I had not worked for with the sweat of my brow. 'Eureka!' I cried. Here's the goose that lays the golden eggs."[11]

In 1859 Scott promoted Carnegie to superintendent of the western division of the Pennsylvania Railroad at a salary of $1,500 a year. And when Scott became Assistant Secretary of War in 1861, he appointed Carnegie superintendent of military transportation and director of the Union's telegraph communications.

Meanwhile, another goose came his way. Riding the railroad in 1860, Carnegie was approached by a stranger carrying a green bag. The stranger introduced himself as T. T. Woodruff and inquired if Carnegie was connected with the railway. Woodruff then opened his bag and showed Carnegie a small model. It was, in miniature, the first sleeping car. Carnegie arranged for Woodruff to meet Scott, and soon a company was formed in which Carnegie was given a one-eighth interest for his services. Within two years the Woodruff Palace Car Company was paying Carnegie dividends of over $5,000 a year.

Investments now became the center of Carnegie's interest and the means to his initial fortune. The Palace Car Company was followed by an interest in the Keystone Bridge Company, the first successful manufacturer of iron railroad bridges, which were needed to sustain the weight of ever heavier locomotives. Next came a share in the Pittsburgh Locomotive Works; thereafter a share in a local iron foundry that would become the nucleus of Carnegie's steel empire.

By 1868 Carnegie was already rich. Yet, unlike the great majority of his fellow budding captains of industry, he was troubled by his wealth. In a suite in the opulent St. Nicholas Hotel in New York he wrote a memorandum to himself:

> Thirty-three and an income of 50,000$ per annum. . . . Beyond this never earn—make no effort to increase fortune, but spend the surplus each year for benevelent *[sic]* purposes. Cast business forever aside except for others. . . .
>
> Man must have an idol—the amassing of wealth is one of the worst species of idolitry *[sic]*. . . . To continue much longer overwhelmed by business cares and with most of my thoughts wholly upon the way to make more money must degrade me beyond hope of permanent recovery.
>
> I will resign business at Thirty-five. . . .[12]

Odd thoughts for a robber baron! And of course Carnegie did not "resign business." On the contrary, his real business career was soon to begin; everything previous had been a harbinger of what was to come. While vacationing in England he had a chance to see the astonishing new way of making steel invented by Henry Bessemer (we will find out more about that method in our next chapter). Although he had known about this method of making steel for some time, it was not until then that Carnegie became convinced that the day of cheap steel had arrived. Perhaps something about the spectacular volcanic eruption of Bessemer's "converter" appealed to his fiery temperament. Carnegie rushed home and built the largest Bessemer plant in America. It is interesting that the year of his return was 1873, and that the United States was in the throes of the most severe business depression it had ever experienced. But Carnegie was convinced that the future was bright. In addition, because of the depression, he was able to build a large up-to-date mill for $1.25 million, about 25 percent less than the cost in normal times. By 1875 the plant was in production and he was on his way to becoming the most renowned industrial businessman in the world.

The Rise of the Business Manager

Carnegie's career is a corrective to that of Jay Gould in that it gives us a sense of the men and motivations that lay behind the market mechanism. But before we are finished with our study of businessmen, we must pay heed to one extremely significant development of the sixty-year period in which we are interested. This is the gradual emergence of a new "style" of businessman—no longer a robber baron, or even a captain of industry, but a corporate manager, indeed a business bureaucrat.

Sociologist Reinhard Bendix describes him this way:

> Entrepreneurs start firms of their own at some point in their careers; bureaucrats do not. At the climax of their careers entrepreneurs are substantial owners of a firm, while bureaucrats are typically salaried executives. Entrepreneurs sometimes spend parts of their careers as salaried employees, bureaucrats do so invariably and for a major portion of their careers.[13]

Bureaucrats are peculiarly creatures of organizations, and it was inevitable that a business bureaucracy should develop as the size of industry grew. A Lowell cotton mill or a Pittsburgh rolling mill was an operation that could still be housed in a single large shed or in a small complex of buildings, where the owner or his mill foreman could take in the entire works in an hour's tour of inspection. But once a certain size of endeavor was reached, the possibility for direct supervision disappeared and an effective *organization* became essential. By the 1850s Henry Varnum Poor, editor of the *Railway Journal* (and later the founder of the first manuals of statistical information for investors), was tracing the misfortunes of the railroads to the fact that the owners of the roads could not manage them, and that the managers did not own them. What was lacking, in other words, was a managerial element—a group of executives subordinate to the ultimate decisional authority of the owners in matters of grand strategy, but possessing the authority to run complex organizations according to their own expertise.

The First Table of Organization

As we might expect, we find the first efforts to create systems of administration in the largest industry of the times, the railroads. The pioneer of industrial organization was Daniel A. McCallum, a talented engineer and inventor who was asked in 1854 to become general superintendent of the Erie Railroad. (It is ironical that the railroad that would one day belong to the greatest industrial pirate, Jay Gould, was also to be the locus of a profound managerial reorientation.) McCallum's task was to establish a system to assure better accountability of both managers and men. He responded to the challenge eagerly. As he pointed out in his report a year later:

> A Superintendent, if a road is fifty miles in length, can give its business his personal attention and may be constantly on the line engaged in the direction of its details; each person is personally known to him, and all questions in relation to its business are at once presented and acted upon; and any system, however imperfect, may under such circumstances prove comparatively successful.
>
> In the government of a road five hundred miles in length, a very different state exists. Any system that might be applicable to the business and extent of a short road would be found entirely inadequate to the wants of a long one; and I am fully convinced that in the want of a system perfect in its details, properly adjusted and vigilantly enforced, lies the true secret of [the road's] failure; and that this disparity of cost per mile in operating long and short roads, is not produced by any difference in length but is in proportion to the perfection of the system adopted.[14]

To achieve his desired system, McCallum drew up what is probably the first table of organization for an American company—a tree with the roots representing the president and the board of directors, and five branches showing respectively the main operating divisions— engine repairs, cars, bridges, telegraph, printing—plus the service division. On the branches, leaves represented the various local agents, train crews, foremen, and so on. Furthermore, within the smaller units of the system, such as the machine shops, the same hierarchical system prevailed, with duties prescribed for each grade, and the grade of each individual indicated on the uniform he wore.

Orders were to go from roots to leaves, but as economic historian Alfred Chandler points out, "McCallum realized that the most essential communication in his organization was from subordinate to superior rather than vice versa."[15] Thus a continuous flow of upward-rising reports constantly informed the managers as to the day-by-day, and sometimes hour-by-hour, location of rolling stock, or the occurrence of tie-ups or accidents, and provided them with a detailed, regular scrutiny of the costs of operating the system, not alone as a unit, but in each of its numerous constituent parts.

Henry Varnum Poor considered McCallum's work so remarkable that he had the organizational tree lithographed and offered it for sale at one dollar a copy; the tree was reported on in Parliament and was even popularized in the *Atlantic Monthly*. Thus its influence on the development of internal business organization was widespread.*

Organization Enters Business

Other large enterprises soon followed suit by "rationalizing" their own internal structures of command. In *The Inside History of the Carnegie Steel Company,* James Howard Bridge describes the metamorphosis there. Of the early days of the company, he writes:

> While the workings of every furnace and every machine were carefully watched and tabulated, the operations of the greatest machine of all, its brain, were spasmodic, unmethodical, and for the most part unnoted. The Board of Managers met by chance, there being no fixed time for meetings. Consultations and deliberations were conducted in a haphazard way, and often no minutes of them were taken. If an important change was to be made, perhaps a meeting would be called; or it might happen that the managers most interested in it would have an informal meeting at the works, when the matter would be decided. The old books of the various companies often show a gap of several months without an entry.
>
> With the accession of Mr. [Henry Clay] Frick to the headship of the concern, this was promptly changed. A rule was made that the Board of Managers should meet every Tuesday at lunch, and that a full report of their subsequent deliberations should be kept. Similarly, every Saturday at noon, the different superintendents and their assistants, some foremen, purchasing and sales agents and their principal assistants, to the number of thirty or more, met about a larger table, and after lunching together, talked over all matters of common interest.[16]

---

*Curiously, the actual illustration itself has disappeared. The once famous ubiquitous lithograph is today only a memory: no known exemplar exists.

We find the same organizational scaffolding arising elsewhere. In Standard Oil, for example, an elaborate system of committees superintended the various aspects of the company's affairs. Each day at lunch at 26 Broadway their work was coordinated and supervised by the management committee that provided the central guidance for the whole concern. Similarly in the very large merchandising and manufacturing operations of Swift or Armour, of Duke, of Preston (who created a merchandising operation for refrigerated bananas similar to that of Swift's for meat), in the promotion of McCormick's reaper and Singer's sewing machine, the functional requirements for growth and success were first and foremost the creation of effective and smoothly running organizations.

Bureaucrats versus Barons

What relationship did these committee men have to the robber barons, whose presence still dominated the years during which the committees were proliferating? At first they tended to assume subsidiary roles in which their rise to power depended on the patronage of the central figure. Thus Carnegie steadily promoted men like Charles Schwab and W. E. Corey, and J. P. Morgan assisted the rise of Charles Mellen to become "Railroad Lord of New England." Mellen candidly admitted that he wore the Morgan collar, saying after Morgan's death, "I did what I was told."[17] Others, such as H. H. Rogers of Standard Oil, served their terms as organization men and then left to become independent capitalists on their own. Still others rose to high rank and salary, while never quite emerging as leaders in their own right.

But the change induced by the need to administer the larger scope of enterprise did not end with the production of internal bureaucracies. Soon we find that the bureaucracy itself was producing the leading business figures—the route to power had changed from the assumption of capitalist risk to the exercise of organizational expertise. A study of over 1,000 biographies of prominent businessmen shows that only 5 percent of the business leaders born before 1800 rose to success by way of the bureaucratic route; 16 percent of those born between 1801 and 1830; 21 percent of those born in the 1831–1860 period; 29 percent of the group born from 1861–1890, and 48 percent of those born between 1891 and 1920.[18] A study by William Miller of 185 business leaders in the decade 1901–1910 confirms this finding (see table on following page).[19]

AMERICAN BUSINESS LEADERS BY TYPE OF CAREER

Type of Career	Number	Percent
Professional (lawyers)	23	12
Independent Entrepreneur	25	14
Family	51	27
Bureaucratic	86	47

Thus by the end of the period we are interested in, *nearly half of the great industrial leaders were products of the organizational structure of industrial enterprise.* The managerial-minded men desired by Henry Varnum Poor had moved from a subsidiary to a primary function, no longer merely assisting the personal aggrandizement of the great barons but now taking into their own hands the direction of the great corporations within which they had climbed to the very top.

Their advent brought with it a change in the character of business leadership. The piratical tactics, the zest for competitive combat, the personal generalship so characteristic of the robber barons were not the style of men who had patiently worked their way up the organizational ladder. The new captains of industry were not practiced in the arts of risk but in the arts of negotiation—80 percent of the bureaucratic business leaders studied by Miller had never in their entire careers headed a company or assumed any significant risk of financial responsibility for their business enterprises. Significantly, they were also less successful financially. Of the 303 leading entrepreneurs studied by Gregory and Neu, only fifty-four were considered millionaires. Hence, despite the lingering presence of a few baronial types, the dominant businessmen of the twentieth century would be men who built organizations, not monuments. Theodore Vail, who guided AT&T; Gerard Swope, who made (but did not start) General Electric; Alfred Sloan, who rebuilt General Motors—all were representatives of an entrepreneurial type very different from the dominant figures of the previous generation.

This is by no means to say that they were less successful as businessmen. Indeed, the very point of the shift in the locus of power was that it reflected a changing attribute of the business system itself. Bureaucratization did not mean the slowing down of industrial growth, but rather its adaptation to an environment in which the buc-caneer's mode of operation was no longer the mode best suited to the survival of the system.

What is striking is that the profoundly significant rise of business bureaucracy was rooted in the very period when the robber baron seemed to occupy the center of the stage. Thus, at a time when every American knew the names of the greatest enterprisers of the time, the age was already foreshadowed when no one would know any names except those of the great enterprises themselves.

Notes

[1] Harold C. Livesay, *American Made* (1979), p. 148.

[2] Francis W. Gregory and Irene D. Neu, "The American Industrial Elite in the 1870's: Their Social Origins," in William Miller (ed.), *Men in Business* (1962), pp. 193–211.

[3] Matthew Josephson, *The Robber Barons* (1934), pp. 192–3.

[4] Quoted in Edward C. Kirkland, *Dream and Thought in the Business Community* (1956), p. 40.

[5] Quoted in John Tipple, "The Robber Baron in the Gilded Age," in H. Wayne Morgan (ed.), *The Gilded Age* (1963), p. 36.

[6] *The American Mind* (1950), p. 13.

[7] Charles and Mary Beard, *The Rise of American Civilization* (1933), 2:395.

[8] *North American Review* (February 1889), 141ff.

[9] Quoted in W. J. Ghent, *Our Benevolent Feudalism* (1902), p. 29.

[10] Quoted in Matthew Josephson, *The Politicos* (1938), p. 445.

[11] *Autobiography* (1920), p. 80.

[12] Quoted in Joseph Frazier Wall, *Andrew Carnegie* (1970), pp. 224–25.

[13] *Work and Authority* (1956), p. 229.

[14] Quoted in Alfred Chandler, "Henry Varnum Poor," in Miller (ed.), *Men in Business,* p. 260.

[15] *Men in Business,* p. 262.

[16] (1903), pp. 275–76.

[17] Quoted in William Miller, "The American Business Elite in Business Bureaucracies," in *Men in Business,* p. 290.

[18] Reinhard Bendix, *Work and Authority,* p. 229.

[19] "The American Business Elite," in *Men in Business,* p. 290.

Chapter 3
THE TECHNOLOGY OF INDUSTRIALIZATION

THE RISE OF STEEL

We have become familiar with the men who guided the process of industrialization—barons, captains of industry, and, later, bureaucrats. But we have not yet explored the process itself. We are interested, of course, in the gradual introduction of machines and capital goods throughout American life. But we need to examine the technology of industrialization as closely as we examined the reality of the market mechanism if we are to gain a clear sense of what was happening in the eventful years of our study.

Technical Problems

A good place to begin is with steel, for the age of industrialization can almost be summed up as the age of steel. The reason is that machinery requires steel. You can make machines of wood, as in medieval times, but wood has limited strength. You can make them out of iron, as in the early Industrial Revolution, but iron snaps and bends. Hence from earliest times men have sought to improve iron by heating it, combining it with other materials, or cooking it at high temperatures to make what we call steel—a metal of tremendous strength, resiliency, and versatility.

But the cost of converting iron into steel was tremendous. Steel swords were treasures in medieval Europe, rarities to be handed down from father to son. Moreover, not only was the product extremely expensive, but it could not be made in large quantities. At the time of the American Revolution steel was made in crucibles not much larger than a vase. At the great Crystal Palace Exposition of 1851 a 2½-ton ingot of steel (made by combining the outputs of many crucibles) was a sensation.

The steel bottleneck was broken by an extraordinarily versatile English inventor, Henry Bessemer. Bessemer was an inspired tinkerer who had already made his fortune by inventing a way of using brass to make "gold" paint. Thereafter he became interested in increasing the range and accuracy of artillery by designing a projectile that would spin. The projectile, however, required a rifled gun barrel that would far exceed the strength of wrought iron. Since steel barrels were much too expensive, Bessemer set to work to make his projectile practical by inventing cheap steel.

Bessemer devised a solution of amazing simplicity—once it was discovered.* Instead of refining pig iron into steel by heating its surface, he blew air right through the molten metal. The heat generated by the oxidizing iron kept the iron liquid, and the enormous temperatures rapidly burned out the carbon that made untreated iron brittle. Through the Bessemer process three to five tons of iron could be converted into steel in ten or twenty minutes, compared with the laborious process of heating and stirring and reheating, which used to take a day or more. Meanwhile, as the air shot through the container, a veritable volcano of sparks and fire erupted. Then when the miniature hell subsided, pure steel could be poured out.

That was the process that captured Carnegie's imagination. But it was only the beginning of the new steel technology. When Carnegie built his first plant, its converters held five tons of molten iron. Within twenty-five years they held twenty tons—converters as large as small houses were cradled by immense gantry cranes that raised and lowered and tilted them as easily as sandbox toys. Equally important, machines also performed the operations before and after the conversion into steel. Mechanization began at the mines, where the ore was scraped up by shovels capable of loading a freight car in a few swings. The cars themselves rolled directly into the mills, where a giant dumper picked them bodily off the tracks and cascaded their products into vast bins. Electric cars then hauled the ore to the tops of furnaces ten stories high. Emerging from the converters in a Niagara of

---

*In fact, the process was independently discovered by William Kelly, an American ironmaster. Kelly made the great mistake of keeping it secret.

molten metal, the white-hot steel was sent through a succession of rollers that squeezed the glowing metal thinner and thinner and faster and faster until finished rails shot from the last pair of rollers at speeds of forty to sixty miles an hour.

The Birth of an Industry

The Bessemer process did more than revolutionize the making of steel. As costs fell, steel became the basic building material of a host of other industries. In 1873, steel was selling at over $100 a ton. Although railroad executives badly wanted to replace their iron rails with steel— the iron rails were splintering under the weight of the big new engines—they could not afford to do so at that price. But the Besse- mer process reduced the cost of steel dramatically. When Carnegie's new plant (thoughtfully named the Edgar Thomson works in honor of a top official of the Pennsylvania Railroad) began production in 1875, it cut the cost of rails to fifty dollars per ton. Two years later the cost had fallen to forty dollars. By 1885 it was reduced to twenty dollars; by the late 1890s, to twelve dollars. Selling his rails at eighteen dollars a ton, Carnegie made a very large profit and still offered the railroads an unprecedented bargain.

The new low-cost steel did more than open a vast market for steel rails ten or fifteen times stronger than iron rails and lasting twenty times as long. Carnegie soon saw the versatile possibilities of steel and converted another mill from steel to structural shapes. Again he was right. By the mid-1870s steel began to edge iron out as the material used for railroad bridges: in 1879, for instance, the builders of New York's famous Brooklyn Bridge decided to construct the entire middle section of steel. Within a few more years another market opened. The Masonic Temple in Chicago, which was to rise a dizzying twenty sto- ries into the sky, gave rise to an order for 4,000 tons of girder, all to be made of steel.

After steel beams came steel nails, steel wire, steel tubes. Total steel output, which amounted to barely 157,000 tons the year before the Thomson works opened, grew to twenty-six million tons by 1910. Carnegie's plants did not produce all of this steel; Carnegie had formi- dable competitors, and in our next chapter we will be looking into the problem that this competition caused. But the Carnegie complex of mills, valued at $700,000 when the Thomson works were opened,

The Bessemer process

doubled in value in five years, doubled again in three more years, rose to an official valuation of $300 million by the turn of the century. Indeed, by 1901 Carnegie was producing more steel than was produced in all of Great Britain.

Technology and Growth

How did the business grow? In large part, as we have seen, it grew because the master key of technology opened vast new market demands for a commodity that had previously been too expensive for extensive use. First the 100,000 miles of railroad trackage, as of 1881, was converted to steel; then the 100,000 miles of new trackage laid down in the next decade was built of steel; thereafter the entire national network had to be relaid in a heavier grade of steel rail as locomotives continued to grow in weight. In 1907 the Tennessee Coal, Iron and Railway Company placed an order for 150,000 tons of rail, which was only 3 or 4 percent of the nation's steel output.

The demand for structural steel provided another vast new market. When the Thomson plant opened there was very little demand for steel beams, but within twenty-five years over 2.5 million tons of steel went into girders and plates for bridges and buildings. Steel nails alone took 300,000 tons of output by 1889; steel wire soon approached 1 million tons a year as telephone poles festooned railroad tracks and as barbed wire enclosed hundreds of thousands of farms.

In this process of expansion, the Bessemer method paved the way. Without it we would not have had the steel rails, wires, nails, girders, plates, bolts, needles, screws, and springs that gave us the skyscraper and the steamship, the scalpel and the jackhammer, the train and the sewing machine, the tin can (actually made of steel) and the "tin lizzie" (motor car). Yet it must be clear that steel alone could not have changed the face of America. Industrialization also required power— the electric dynamo, the internal combustion engine, gasoline. It required communication—the telegraph and the telephone, the typewriter and the high-speed press. It required enormous supplies of materials to be wrested from the earth and used as inputs into the production process—sulfur, tin, lead, zinc. It required complex processes that were invisible to the eyes of consumers but indispensable to the production of the goods they bought—of making chemicals, for example, without which rubber tires or photographic film or dyed cloth could not be made.

Industrialization was the sum total of all these technological advances, most of them first invented by some gifted individual like Bessemer and then launched into economic importance under the business generalship of a man like Carnegie. Without the generalship the technology would have lain dormant or would have been diffused only very slowly into the bloodstream of the nation. Carnegie threw into it the force of his dynamic, driving personality. Carnegie once remarked that a fitting epitaph for him would be: "Here lies a man who knew how to get other men to work for him."[1] He pitted one manager against another, paying big bonuses for higher output, shaming laggards with telegrams: "Puppy dog Number Two has beaten puppy dog Number One on fuel."[2] Carnegie recognized no substitute for success; and success meant expansion, expansion—and then more expansion.

THE ECONOMICS OF SIZE

The new technology and the aggressive tactics of the age provided a powerful mixture for economic growth. But they were also a dangerous mixture for economic stability. For the technology and the tactics combined to alter the organizational structure of industry quite as profoundly as it altered its physical configuration.

The table below indicates that change:

IRON AND STEEL FIRMS: 1870 AND 1900

	1870	1900
No. of firms	808	669
No. of employees	78,000	272,000
Output (tons)	3,200,000	29,500,000
Capital invested	$121,000,000	$590,000,000

SOURCE: U.S. Department of Commerce, *Census of Manufactures, 1900, Part IV.*

The Increase in Size

The effect of technology is not immediately apparent in these figures, but it quickly becomes apparent when we relate the number of firms to the figures for employees or output or capital. Then it becomes clear that the thirty-year span is marked by a *dramatic increase in the size of the average enterprise.*

In 1870 the average iron and steel firm employed fewer than 100 men; in 1900, over 400. During the same period, average output per firm jumped from under 4,000 tons per year to nearly 45,000 tons, and the capital invested in an average company rose from $150,000 to almost $1 million. Moreover, these figures understate the "look" of what was going on, because the statistics include numerous small but unimportant firms. We get a clearer picture of the change when we learn that it cost about $156,000 to build a new rolling mill in Pittsburgh at the time of the Civil War whereas a new rolling mill in 1890 cost $20 million.

It was not only in iron and steel that the size of the typical industrial establishment grew. A glass furnace in the 1860s was deemed an adequate size if it had the capacity of six tons. By 1900, an efficient glass furnace had to produce 1,000 tons. Between 1865 and 1885, the typical railroad grew in length from 100 to 1,000 miles. The cost of an oil refinery in the 1850s, when a "refinery" was little more than a shed with distilling equipment, came to less than $500. By 1865, when Rockefeller bought his first refinery, he paid $72,500—a sizable fortune for those days. (By the end of the year that one refinery grossed over $1.2 million!) By 1900 a refinery cost over $1 million.

Thus in nearly every industry we witness a vast increase in size. Already in 1888 a middle-sized railway with headquarters in Boston employed three times as many people and enjoyed six times as much revenue as the state that had created it. By 1891 the Pennsylvania Railroad employed over 110,000 workers. The largest U.S. government employer, the post office, then had only 95,000 on its payroll. In manufacturing, an "enterprise" came to mean not a single modest building but a multiacre complex of structures; machinery grew in size from assemblies that fitted comfortably into a room to constructions that required immense sheds; the work force swelled from troops or companies to regiments and divisions that thronged the streets as they entered or left the factory gate. From one industry to the next, this increase in size varied according to the technology of the product or process, but when we look at the country as a whole, and especially at its industrial core, we cannot mistake the phenomenon of business growth.

The Pattern of Growth

Moreover, the growth of business followed certain common patterns. Much as we have seen in steel, businesses in many fields diversified their products, multiplied their sites, expanded their size of plant. In this way the one-man, one-plant enterprise grew into the bureaucratic organization that we have already studied. And the pattern of growth did not merely involve diversification or geographical extension. Companies grew vertically as well as horizontally, buying up sources of supply or reaching forward to the final sale of their products. The arch-example of successful vertical integration was the oil industry.* Standard Oil began in 1870 as a refining company. Shortly thereafter it expanded "backward" into the actual drilling for oil, and it was also extended "forward" as a direct seller of products such as kerosene to the consumer.

Not every enterprise pushed its vertical integration that far. But in many industries we see an effort to grow in "depth" as well as in "extent." Carnegie's great steel plants, for example, were only the dis-gorging end of a still larger organization that extended far behind the making of steel to a variety of industrial undertakings that fed into the final steel complex. Behind the Thomson and Homestead and Key-stone plants were the famous Lucy and Carrie furnaces for making pig

---

*Of the many *new* industries that emerged after the Civil War, none was more important than oil refining. Although people had been watching crude oil, or petroleum, ooze from the earth for hundreds of years, they did not know how to reach it. The man who proved that petroleum could be drilled for like water was E. L. Drake, a retired railroad conductor. In 1859 Drake began what observers called "Drake's Folly" in Titusville, Pennsylvania. When he had drilled down seventy feet he struck oil. Drake's well yielded twenty barrels of crude oil a day. News of Drake's success brought other drillers to the region. By the early 1860s "wildcatters," as oil prospectors were called, were drilling for "black gold" all over western Pennsylvania. A decade later, the oil fields covered 2,000 square miles of Pennsylvania, West Virginia, and Ohio, and production had soared to forty million barrels. Interestingly, the cost of drilling a well was very modest, about $5,000 throughout most of the post–Civil War period.

iron; and behind them was the enormous Henry Clay Frick Coke Company with its 40,000 acres of coal land, its 2,688 railway cars, and its 13,252 coking ovens; and behind this in turn were 244 miles of railways (organized into three main companies) to ship materials to and from the coking ovens; and then at a still more distant remove were a shipping company and a dock company with a fleet of Great Lakes ore-carrying steamers; and then, at the very point of origin of the steel-making process, was the Oliver Mining Company with its great mines in Michigan and Wisconsin.

Pittsburgh steel mills, c. 1880–1890

What was the point of this vertical organization? Partly it was an effort on the part of business managers to assure a steady flow of necessary raw materials, or to head off the possibility of being "held up" by some strategically placed railroad or mine company. In part it was also a natural avenue of expansion for companies that were seeking profitable areas for investment but feared to extend themselves further in their own markets. And in part the vertical organization of business expressed the "logic" of a technology that was increasingly knitting the production activities of industrial society into one vast, interconnected process.

The Visible Hand

Surveying these motives and maneuvers, historian Alfred Chandler described the entire process in a vivid phrase. It was, he said, "the visible hand of management [replacing] the invisible hand of market forces . . ."[3] What Chandler meant was that the forces of technology were bringing out ever larger and more rapid flows of production, thereby forcing business units to seek ever wider and deeper forms of organization. They did so because horizontal expansion and vertical integration offered corporate managers the opportunity to *administer* the productive process from start to finish, rather than having to deal with the surprises and possible disruptions of the market as that process moved toward completion.

Thus the vertical integration of Carnegie Steel not only assured the steady physical transformation of ore into finished steel, but also removed the necessity of buying and selling, with all its attendant uncertainties, at each linkage along the way. Without the organization that Carnegie (and other entrepreneurs) built, the raw material would have had to be purchased, and then the shipping services that transported it, and then the equipment that processed it, and so on until the final product was made. *Once vertical integration was achieved, no market forces intruded within the long chain of operations from start to finish.* In this way the visible hand of management replaced the invisible hand of the market.

Changing Structures

Recently, Chandler has described in detail the economic pressures that gave rise to the visible hand, not only among firms in the United States but in Germany and England as well.[4] The first of these was the huge savings in cost—"economies of scale"—yielded by massive machinery and equipment. As the rolling mills and blast furnaces increased in size, the river of output swelled out of all proportion. By the late 1890s a dozen men on the floor of a Pittsburgh rolling mill were able to turn out three thousand tons of steel a day, as much as a mill employing several hundred men forty years earlier. The result, as we have seen, was a dramatic drop in the cost of producing steel.

A second impetus to the rise of managerial organization were economies of "scope"—that is, an ability to widen the range of outputs as the sheer size of enterprises grew. In Germany, for example, dye factories first gained cost-cutting economies of scale similar to those of U.S. steel mills, and then used their vast facilities to broaden their markets with new varieties of dyes. By 1913 the Bayer company alone was producing over 2,000 different chemical products. Last, but by no means least, was the replacement of one-man leadership by elaborate managerial teams. The gigantic enterprises were too ramified in their inner workings, and too complex in their connections with the larger economy to be efficiently, or even effectively, run by a single person or a small group of partners. Enterprises were now the size of small armies, and required, as do armies, not only a single general but generals, each with his staff, and not only clear directives but manuals of rules and regulations. Little by little the era of the boss gave way to that of the business bureaucrat.

Did all this mean that the importance of the market mechanism was thereby lessened within capitalism? Unquestionably it meant that the internal organization of business was becoming more and more organized—planned, if you will—by the very actions of businessmen themselves. But still the market retained its powerful influence in the system. For eventually the rivers of output, now part of an engineered flow, met the sea where other rivers of similar outputs also debouched, and there great battles of competition took place—battles that could not be avoided by vertical envelopment. Later in this chapter, and even more intensively in our next chapter, we will see what were the consequences of this battle of competing commodities.

The Leap Overseas

First, however, we must pay heed to a hitherto unnoticed aspect of business expansion. This was the extension of the expansive thrust of business overseas.

Such expansion typically began with exports. As a firm grew larger, its market expanded from locality to region, from region to the nation. But why stop at the frontiers of a nation? Would not Canadians and Mexicans, English and Germans also consume the goods a firm could produce if it could manage to sell them cheaply enough to cover transportation costs and meet competition abroad? That was clearly the trend by the late 1800s. Between 1870 and 1900, total United States exports tripled from $450 million to $1.5 billion, and, even more significant, the percentage of those exports that consisted of manufactures (rather than agricultural or raw materials) jumped from 15 percent to 32 percent.

Thereafter only one avenue of expansion remained to be explored. This was actual production overseas—that is, the establishment of branches abroad, not to sell goods but to produce them. Thus by 1897 American companies had invested some $635 million abroad—in oil wells, railway ventures, mines, plantations, and—most interesting of all—in manufacturing. By that date $94 million was already invested in foreign factories, such as the giant Singer Sewing Machine factory at Kilbowie, Scotland, as large as the company's largest domestic plant. Because Singer was selling half its output overseas, foreign production, rather than exports, made economic sense. It came to make the same sort of sense to a wide variety of industries, some of which expanded overseas "horizontally" (like Singer), some of which expanded "vertically" (like Standard Oil, seeking oil wells).

Thus from an early date business exerted an expansive thrust that brought the American economy into involvement with economies throughout the world. Moreover this internationalist, "imperialist" impulse was strongly encouraged and supported by American government policy. The Caribbean became an American lake. American troops policed the region to guarantee U.S. security and prosperity. From 1900 to 1917 U.S. Marines were landed in Cuba, Panama, Mexico, Haiti, Nicaragua, and the Dominican Republic. American officials took control of the customs houses to ensure that tariff revenues were properly collected and spent; they renegotiated foreign debts with U.S. banks; and they even ran elections. In 1900 the United States dispatched 2,500 American soldiers to join an international European "rescue" expedition aimed at suppressing the Boxer Rebellion—a Chinese uprising against foreign economic influence in Chinese affairs.

Within a few years American foreign policy would openly be called "Dollar Diplomacy." President William Howard Taft was not reluctant to admit—indeed, to advertise—the close association of American military might and the promotion of American commercial interests. In his annual message of December 3, 1912, Taft spoke of the new diplomacy as "an effort frankly directed to the increase of American trade upon the axiomatic principle that the Government of the United States shall extend all proper support to every legitimate and beneficial American enterprise abroad."

In this book we shall not trace the complex story of the expansion of American economic influence abroad. But at least we can see that the roots of the modern multinational corporations can be discovered almost 100 years ago—and that the pressures for international growth were only the final expression of an expansive process of capitalism whose domestic aspects we are now familiar with.

The Struggle for Market Shares

Now we must return to our central theme—the economic transformation of the country. For we have hitherto only attended the causes of the change in size that marked the post–Civil War years. We have yet to investigate the consequences of that change.

The most important immediate effect was a devastating new form of competition. Competition, we recall, was the disciplinary process of the market system. But this disciplinary effect held true only in a milieu of small firms, none of which could take over the entire market. With the coming of the new technology the nature of this disciplining process altered completely. A firm with great economies of scale—the economist's term for the advantages in cost per unit of output resulting from large-scale production—often had the ability to take away the entire business of a competitor. Competition thus awarded to the more efficient firm* the power not merely to "discipline" the prices of a laggard or overly avaricious firm, but literally to wipe out such a firm.

---

*Economies of scale, it should be noted, are available only to those firms that can afford the equipment needed to achieve them. Between 1850 and 1900 the average amount of capital invested in a manufacturing firm more than doubled, rising from $700,000 to $1.9 million.

Fixed Costs

Moreover, technology changed competition in another way. Typically, the expensive new machines and equipment added to the "fixed costs" of business—a steel mill that put in Bessemer converters, for example, had to pay interest on the money it borrowed to pay for them and had to bear the cost of the depreciation of the new investment. These large fixed costs also served as a powerful stimulus for aggressive business behavior.

Suppose, for example, that a steel plant put in a Bessemer process and thereby incurred new interest and depreciation costs of $1 million per year. Those costs had to be paid whether the plant was running or not. Therefore there was a tremendous temptation, whenever business was dull, to cut prices in order to bring in *some* revenues, even if they were not enough to make a profit. Carnegie put the matter in a nutshell when he said that it cost less to keep the machines running, even when there was no market in sight, than to shut down the factories.

Cutthroat Competition

Thus the growing investment in new technology exerted a powerful inducement to price-cutting as a means of stealing a march on competitors. Price-cutting was all right—until the going got rough and the bigger firms, with more wealth, began to cut prices *below* costs, accepting a loss in order to keep revenues coming in. As Carnegie wrote in 1902, "Political economy says that . . . goods will not be produced at less than cost. This was true when Adam Smith wrote, but it is not quite true today."[5]

Not just in steel, but in virtually all industries with heavy fixed costs—railroads, oil, coal, copper—"cutthroat" price wars repeatedly broke out as producers desperately struggled to find markets for their products when business was slack. By the 1880s fixed costs averaged *two-thirds* of a railroad's total annual cost. "A starving man will usually get bread if it is to be had," said James J. Hill, president of the Great Northern Railway, "and a starving railway will not maintain rates."[6]

As we would expect, this cutthroat competition soon forced smaller firms, with less wealth, against the wall. We can see this tendency if we examine the statistics of the iron and steel industry once again. Notice that there were *fewer* firms in operation in 1900 than in 1870, even though the industry's output had increased enormously. Obviously some firms had grown at the expense of others.

It was not just in iron and steel that dog-eat-dog competition winnowed the ranks of the firms. In 1900, for example, the number of textile mills in the country was one-third fewer than in the 1880s, although textile production was up threefold. In similar fashion, the number of manufacturers of agricultural implements had fallen by 60 percent despite a rapid increase in the use of farm machinery.

We can sum up the change in a sentence: *Competition became a process in which firms struggled for shares of the market.* The result was a desperate contest whose consequences would have profound effects on the workings of the entire economy. We shall trace those consequences in our next chapter. But first, while we are still focused on the role of technology in the economic transformation, we must stop to consider another change, without which the thrust of economic growth would have been expressed in very different fashion. This is the *social technology of organization,* and specifically the development of the organizational form we call the corporation.

THE TECHNOLOGY OF ORGANIZATION

Corporations and Proprietorships

The corporation can be traced very far back into history. The early colonial settlers had corporations for the performance of certain activities, such as charity work and other activities that were associated with the public welfare. These corporations were entities organized by the state or colony—that is, organizations that received a corporate "charter" from the local government permitting them to carry on their business.

But certainly the corporation was very much the exception rather than the rule until well into the nineteenth century. Corporations required the approval of legislatures and therefore entailed a degree of government intervention into economic life that appeared both unnecessary and burdensome to enterprisers in the eighteenth and early nineteenth centuries. The typical enterprise was a proprietorship or a partnership—forms of organization in which the principals of a business "owned" it very much as they owned their private assets, such as their house or other personal effects.

There were obvious conveniences to such a simple mode of establishing a business, but there were also difficulties and problems. For if a proprietorship or a partnership failed, its creditors could sue the

WITHDRAWN

SCCCC - LIBRARY
4601 Mid Rivers Mall Drive
St. Peters, MO 63376

owners personally, forcing them to pay any debts of the business from their personal assets. Proprietorships thus exposed their owners to considerable financial risk in case of business failure. Moreover, they were ill-suited to businesses that were expected to last beyond the life of the proprietor, because the enterprise had to be legally reorganized every time its owner or partners died.

Corporate Advantages

The corporation avoided those difficulties. Because it was an entity created by the state, it existed in its own right as a "person" created by law. As such a legal person, the corporation could do anything that a private person could—own, buy, or sell property, carry on business affairs, sue or be sued. But it had two extraordinary features:

1. *The "person" of the corporation did not die when any official or shareowner of the corporation died.*

It went on forever—or at least until the state that issued its charter revoked it.

2. *The corporate person was responsible only for "its" own obligations.*

If a corporation went bankrupt, it met as much of its debts as it could from its own assets, but neither its officials nor its shareowners could ordinarily be asked to pay any remaining debts from their personal wealth.

Corporate Ownership

Clearly the corporation had substantial advantages over proprietorships and partnerships. But who owned it? How did it run?

A corporation today as in the past is owned by individuals who buy "shares" in it. Suppose that a corporation is granted a charter to carry on a business, say in retail trade. The charter also specifies how many shares of stock this business enterprise is allowed to issue. For example, a corporation may be formed with the right to issue 1 million shares. If these shares are sold to individuals at a price of ten dollars each, the original shareholders (also called stockholders) will have put

$10 million into the corporation. In return they will receive stock certificates indicating how many shares each person has bought.

These stock certificates are somewhat like a partnership agreement, although there are very important differences. If someone buys 1,000 shares in our imaginary corporation, he or she will own .1 percent of the corporation. He will have the right to receive .1 percent of all income that it pays out as "dividends" on its stock. He will also be entitled to cast 1,000 votes at the meetings of shareholders that all corporations must hold. In this way a shareholder is very much like a junior partner who was given a one-tenth of one percent interest in a business.

But there are critical differences. As we have already said, a stockholder is not personally liable for any debts that the corporation cannot pay from the money it has taken in from its stockholders or from its earnings. If the company goes bankrupt, the shareholder will lose his investment of $10,000 (1,000 shares at ten dollars), but no one can sue him for any further money. *His liability is thereby limited to the amount he has invested.*

Moreover, unlike a partner, who usually finds it very difficult to sell his shares, a stockholder may sell his shares to anyone he likes, at any price he can get. If our imaginary corporation prospers, he may be able to get twenty dollars for each share. He is perfectly free to sell as many of his shares as he wishes at that price. Moreover, marketplaces for stocks and bonds have developed along with the corporation to facilitate sales of stock. The most important of these markets, the New York Stock Exchange, was organized in 1817. By 1900 over 100 million shares a year were being traded on its floor. *Thus with the corporation came the advantage of a much greater "liquidity" of personal wealth.*

Finally, shares of stock entitle the stockholder to the dividends that the directors of the corporation may decide to pay out for each share. But as a stockholder he is not entitled to any fixed amount of profit. If the corporation prospers, the directors may vote to pay a large dividend. But they are under no obligation to do so—they may wish to use the earnings of the corporation for other purposes, such as the purchase of new equipment or land. If the corporation suffers losses, ordinarily the directors will vote to pay no dividend, or only a small one, to be paid from past earnings. *Thus as an owner of ordinary*

The New York Stock Exchange

*"common" stock, the stockholder must take the risk of having his dividends rise or fall.**

---

*Corporations are allowed to issue bonds, as well as common stock. A bond is different from a share of stock in two important ways. First, a bond has a *stated value* printed on its face, whereas a share of stock does not. A $1,000 bond is a certificate of debt issued by the corporation. It makes the bondholder not a sharer in the profits of the company but a creditor of the corporation—someone to whom the corporation is in debt for $1,000.

Second, a bond also states on its face the *amount of income* it will pay to its bond-holders. A $1,000 bond may declare that it will pay eighty dollars a year as interest. Unlike dividends, this interest payment will not rise if the corporation makes money,

Ownership and Control

One last matter is also of significance in discussing the organization of the corporation. The new mode of structuring enterprise brought a development of great moment for the captains of industry and their successors, the business managers and the bureaucrats. It enabled a small group of men to direct the affairs of an enterprise *even if they did not personally own it.*

As we have seen, stockholders are the actual owners of a corporation. But it is obviously impossible for large numbers of stockholders to meet regularly and run a company. Many large corporations have over a million stockholders. Where could they meet? How could they possibly decide what the company should do? Even in the 1870s, how could shareowners of a large railway company have gathered to run their enterprise?

Therefore all corporations are run by boards of directors elected by the stockholders. At regular intervals, all stockholders are asked to elect or reelect members of the board, each stockholder casting as many votes as the number of shares he or she owns. In turn the board of directors appoints the main officials of the corporation—for example, its president and vice-presidents. In turn the main officials hire the rest of the employees.

As a result, a corporation is something like a private government. It has an electorate—its shareholders. It has an elected governing body—its board of directors. It has an executive—its officials. Needless to say, there are very important differences between a government and a corporation, but it is not too misleading to think of corporations as a means of governing the complicated affairs of a business enterprise.

Moreover, as the number of shareowners grows, power tends to drift into the hands of the board of directors and the officials whom it

---

nor will it fall if it does not. Thus there is no element of profit-sharing in bonds, as there is in stocks. However, there is compensation for this. The risk of owning a bond is much less than that of owning a stock. A bond is a legal obligation of the corporation, which *must* pay interest, and which must buy back the bond itself when a fixed term of years has expired and the bond becomes "due." (If it fails to do so, the bond-holder can sue the corporation.) A stock has no such obligations attached to it, and a share of stock never comes "due." No stockholder can sue a corporation if it fails to pay a dividend. Last, bondholders' claims come ahead of stockholders' if a corporation goes out of business or becomes bankrupt.

appoints. Consequently, it becomes extremely difficult to round up enough votes to elect a slate of directors different from the directors in office. Who, after all, has the money and the time to write to a thousand—much less a million—shareowners, recommending a special candidate? Thus boards of directors tend to become self-perpetuating, each year mailing to the company's stockholders a mail ballot (called a proxy) on which are printed the names of their own candidates—usually themselves. Except in unusual circumstances, the shareowners obediently vote the slate that the directors have designated.* It is easier for a shareholder who "wants out" to sell his company shares than to get a new management in place of the old. (This is not to say that the directors are indifferent to stockholders' opinions, for they are not. All directors are concerned about their company's image, especially if they plan to offer more stocks and bonds for sale at a future date.)

Thus power comes to settle in the hands of a board of directors whose members may own only a tiny fraction of the total outstanding stock of the company. We do not have statistics for the early years of corporate activity, but in 1929 the board of directors of the United States Steel Corporation held in all only 1.4 percent of the company's stock. In contrast, in 1900 Andrew Carnegie had personally owned over half of Carnegie Steel, Ltd. Needless to say, the passing of effective control from the hands of a few wealthy capitalists into the hands of a small group of self-chosen directors further enhanced the change from the captain of industry to the industrial manager.

The Corporation and Economic Growth

The development of the modern corporation did not take place overnight. In Pittsburgh in 1860 there were seventeen foundries, twenty-one rolling mills, seventy-six glass "factories," and forty-seven other manufacturing establishments to be seen, but not a single one of them was incorporated. As late as 1878 in Massachusetts there were only

---

*Once in a while shareholders may receive letters urging them to vote their stock in a certain way. Usually this is when a corporation is the target of a "takeover" attempt—an effort by another corporation to buy enough of its shares to control the company, or even to merge it in its own company. Takeovers are dramatic battles, but they did not stir up the corporate world in its early days because, as we shall subsequently see, corporations were not yet legally authorized to buy stock in other corporations.

520 businesses organized as corporations out of 11,000 manufacturing enterprises, but those 520 corporations already produced one-third of all the state's manufacturing output. By the turn of the century, 70 percent of the industrial labor force worked for corporations and two-thirds of the nation's industrial output was the product of incorporated enterprise. As we will see in our next chapter, the legal powers and flexibility of the corporation changed considerably as various state legislatures altered the requirements for corporate charters. But we can already understand how this enormously important development in social technology assisted in the growth of the economy.

To the robber barons and the captains of industry the corporation offered immediate advantages. The corporation limited their personal financial risk and increased their liquidity—that is, their ability to raise cash by selling their stock. Therefore their ability to move into and out of businesses was vastly increased. The possibility of steering the policy of a large enterprise without necessarily owning a majority of its shares was still another gain for them.

More important in terms of economic growth was the possibility for successful businesses to tap a source of capital that would have been impossible to reach without the limited liability and high liquidity of stocks and bonds. In the early days of enterprise, businessmen had to look to their own resources, or to those of capitalists at home or abroad, to raise the money needed for their operations. Once the market for stocks and bonds was organized, a whole new layer of capital became available among small merchants or moderately well-to-do citizens who were eager to share in the rising fortunes of the great railways and major companies, or who simply wanted a chance to "play the market" in the hope of getting rich quick. Indeed, many of the early railroads were financed by sales of stock to small stockholders.

Fortunately for the captains of industry there was an enormous pool of capital that was available to underwrite industrial expansion in these years. During the last half of the nineteenth century, as a consequence of their increasing real incomes, Americans began to set aside a larger share of their revenues as savings. Before the Civil War, households and businesses channeled about a seventh of their receipts into savings and investment—that is, into the building of new capital. By the 1870s that share had more than tripled.

To put this money to work, a host of new financial institutions emerged—savings banks, commercial banks, life insurance companies, investment houses—to serve as intermediaries between the investors and the corporations. By 1880 well over two million depositors had placed roughly $819 million in savings banks. Two decades later depositors exceeded six million and funds fell just short of $2.5 billion. Because of the role they played in capital formation, financial intermediaries soon became essential for economic expansion. Like the businesses they served, they were themselves incorporated enterprises.

A last, but important, source of capital was foreign investment. Between 1870 and 1900 foreign investment in the United States rose from $1.4 billion to $3.6 billion. Most of this foreign money, writes economic historian Stuart Bruchey, "went into municipal and other local bonds, and into railroads and public utilities, although a few manufacturing firms were also among the recipients."[7]

The Corporation and Capitalism

The corporation was therefore an indispensable adjunct to the machine technology. It was a social invention every bit as powerful as the technical inventions it controlled. To put the rise of the corporation into Fernand Braudel's organizing framework, we can say that the corporation represented a development of economic life that was the cause of vast changes both in material life and in the dynamics of capitalism.

Without the possibilities of management and discipline brought by the corporation—a discipline that extended from managerial heights down to the factory floor—the dazzling advances in speed and volume of output never could have been achieved. Without the vast market for capital that the corporation brought into being and then tapped, the extraordinary increase in physical capital never could have been financed. And without the organizational focus of creative energies that the corporation made possible, the accumulation of capital on so vast a scale never could have taken place. Thus the corporation changed the pace and the dynamics of capitalism as dramatically as it changed the pace and dynamics of business life, for capitalism is, in fact, the larger shape of historical change that emerges from the business process itself.

Notes

[1] David Brody, *Steelworkers in America: The Nonunion Era* (1960), p. 48.

[2] Quoted in J. H. Bridge, *The Inside History of the Carnegie Steel Company* (1903), p. 113.

[3] *The Visible Hand* (1977), p. 121.

[4] *Scale and Scope: The Dynamics of Industrial Capitalism* (1990).

[5] *The Empire of Business* (1902), p. 154.

[6] Quoted in Thomas Cochran and William Miller, *The Age of Enterprise* (1942), p. 141.

[7] *Growth of the Modern American Economy* (1975), p. 87.

Standard Oil gas station, New Jersey, 1927

Chapter 4

FROM TRUST TO ANTITRUST

Thus far we have examined particular elements of the industrialization process—the evolution of the businessman who was its main human agency, and the development of the technologies that were its most powerful material agencies. Now we must put these elements together, watching what happened as the aggressive drive of the business search for profit combined with the new industrial techniques and the new forms of social organization.

THE SPIRIT OF THE AGE

A good way to begin is to put ourselves into the business frame of mind of the late nineteenth century. We tend to think of those years as a time of easy money-making, when everyone prospered and businesses grew effortlessly from small firms into large enterprises.

But that is not at all how things looked to the businessmen of the time. The "Gilded Age"* was a period of extreme business uncertainty. Periods of prosperity were interrupted by long and frequent stretches of business depression. Indeed, of the twenty-five years between 1873 and 1897, fourteen were viewed by contemporaries as times of recession and depression.

*The phrase comes from the title of a book written by Mark Twain with Charles Dudley Warner. Published in 1873, it captured many aspects of the age—its coarse materialism, its speculative fever, and above all, its corruption. To Twain the 1870s were a base age, covered over with an ornate veneer, but lacking substance and quality. Ever since its publication, Twain's title has become a catchword for post–Civil War America.

Panic and Pain

The businessmen of that time were not mistaken: those *were* difficult years. In the terrible debacle that began in 1873 the general price level dropped by a quarter; the rate of business failures doubled; more than half the nation's steel furnaces and rolling mills were idle; the New York Stock Exchange was even shut down for ten days. "Business since 1873," said the *Commercial and Financial Chronicle* at the beginning of 1879—*six years* after the onset of the recession—"has been like a retreating army on the march."[1] Worse still was the depression of 1893, which has been adjudged the most severe in American history, save only for the Great Depression of the 1930s. On December 30, 1893, *Bradstreet's* wrote: "The business year 1893 promises to go into history with heavier net losses in financial, commercial, and industrial circles throughout the United States than in the more severe panic periods in the past eighty years." Indeed, reflecting on his years in the oil business John D. Rockefeller later wrote:

> [I wondered] how we came through them. You know how often I had not an unbroken night's sleep, worrying about how it was all coming out. All the fortune I have made has not served to compensate for the anxiety of the period. Work by day and worry by night, week in and week out, month after month.[2]

Hence business enterprisers did not enter on their search for profit and expansion confident that all would end well. As a guiding mechanism the market was a harsh pacesetter, urging business into hell-for-leather expansion when the outlook seemed bright, exacting terrible penalties when the outlook changed. The expansion of output and the accumulation of wealth took place, not in an atmosphere of security, but in one of "panic and pain," as historian Edward Kirkland has described it.

The Business Cycle

In a word, economic growth did not proceed along a smooth upward path but took the form of booms and busts. Economists call this irregular wavelike motion the *business cycle:* and they attribute it to the very phenomenon we have seen—a rush of business expansion in one period, normally lasting four to five years, followed by a period of doldrums typically lasting another three, four, or five years.*

These business cycles were not a totally new experience in economic life, for we can trace waves of faster and slower growth back to the years before the Civil War. But the industrialization process brought much sharper swings in prosperity and recession. "In the three decades after the Civil War," write Thomas Cochran and William Miller, "as confident entrepreneurs raced to take advantage of every ephemeral rise of prices, of every advance in tariff schedules, of every new market opened by the railroads and puffed up by immigration, they recklessly expanded and mechanized their plants, each seeking the greatest share of the new melon. The more successful they were in capturing such shares and the more efficient they were in promptly satisfying the new market, however, the greater was the number of buildings and machinery left idle when the new market approached the saturation point and the rate of expansion declined."[3]

But the business cycle was more than just the cause for "panic and pain." It was also a prime factor in that concentration of business in fewer hands that we noted in our last chapter. During the years of panic and depression, many smaller, weak firms went under, and bigger, rich firms survived; so that when the cycle was over and the forward movement resumed, the new (and usually larger) volume of production was lodged in a smaller number of firms than before. And then, quite independent of the cycle, the bigger and more aggressive firms pursued expansive strategies of the kind we have seen, forcing competitors to the wall and further accelerating the "concentration" of industry.

Competition and Combination

Thus the struggle for markets brought fear in its wake. "Competition is industrial war," wrote a large manufacturer of envelopes in 1901. ". . . [U]nrestricted competition, carried to its logical conclusion, means

---

*Actually, there is more than one cycle in the pattern of growth. Statisticians identify at least three different cycles: a short one, of one to three years' duration, commonly associated with swings in inventories; a very long cycle of about twenty years, probably the result of swings in housing construction and household formation; and the "regular" seven-to-ten-year cycle we mention above.

death to some of the combatants and injury for all. Even the victor does not soon recover from the wounds received in combat."[4]

The Pittsburgh *Commercial,* a newspaper concerned with the oil industry, bemoaned "a ruinous competition between refineries, by which all parties have lost money."[5] Even the Social Darwinists, who extolled the virtues of the competitive struggle, felt the strain was too much: "The struggle for existence and survival of the fittest is a pretty theory," said George W. Perkins of the Chicago, Burlington and Quincy Railroad, "but it is also a law of nature that even the fittest must live as they go along."

An obvious response to the anxiety and threat of cutthroat competition was for the firms in a given industry to get together and to agree not to undercut one another—to "live and let live." From pre-1865 days—indeed, back to colonial times—this had been a constant aim of businesses in many fields, who formed "pools"—informal agreements on prices—to avoid their suicidal race for markets.

In 1876 the Cleveland *Gazette* described how a pooling arrangement worked on a local steamboat route:

> The object of the pool line (so called because each boat is required to put up a certain amount of its receipts—about 45 percent—each trip into the hands of the treasurer, when it becomes the property of the line) . . . is to maintain a regular rate on freights at Cincinnati and all points on the river, to, and including, Cairo.
>   . . . In case of opposition, the pool boat on "berth" will take freight at figures so low that the opposition will lose money, and the regular boat's rate is made up to the established rate out of the pool's fund. . . . After 60 days a division of the pool money is made, retaining 20 percent of the whole amount to maintain organization. The assessment of the pool is very heavy . . . so that it does not take long to get enough money on hand to make all boats "stick," for, if they do not live up to their agreement, they forfeit all the money they have paid into the pool.

By the 1880s there was a cordage pool, a whiskey pool, a coal pool, a salt pool, and endless rail and other pools. For the growing scale of individual firms provided a strong new impulse to avoid the mutual bloodletting of cutthroat competition. As fixed costs grew, the incentive to take in business at any price was often irresistible.

Yet, none of the pools worked. As soon as business worsened, the need to assure revenues led one firm after another to reduce its prices.

At a meeting of railway managers called to agree on a schedule of freight rates, the president of one railroad slipped out during a brief recess to wire the new rates to his company so that it could be the first to undercut them. "I suppose they will cheat," sighed one railroad executive, "but we can stand a great deal of cheating better than competition."[6]

Trusts and Mergers

The basic reasons that pools could not prevent all-out competition was that they were illegal. A long tradition in English and American law forbade *contracts* in "restraint of trade." Therefore no company could sue another for breaking its "gentleman's agreement."

The failure of the pools did not, however, bring to an end the search for a means of enforcing price discipline. It merely turned that search in a new direction—a direction happily provided by the growing predominance of the new corporate means of organizing business. For the corporation was soon discovered to offer a highly effective way of avoiding the internecine economic wars that upset the business community.

The first businessman to benefit from the new method was John D. Rockefeller. Rockefeller was born in Richford, New York, in 1839. After making a modest fortune in the grain and meat business in Cleveland, he decided to go into the oil business. Rockefeller was an extraordinary businessman. Those who worked with him could not help but admire his decisiveness, his sureness of touch, and his infinite resourcefulness. Rockefeller knew how to fasten upon and make the most of the opportunities that were presented to him. When his inner clock told him that the time was ripe, he was capable of acting with a speed, an authority, and, if it was needed, a ruthlessness that never failed to impress his subordinates.

Rockefeller was a deadly competitor. He forced railroads to give him rebates on his huge oil shipments. He sold below cost in particular communities to steal business from local refiners. Then he gave the refiners a choice: sell out to Standard Oil or face destruction. He also paid bribes to informers to gain information about his competitors' activities.

Because he detested waste, Rockefeller kept close track of every aspect of Standard Oil's complicated affairs. His plants were so

John D. Rockefeller (1839–1937)

efficient that he could undersell competitors and still make enormous profits.* Rockefeller's principal objective was to combine all the refineries in the country into one supercompany. Then the industry could develop in a safe, orderly manner. The architect of Rockefeller's supercompany was Samuel C. T. Dodd, the chief counsel of Standard Oil. Dodd saw that the corporation, with its control vested in a small number of directors, provided a legal means of achieving what could not be done under the common law. His brainchild was the trust—a legal arrangement under which stockholders in a corporation gave their stock to a central board of directors "in trust." The board members were authorized to vote the stock as they wished, while the dividends on the stocks continued to be paid to the shareholders, who had surrendered their stock for trust certificates.

In 1882 Dodd established a trust for Standard Oil that permitted its board of directors to control the overall policies of forty corporations from Standard's headquarters in New York City. Soon the trust idea spread to other industries: there was a sugar trust, a cottonseed oil trust, and a dozen more. By the late 1880s, trusts were a well-nigh ubiquitous feature of industry, much talked about in the press. One commentator said that an average citizen was born to the profit of the milk trust and died to the profit of the coffin trust.

The voting trust was, however, only a stepping stone to a still more effective means of avoiding competition. This was the corporate merger, a very simple device by which one corporation bought up the stock of another, thereby winning control of its price and other policies. Why was such an obvious means not used before? The principal reason was that corporations were not at first allowed by their charters to own stock in other companies. Then in 1889 New Jersey amended its incorporation laws to make mergers possible, and businessmen quickly took advantage of the new law.

Morgan and U.S. Steel

One such businessman was John Pierpont Morgan, the dominant (and domineering) figure of finance at the turn of the century. Morgan lorded over the financial world with a passion for order and a fierce hatred for the financial havoc that competition brought. He also had a

---

*In 1892 Rockefeller's fortune was reported as amounting to $815,647,796.89.[7]

shrewd eye for the profits that could be made by merging warring corporations into one giant firm and then selling the stock of the new giant for more than the combined values of the corporations that comprised it. "I like a little competition," he was quoted as saying, "but I like combination better."[8] Between 1892 and 1902 Morgan was instrumental in merging competitive firms to create such new giant corporations as General Electric, American Telephone and Telegraph, and International Harvester. But the capstone of his career was the formation of the United States Steel Corporation, the first billion-dollar company in American history.

One evening in 1900 Morgan was invited to a dinner of leading industrialists, where Charles Schwab, the dynamic young operating president of Carnegie Steel, sketched out his vision of a unified steel

J. P. Morgan (1837–1913)

industry. We have already mentioned that Carnegie had competitors. Other capitalists had also formed Bessemer-based operations that fought Carnegie in every aspect of his operations. There was the American Can Company, American Steel and Wire, Federal Steel, National Steel, National Tube, American Bridge—a whole regiment of steel-producers. Schwab painted the picture of an industry rid of this competitive duplication of factories and mills, guided by a single great corporation charged with the orderly development of American industrial power. Needless to say, such a vast steel corporation would also be immensely profitable.

Morgan's imagination was kindled. He took Schwab aside and plied him with questions about his absent master. On what terms would Carnegie sell his interests? What companies would be inside the new supercorporation; what ones could safely be left outside? In turn Schwab conferred with Carnegie, and the veteran steel-maker, tired of business, agreed on a price for selling out to Morgan: $492 million, of which $250 million would go to Carnegie, the rest to his partners. Morgan looked at the scrap of paper on which the number was scrawled and brusquely said: "I accept."

Morgan then set about acquiring the other firms he needed for his supercorporation. One of them was American Steel and Wire, controlled by John Gates, a swashbuckling robber baron whose latest scandal had been to risk a million dollars on the turn of a single card. (He lost.) Gates was reluctant to sell. At last Morgan stormed into his office, pounded on the table, and, fixing Gates and his associates with his fierce eyes, said, "Gentlemen, I am going to leave this building in ten minutes. If by that time you have not accepted our offer, the matter will be closed. We will build our own wire plant." Gates capitulated.

The firm assembled by Morgan consisted of Carnegie Steel and its eight largest competitors. It had a capacity of two-thirds of the nation's steel castings and ingots. It embraced every aspect of steel-making from ore beds to finishing plants. It had 156 major factories. It was the largest industrial company the world had ever seen, and the wealthiest. For Morgan sold the shares of the new United States Steel Corporation for $1.4 billion. Of this enormous sum, perhaps $700 million was "water." The shares were bought at their inflated price only because Morgan's prestige convinced investors that their value was real.

THE MERGER MOVEMENT

What Morgan brought to pass in steel was also rapidly coming about—often at Morgan's doing—in many other industries. For beginning in 1898, the merger device was producing a tremendous wave of amalgamation.

The effect of the merger wave was to change the structure of American industry almost overnight. In 1865 most industries were competitive, with no single company dominating any field. By 1904 one or two giant firms—usually put together by merger—controlled at least half the output in seventy-eight different industries. In the locomotive field nineteen firms had shared the market in 1860. Two merger-created firms ruled the roost in 1900. In the biscuit and cracker market—formerly a scatter of tiny companies—one giant merged firm, the National Biscuit Company, controlled the great preponderance of the industry's market. In oil, the Standard Oil Company, under the shrewd and aggressive leadership of John D. Rockefeller, grew from insignificant beginnings in the 1860s to a supercorporation that owned well over 80 percent of the nation's refining capacity by the turn of the century.

Another way of looking at the transformation is to note the change in sheer size. In 1865 it is doubtful if there was a single firm in the

	THE MERGER WAVE	
Year	**Number of Firms Bought**	**Capitalization of Firms Bought (in $ millions)**
1895	43	40.8
1896	26	24.7
1897	69	119.7
1898	303	650.6
1899	1208	2262.7
1900	340	442.2
1901	423	2052.0
1902	379	910.8
1903	142	297.6
1904	79	110.5

United States worth $10 million. In 1896, except for the railroads, there were not a dozen $10-million companies. In 1904, after the merger wave, there were 300 such firms which together owned $20 billion—over 40 percent of all the industrial wealth of the nation. In 1913, two banking groups, one controlled by Morgan and the other by Rockefeller, held thirty-four directorships in twelve corporations with an aggregate capital of more than $22 billion. As two of America's leading economists wrote in 1912, "If the carboniferous age had returned and the earth had repeopled itself with dinosaurs, the change in animal life would scarcely have seemed greater than that which has been made in the business world by these monster corporations."[9]

The Results of Combination

Did the trusts achieve their end? Yes and no. Investigating the course of steel prices from 1880 to 1901, one scholar has discovered that the monthly average price per ton for standard Bessemer rails ranged from $16.50 to $85. For the next fifteen years, following the merger that produced the United States Steel Corporation, they sold for $28 a ton without deviation, save for occasional rush orders. During this period steel prices still fluctuated considerably, and once or twice the price of pig iron rose *above* the price at which rails sold. But rails, which were the main focus of cutthroat competition, held firm. The perils of competition had been effectively eliminated.

In oil, farm machinery, lead, biscuits—in short, in most heavily concentrated industries—one large corporation now emerged by tacit consent as the price-maker, the remaining firms following closely or exactly in its tracks.

We should note, however, that price leadership did not necessarily ensure price stability, despite the extraordinary results in steel rails. Indeed, according to a study prepared by the National Industrial Conference Board in 1929, the trusts as a whole did not diminish the scope of price swings over the business cycle. But we must remember that the purpose of the consolidation movement was not to counteract the business cycle (which was then regarded as beyond the intervention of man), nor was it even to raise prices "unduly." Above all, *the aim of consolidation was to remove the threat of the unrestricted price competition that proved so dangerous for a world of large-scale enterprise.*

Viewed in this light, the combination movement was a considerable success, for it did mute price competition. Yet, surprisingly, the merger movement never succeeded in wholly stamping out competition by other means. In fact, one of the most interesting findings about the trusts is that the shares of the market commanded by the great corporate giants steadily declined, as smaller and more aggressive firms stole business away from the large conservative monoliths, or as new firms were formed to enter the industry. In the following table we see the steady erosion of the market share of the biggest firms over time:

SHARE OF MARKET OF LEADING MERGERS		
	At Time of Merger	Later Date
U.S. Steel (1901)	62%	40% (1920)
Standard Oil (1882)	90+	64 (1911)
Int'l. Harvester (1902)	85	64 (1918)
Anaconda Copper (1895)	39	12 (1920)
Am. Can Co. (1901)	90	50 (1913)

Thus the trusts were a mixed success. They did mitigate the severity of the price competition that had demoralized business for so long. They did not, however, secure monopoly positions, or even commanding shares of the markets, for the biggest firms. And perhaps most important of all, by their very efforts to achieve economic success, the trusts brought upon themselves the political animus of the nation. Let us next follow that development.

THE ANTITRUST MOVEMENT

Popular Opposition to the Trusts

Grass-roots opposition to the trust movement was a sentiment of long standing. What historian Arthur Dudden has called a "simmering ferment of anti-monopolistic ideas" was discernible through most of the late nineteenth century: "The corners and pools of the eighteen sixties and seventies," he wrote, "the oil trust of the seventies together with its imitators of the eighties, and the multitudinous mergers and consolidations throughout, were assailed by their detractors not only as particular evils but as overall manifestations of foreboding portent."[10]

These antitrust feelings were at first of little importance. Then, as the railway pools began to squeeze the small businessman and the farmer, voices began to rise in protest. A resolution passed in 1873 by the Illinois State Farmers Association read:

> Resolved, that the railways of the world, except in those countries where they have been held under the strict regulation and supervision of the government, have proved themselves arbitrary, extortionate, and as opposed to free institutions and free commerce between states as were the feudal barons of the middle ages.[11]

Labor organizations, such as the Knights of Labor and the American Federation of Labor, also feared the rise of mighty concentrations of business power: "The great corporations, the trusts, with their capital, their machinery, special privileges and other advantages, are overwhelming the individual, reducing him to the condition of a mere tool, to be used in their great undertakings for their individual profit, and of no more consequence than a dumb piece of machinery," wrote John Hayes of the Knights.

And by no means least influential, a group of journalists began to call attention to the practices of the robber barons. Probably the most important critic of monopoly in these years was Henry George, a San Francisco journalist. His *Progress and Poverty,* published in 1879, was not merely a tract for the times but a major text in American social criticism. The central question to which George addressed himself was one that Americans are still wrestling with: why is economic progress accompanied by poverty? George blamed poverty on the fact that private individuals could own advantageously situated land. Because this land was strategically located, landlords could charge exorbitant rents for their property, even if they had not done anything to improve it. This was immoral, George argued. Land was valuable only because people lived on it and used it. An acre in an empty desert was worthless. Expressed differently, society was the true creator of wealth. The rent that landlords charged for unimproved land should be taken by the government and used for public purposes. This single, massive tax on land, George believed, would destroy monopolies, distribute wealth more equitably, and eliminate poverty.

In *Wealth Against Commonwealth,* published in 1894, Henry Demarest Lloyd excoriated big business in general and the Standard Oil Company in particular. Lloyd's book, detailing the transgressions of the great oil company, was the first of a series of what would later be called "muckraking" exposés that would do much to mobilize outrage against the tactics of business aggrandizement and the general indifference, not to say contempt, evidenced by business for the public.*

As a consequence of all these protests, public sentiment began to change. Significantly, whereas the Anti-Monopoly Party polled but 173,000 votes in the election of 1884, four years later even the Republican Party declared itself against "all combinations of capital organized in trusts," and Democratic President Grover Cleveland asserted that the people were being "trampled to death" beneath the iron heels of the trusts. Clearly a new political theme was being sounded; as Henry Demarest Lloyd wrote, "If the tendency to combination is irresistible, the control of it is imperative." By 1890 twenty-one states had attempted to curb monopoly with antitrust statutes of varying kinds.

The Regulation of Enterprise

The question was: What to do? By the early 1890s one remedy had been tried and was found wanting. Many states had gone to court to sue the trusts on the grounds that they were "restraining" trade— Louisiana sued the cottonseed trust, Nebraska the whiskey trust, New York the sugar trust, Ohio the almighty oil trust. Yet, although the states generally won their court cases, the trusts were not so easily

---

*Muckrakers were investigative journalists who dramatized the need for reform by casting a searching light on dark corners of American life. These writers dug into public records and interviewed anyone with knowledge about whatever subject they were investigating. They were given their name by Theodore Roosevelt, who compared them to the man with the muckrake in John Bunyan's *Pilgrim's Progress,* whose attention was so fixed on "the filth of the floor" that he could not notice the "celestial crown" that was offered him in exchange. Despite the implication, "muckraker" became a term of honor.

vanquished. As we have seen, they abandoned the "trusteeship" idea, only to achieve the same dominating effect through mergers and other corporate devices, or simply by moving their headquarters from a state in which they were being attacked to another, more obliging one.

It was the failure to achieve control over the trust at the state level that brought pressure on Congress to intervene at the federal level. The first target was the railroads, now accused by merchants all over the country of charging exorbitant rates. One newspaper in Sacramento, California, for example, published a schedule of freight rates between that city and a number of points in Nevada, showing that far lower rates had been charged by wagon-teams before the railroad was built! In addition, there was growing outrage at such practices as charging more for some short hauls than for long hauls, or for the nefarious granting of secret rebates or kickbacks to favored shippers.

The Interstate Commerce Commission

In a mood of indignation Congress passed the Interstate Commerce Act of 1887, establishing the first federal *regulatory agency,* the Interstate Commerce Commission. As its title makes clear, the commission was limited to the regulation of railroad rates in interstate commerce, for the Constitution had specifically provided Congress with the authority only to regulate commerce between the states. The act declared that railroad rates must be "reasonable and just," that railroads had to publish their rate schedules, and that most of their shadier practices, such as granting rebates, were unlawful.

The ICC had immense obstacles to overcome. To begin with, the law itself was obscure: What was a "reasonable and just" freight charge? In its *First Annual Report,* the Committee stated:

Of the duties devolved upon the Commission by the act to regulate commerce, none is more perplexing than that of passing upon complaints made of rates as being unreasonable. The question of the reasonableness of rate involves so many considerations and is affected by so many circumstances and conditions which may at first blush seem foreign, that it is quite impossible to deal with on purely mathematical principles, or on any principles whatever, without a consciousness that no conclusion which may be reached can by demonstration be shown to be absolutely correct.[12]

Yet another difficulty the commission had to contend with was the flood of requests for action that it received. Over a thousand cases were presented to its tiny staff in its first few months of existence. And not least, the ICC had no way of enforcing its decisions except to sue in the federal courts.

Taking advantage of the confusion, the railroads paid little attention to the commission, often continuing to charge their high rates even after the commission had directed them not to. Four or five years later, when the erring railroad was finally brought to court, the roads generally gained from judicial interpretations of the law that gave the benefit of every doubt to the railroads and that regarded the new federal authority with grave suspicions. Of sixteen cases brought to the Supreme Court between 1887 and 1905, fifteen were decided in favor of the railroads. One railroad executive announced that "there is not a road in the country that can be accused of living up to the rules of the Interstate Commerce Law."[13]

In time the situation changed. The powers of the ICC were gradually expanded and its staff enlarged. By the beginning of the twentieth century the commission was effectively regulating the rates on virtually all rail transportation, and no railroad dared flout its rulings.* Ironically, by the midpoint of the twentieth century, the ICC had become the *protector* of the railroads, establishing freight schedules for trucking that prevented this new, aggressive form of freight-handling from undermining the dwindling profits of "their" industry. This conversion of an agency charged with the suppression of abuses into an agency concerned with the protection of its client industry has since been many times repeated, as the ICC model was extended into other fields—banking, food inspection, communications, drugs, airlines.

The Sherman Act

Regulation, however initially ineffective, was not the only sign of a gradual swing of public sentiment against the big corporations. Equally important was the growing movement that we call

---

*This was largely due to the passage of the Hepburn Act (1906), which, among other powers, gave the ICC the authority to inspect the books of railroad companies and reduce unreasonable rates on the complaint of a shipper, subject to the review of federal courts.

"antitrust"—a movement designed to break up the big companies and to restore competition rather than to restrain it.

Like the simmering discontent against the trusts because of their abuse of power, there had long existed an undercurrent of mingled fear and dislike directed against them sheerly because they represented a threat to the ideal of democratic equality. A strain of "populist," anti-wealth, anti-big-business ideas had always tinctured American thought, even in the years of all-out celebration of wealth. Gradually that strain received popular support as the trusts waxed fat and the books of the muckrakers began to make a deep popular impression. By 1890 the political feeling had swelled to such an extent that a bill directed against the trusts—the Sherman Antitrust Act—passed Congress without a murmur of dissent: 52 to 1 in the Senate, unanimously in the House.

The Sherman Act declared that "every contract, combination in form of trust or otherwise, or conspiracy in restraint of trade among the several States . . . is hereby declared to be illegal," and "that every person who shall monopolize or attempt to monopolize or combine or conspire with any other person to monopolize any part of trade or commerce among the several States . . . shall be deemed guilty of a misdemeanor." This surely seemed a radical departure for a nation that had always extolled its business leaders and admired their exploits. How did such a bill pass through a highly conservative Congress whose Senate was called—with good reason, as we have seen—"The Millionaires Club"?

Looking backward we can see a number of explanations. The mood of the country was strongly "antitrust," and the bill satisfied the need of Congress to go to the electorate and declare that it had passed a bill to punish the trusts. Then, too, the bill did not really break new ground in its economic philosophy but merely moved the long-standing disapproval of monopoly from the exclusive concern of the states to the mixed concern of the states and the federal government. Another reason was the genuine desire of Congress to "do something" about the trusts, although no one was able to say exactly what should be done: the bill in its general condemnation of monopoly seemed as good an answer as any. And then there was the knowledge that the actual impact of the law would depend on the interpretation of the judiciary, which in turn could be depended on for a conservative reading of the law.

Business Ignores Antitrust

Certainly Congress was correct in not expecting the law to make a great change. Most business leaders simply ignored it. Testifying before the Stanley Committee investigating the United States Steel Corporation, Carnegie was nonchalant about the Sherman Act: "Do you really expect men engaged in an active struggle to make a living at manufacturing to be posted about laws and their decisions, and what is applied here, there, and everywhere?" Pressed further, as to whether his lawyers might not have advised him about the law, he answered: "Nobody ever mentioned the Sherman Act to me, that I remember."[14] Carnegie's indifference must have been widespread, for, as we have seen, the merger movement gained its greatest impetus in the decade *following* the passage of the Sherman Act. Thus if the act was supposed to halt the growth of trusts, it clearly failed.

The failure was traceable in large part to the extremely conservative interpretation that the Supreme Court put on the law, as expected. In the first important case in 1895, *U.S.* v. *E.C. Knight Co.,* involving the American Sugar Company's control over 98 percent of the nation's refining capacity, the judges decreed 8 to 1 that the company's mergers concerned *manufacture* and therefore did not fall within the scope of interstate *commerce.* How the trust could have disposed of all that sugar without selling it in many different states the high court did not say. In the face of such decisions, we can understand why a humorist of the times wrote, "What looks like a stone wall to a layman is a triumphal arch to the corporation lawyer."

Following the Court's conservative interpretation, the Sherman Act lay dormant, having virtually no effect in breaking up the trusts or slowing down the process of business amalgamation. Then, in 1902, the act was rejuvenated. In that year President Theodore Roosevelt ordered his Attorney General to prosecute the Northern Securities Company under the Sherman Antitrust Act. The Northern Securities Company was a corporation formed by J. P. Morgan to control the Northern Pacific, the Great Northern, and the Chicago, Burlington and Quincy railroads, giving it a monopoly of western transportation. The Court dissolved the Northern Securities Company in 1904, earning for Roosevelt the sobriquet "trust-buster." Roosevelt also initiated a suit against the Standard Oil Company, which was adjudicated under Taft in 1911. Although the Court dissolved the Standard Oil Trust, the Standard

Oil Company of New Jersey promptly reorganized as a holding company (a corporation that owned stock in other corporations) to re-establish direct control over some seventy companies that had been severed from it by the antitrust decision.*

The Effect of Antitrust

Thus, just as in the case of regulation, it is difficult to claim that the immediate aims of the antitrust movement were achieved. Even today, after the Sherman law has been strengthened by other legislation, many economists doubt whether the dynamics of industrial concentration have been much affected by efforts to curb the tendency toward monopoly. Yet, as is also the case with regulation, perhaps it is possible to see the problem from a perspective that does not focus directly on the success or failure of the legislation.

For in retrospect what seems most significant about the Sherman Act or the ICC and its subsequent regulatory agencies is the expression of a new concern on the part of the national government. We have seen how the expansion of business size was intimately related to the whole process of industrialization. During the early years of that process, the change in the texture and scale of business life was a matter of indifference to the national government. Indeed, the government watched with admiration as the captains of industry built a mighty

---

*Roosevelt, it should be noted, never opposed giant corporations because of their sheer size. Indeed, he believed that big corporations were more efficient than smaller ones, and that competition among behemoths in the same field would be dangerous and wasteful. Such companies, he believed, should be allowed to combine and cooperate, but they should not be allowed to use their size or power to tyrannize small producers and the consuming public. To neutralize the power of the great corporations he supported measures to extend the control of the federal government over the national economy, such as the creation of a Bureau of Corporations (1903) to investigate business practices. Only a forceful government could subject big business to a measure of control, he argued—but he continued to apply subjective standards to differentiate "bad" trusts that should be subject to control from "good" ones that should not.

On the other hand, what Roosevelt did oppose was the arrogance of big-monied men. This personal resentment became particularly clear during the anthracite coal strike of 1902, when 140,000 miners demanded a pay raise, a shorter workday, and recognition of their union, the United Mine Workers. When the coal operators imperiously refused to negotiate, Roosevelt settled the strike by threatening to use federal troops to operate the mines. The miners won a modest raise and a shorter work day, but the owners did not have to recognize the union. According to Roosevelt, everyone had received a "square deal."

President Theodore Roosevelt exterminating the
"bad" trusts and restraining the "good" trusts

industrial economy; and both state and federal legislatures were gener-
ous with help to hasten that process along.

Slowly, however, another view began to manifest itself—a view
quite different from the uncritical approval of business expansion and
private enrichment so characteristic of attitudes at the beginning of the
period of industrialization. In 1890, ex-President Rutherford B. Hayes,
certainly no radical, wrote in his diary about the "wrong and evils of
the money-piling tendency of our country." Theodore Roosevelt,
though deeply concerned about the "socialistic" tendencies of reformers like Henry Demarest Lloyd, nevertheless shared their disdain for
what he called the "malefactors of great wealth": "I am unable to make
myself take the attitude of respect toward the very wealthy men which
such an enormous number of people evidently feel," he wrote. As we
have seen, it was under Roosevelt's presidency that the first efforts
were made to enforce antitrust legislation against the "bad" trusts.

Woodrow Wilson was even more outspoken in his crusade against the trusts. Unlike Roosevelt, Wilson did not believe in government regulation of big business. Rather, he wanted to use the antitrust laws to break up monopolies. This would restore competition, make business more efficient, and release anew the individualism that had made America a rich and powerful nation. "If monopoly persists," he wrote, "monopoly will always sit at the helm of government. I do not expect monopoly to restrain itself. If there are men in this country big enough to own the government of the United States, they are going to own it."[15] Under Wilson the Federal Trade Commission and the Clayton Antitrust Act (both passed in 1914) greatly strengthened the hand of government vis-à-vis the corporation.*

A Final View

How can we sum up this complicated chapter of economic history? It would be wrong to view the tendency to giant size or to monopoly as an indication of evil intentions on the part of business. The captains of industry, seeking to aggrandize their firms by price competition or by merger, were only following the profit incentive that is the legitimate

---

*The Federal Trade Commission was empowered to conduct investigations of huge business corporations. The Clayton Act outlawed interlocking directorates—that is, it made it illegal for directors of one corporation to be directors of other corporations in the same field—and provided that the directors of a company that violated the antitrust laws could be held personally accountable for their actions. In addition, the law stated that labor unions were *not* to be considered "combinations in restraint of trade." This was, of course, a great victory for labor, into which we will look further in our next chapter.

Two other pieces of legislation signed into law under Wilson are worthy of mention. One of these was the Underwood Tariff Act of 1913, which, in addition to lowering the protective tariff, provided for a graduated income tax. This was possible because the Sixteenth Amendment, authorizing federal income taxes, had just been ratified.

Second was the Federal Reserve Act (1913). At the time of its passage the Federal Reserve Act was intended mainly to assure stability and orderliness to the nation's banking system which was then subject only to the regulation of the states. Gradually, however, the Federal Reserve System became a mechanism for regulating the amount of credit (loans) that its member banks could authorize. By the time of the Great Depression in the 1930s, the Federal Reserve System had become recognized as the "monetary authority" of the nation, the central agency responsible for regulating the amount of spending power, mainly in the form of bank deposits, available to the country.

objective of market behavior. Although their tactics were outlandish by present-day standards, their motives were beyond reproach. Rather, we must see the emergence of giant corporations and of trusts and mergers as the natural, even the logical, outcome of this motivation coupled with the new technologies of mass production and corporate organization that we have previously examined.

In a word, mergers (and before them, trusts and pools) sought to accomplish "horizontally" what the integration movement had accomplished "vertically," namely to remove the disturbing influences of the marketplace from the production and distribution of commodities. Mergers, like vertical integrations, were efforts to replace the invisible hand of market forces with the visible hand of managerial administration.

The businessman was not to blame for this turn of events: he was only the agent of economic forces and developments beyond his control. But the businessman was never the only, though he may have been the dominant, figure in the social system. As the reach and power of business organizations increased, other elements within the body politic began to search for effective countermeasures to be applied against the emerging business monoliths. There was only one agency capable of applying those countermeasures—the government. Thus, from many quarters pressure mounted to use the government as a deliberate force to contain or guide or even inhibit business growth.

As we have seen, the application of government power was halting, was at best only partially effective, and was even used, in the regulatory system, to bolster the fortunes of portions of the business world.* This outcome is hardly surprising. The regulation or curtailment of business does not easily accord with the basic beliefs in "free" and "private" enterprise that underlie the capitalist market system. More-

---

*A school of "revisionist" historians, challenging the conventional interpretations of political and economic history, contends that much of the regulatory or antitrust sentiment came from big business itself, eager to establish rules of behavior that would eliminate the smaller concerns nibbling at their markets. Gabriel Kolko has presented the most effective case for this view in *The Triumph of Conservatism* (1963) and *Railroads and Regulation* (1965). His general contention that "big business led the struggle for the federal regulation of the economy" is still under debate. But there is no doubt that some business leaders did cooperate with the government in seeking a means to achieve through legislation what business could not do by itself—namely, to lessen the pressure exercised against major firms by the price and standards-cutting behavior of smaller companies.

over, efforts to interfere with the natural expansive tendencies of business threaten to dampen the expansive forces of the economy itself. A society that depends on the workings of a business system cannot easily interfere with the dynamics of that system.

Yet it would be wrong to conclude this chapter on a note that stresses the unsolved aspects of controlling big business, although that problem is still very much with us. Rather, we should come away with two conclusions:

The first is that the process of economic growth, though lodged mainly within business enterprises, has gradually required the intervention of government—in part to protect the market mechanism from destroying itself, in part to assert the claims of the larger society over the blind workings of that mechanism. The unresolved question is not whether government should intervene, but where, and how far.

The second is that economic growth, which we have hitherto considered mainly as a force for economic expansion, is also a force for profound structural change. With this change come problems for which no immediate or easy social solution may be at hand. More and more, as we proceed with our theme, this disturbing aspect of economic growth will come to our attention.

Notes

[1]Quoted in Norman S. B. Gras and Henrietta Larson, *Casebook in American Business History* (1939), p. 718.

[2]Quoted in Edward C. Kirkland, *Dream and Thought in the Business Community* (1956), p. 9.

[3]*The Age of Enterprise* (1942), p. 139.

[4]Quoted in Gabriel Kolko, *The Triumph of Conservatism* (1963), p. 13.

[5]Quoted in Allan Nevins, *A Study in Power* (1953) 1:96.

[6]Quoted in Thomas Cochran, *Railroad Leaders* (1953), p. 163.

[7]Nevins, *A Study in Power,* p. 613.

[8]Quoted in John Tipple, "The Robber Baron in the Gilded Age," in H. Wayne Morgan (ed.), *The Gilded Age* (1963), p. 26.

[9]J. B. and J. M. Clark, *The Control of Trusts,* pp. 14–15.

[10]Arthur Dudden, "Men Against Monopoly," *Journal of the History of Ideas* (October 1957), 587–88.

[11]Quoted in Jonathan Periam, *The Groundswell* (1874), p. 286.

[12]Interstate Commerce Commission, *First Annual Report* (1887), p. 36.

[13]Quoted in John A. Garraty, *The New Commonwealth* (1968), pp. 119–20.

[14]Quoted in E. C. Kirkland, *Industry Comes of Age* (1961), p. 323.

[15]Quoted in Richard Hofstadter, *The Age of Reform* (1955), p. 231.

Pre-1920 Ford Motor Co. assembly line

Chapter 5
WORKERS AND WORK

The end of our last chapter provides a good beginning for this one. Until now, we have examined economic growth as if it were a process that mainly affected business. This is because business enterprise, as we have seen, was the agency through which the process of growth was expressed and by which the forces of growth were mobilized. Economic growth in a capitalist market system is set into motion by business expansion, and it makes sense, therefore, to focus initially on the individuals, the techniques, and the problems associated with that business effort.

Yet, as our first pages indicated, we mean more by "economic growth" than just the expansion of output that was its most striking result from a business point of view. Growth was also a process that changed American society at every level, bringing new ways of life, new stresses and strains, new difficulties as well as new advantages and improvements. In our next chapter we will look again into some of the social aspects of the process of industrial transformation. But first we must examine an attribute of the changing society that is closely associated with the development of business, though submerged beneath it. This is the effect that economic expansion—specifically, industrialization—exerted on the working men and women whose energies were harnessed within the business system.

THE CONDITIONS OF WORK

Homestead

Let us start by taking a tour of a great new steel mill that Andrew Carnegie built on the banks of the Monongahela River in 1879. When the site was chosen, Homestead, Pennsylvania, was a hamlet of 600 people. By 1892 the population had swelled to 11,000. Almost every able-bodied man and youth worked in the sixty-acre assemblage of sheds—there were 3,800 employees, including the mayor of the town who worked as an assistant roller earning $65 a month. This was a good wage, considerably above the forty dollars per month average earnings of manufacturing workers. And prices were far lower than they are today: One could keep body and soul together on those wages, especially if more than one member of the family worked or if the family had a small vegetable garden or kept a cow.

We do not know what Homestead looked like before the mill was built; in all likelihood it was another sleepy Pennsylvania town, with a few stores, and a generally rural air. By 1892 that rural aspect had vanished. The Monongahela was so polluted with wastes from the mill that it was said no self-respecting microbe would live there (perhaps just as well, since many a typhoid microbe lived in the Ohio River near Pittsburgh). Cinders and dust covered the area—even the trees were gray with soot, except after a heavy rain. Hamlin Garland, a novelist, found the vista depressing:

> The streets of the town were horrible; the buildings poor; the sidewalks were swaying, sunken and full of holes. . . . Everywhere the yellow mud of the street lay kneaded into a sticky mass, through which groups of pale lean men slouched in faded garments, grimy with soot and grease of the mills.[1]

Life was certainly hard in Homestead, and in dozens of industrial towns like it. The men worked every day of the year except Christmas and July 4th, twelve hours each day except for a swing shift every other week when they worked twenty-four hours straight. There were no lunch periods, no shower rooms, only primitive sanitary facilities. When the day was over the men sloshed off the dirt in the same troughs in which they washed their tools and trudged home for an exhausted sleep—perhaps stopping for a drink at one of the many saloons on Eighth Avenue.

Inside the mills a fearful scene greeted Garland's eye. In the furnace room he saw "pits gaping like the mouth of hell and ovens emitting a terrible degree of heat, with grimy men filling and lining them. One man jumps down, works desperately for a few minutes, and is then

Work in a steel mill

pulled up, exhausted. Another immediately takes his place. . . ."[2]
Garland spoke to the men about the heat. They told him he was lucky
he was there in the winter.

A modern historian of the Carnegie mill describes some of the less
arduous jobs as follows:

> Pressure work in the rolling, blooming, and plate mills (as contrasted to
> hot jobs) was cooler but equally nerve-racking, due to the incessant
> vibration of the machinery and the maddening screech of cold saws rip-
> ping through steel. In time the men became hard of hearing. The din
> within the huge sheds forced them to yell to each other all day long.
> They and their clothes were covered with miniscule [*sic*], shiny grains of

steel. They complained about respiratory ailments and drank liquor after work, as one man said, to 'take the dust out of my throat.'[3]

Work was dangerous as well as hard. We do not have precise statistics of industrial safety for those years, but we know that in a single year 195 men were killed in Pittsburgh's iron and steel mills: twenty-two from hot metal explosions, five from asphyxiation, ten from rolling accidents, twenty-four falling from heights or into the pits. Men worked only inches away from white-hot metal; terrible burns were frequent. In the hot departments the steel floors hissed when water was poured on them. In 1893 Homestead alone had sixty-five accidents, seven of them fatal, two necessitating amputations. Not a cent of recompense was paid for most injuries or even for death—not because Carnegie was a mean-spirited employer—on the contrary, "Andy" was admired and even loved by his men—but because the idea of workmen's compensation had not taken hold in American industry.

The United States as a whole had an appalling industrial accident rate, one of the highest in the Western world. Between 1880 and 1900, some 35,000 workers were killed annually and another 536,000 were injured. Coal mining was the most hazardous occupation. According to some estimates, three miners were killed every two days in the anthracite fields. Some died of accidents (roof collapses, faulty explosives, runaway coal buggies); others of gas poisoning or lung disorders.

It is a chilling picture. Of course we must be careful not to assume that work everywhere in America was as arduous, dangerous, and exhausting. Only a small fraction of the total labor force was exposed to the full rigors of the industrial work process. Total employment in all the iron and steel mills of the nation amounted to less than 1 percent of the jobs in the country. Yet, for reasons that will become clear as we go along, the experience of the industrial force was as decisive for our future as was the experience of trustification, which affected far fewer than 1 percent of all the business firms in America.

Immigrant Labor

But we are not quite finished with our tour. As we go about the plant we notice another thing: how "foreign-looking" so many of the work-

ers are. We are right—about a third of all workers in 1870 in manufacturing industries were foreign-born, perhaps more than a third in
"dirty" industries such as steel. By 1907, over four-fifths of the laborers
in the Carnegie plants of Allegheny County were eastern Europeans.*

We have already seen how significant was the contribution of immigrant labor before the Civil War. Now, with the full-scale advent of
industrialization, the role of immigration in providing a labor force
became even more indispensable for the expanding business system.
After the Civil War, the costs and stresses of ocean voyages were
reduced. The cost of a steerage ticket ranged from ten dollars to
twenty dollars, while steamers took only one week to cross the ocean.
Driven by hunger and lured by visions of a promised land, beginning
in the third quarter of the century, immigrants arrived in enormous
numbers: 138,000 in 1878, 789,000 in 1882; in all, over 6 million
between 1877 and 1890; fourteen million from 1860 to 1900! The
immigrants brought extraordinary vitality and sometimes business acumen. But the greater part of them were pressed into the service of the
industrial sector where they helped sustain the momentum of expan-

---

*Before the 1880s most immigrants had come from western and northern Europe, espe-
cially from England, Ireland, Germany, and the Scandinavian countries. In the 1880s the
immigrant stream began to flow from a different source—southern and eastern Europe.
Among the new ethnic stocks were Hungarians, Greeks, Italians, Russians, and Jews
from Poland and Russia. In 1851 one lone Russian immigrant had entered the United
States; in 1890, 35,600 stepped ashore. Between 1881 and 1891, 135,000 Russian Jews
left for America. In 1880 New York held 12,000 foreign-born Italians. By 1900, 145,000
lived in the city. Although many of these newcomers succumbed to waves of nostalgia
for their old homelands, only about 24 percent of the immigrants who arrived between
1870 and 1900 returned to the Old World. In fact, they struggled to save their money in
order to bring other family members over. By 1900, about one-half of all steerage passengers arrived on steamship tickets prepaid by such sacrifices.

To adjust to city life, immigrants from each country or district tended to cluster
together in the same neighborhoods. In 1890, Jacob Riis, a New York reporter, wrote
that a map of the city showing where different nationalities lived would have "more
stripes than the skin of a zebra, and more colors than any rainbow." These ethnic communities took on the character of a small city. They offered people right off the boat in
the strange new world of America a chance to hold on to a few fragments of the world
they had left. There the immigrants could find people who spoke their language,
houses of worship and clubs based on old-country models, and foods they were accustomed to. The ethnic neighborhood also served as a haven against the outside world. It
protected the newcomers while they prepared themselves for the hardships they would
have to overcome.

sion, first by providing sheer labor power, second by holding down wages and thereby enabling businessmen to reap larger profits which were plowed back into still more expansion.

Mainly between the ages of fifteen and forty, poor and unskilled, the immigrants were drawn like iron filings to a magnet toward the growing industrial centers of work. By 1880 immigrants made up 80 percent of the populations of New York, Cleveland, Detroit, Milwaukee, and Chicago. There they took on jobs at pay that native-born American working men and women would not accept. "Immigrants work for almost nothing and seem to be able to live on wind—something which I cannot do," said one American worker. Another objected that immigration brought wages "below the bread line."[4] A reporter, Margaret Byington, inquiring into weekly wages at Homestead in 1907, found that native white Americans averaged twenty-two dollars; English-speaking Europeans (mainly Irish and Scots), sixteen dollars; "Slavs" (Slovaks, Croats, Magyars, Russians, Italians), a miserable twelve dollars.

It was not just in steel that the immigrant played a major role in providing the muscle power and the docility that enabled crushing work to be performed at cheap rates. Upton Sinclair, describing the Chicago stockyards in his famous novel *The Jungle,* published in 1906, wrote about "Hunkies" and "Polacks" who performed their work in a sea of blood and miasma of fetid stench. In the West 9,000 Chinese toiled on the plains and in the mountains, building the Central Pacific transcontinental line. In the cities of the East, sweat-shop industries, such as clothing, were "manned"—we need quotation marks because so many workers were women—by immigrant Jews, largely from Poland and Russia.

Labor's Attitude Changes

Immigrants fitted into the picture in yet another way. Because they were often from peasant backgrounds, unused to the ways of city life, and because they had much less independence than native workers— if they lost a job there was often no family to turn to—immigrants were much less likely to join the labor unions of the time. Not only did employers find it easier to persuade them not to unionize, but American workingmen were reluctant to admit "foreigners" into their union lodges.

Unions were, of course, regarded with suspicion and antipathy by almost all employers. Not only were they regarded as a direct threat to profits, but their very existence was seen as a challenge to the ideal of benign parental authority that employers believed to be the proper relation of the owner to "his" working people. Moreover, these feelings were shared by many workers, some of whom had been trained to look up to and respect their "betters," others of whom believed fervently in the American dream of rising from humble origins to wealth and power, and who saw in union membership the surrender of this ideal.

But the gradual change in the environment of work and the breaking down of the older personal relations between the "boss" and his workers began to make these sentiments outmoded. In 1860 the average factory had fewer than ten employees. By 1900 the McCormick reaper plant had 4,000 employees, the Baldwin locomotive works 8,000. Looking at the nation as a whole in 1900, about 1,100 companies had payrolls of more than 500 workers and 443 had more than 1,000 wage earners. The factories of such big companies had to be run like armies. Like the railroads, they required a chain of command in which the scope and limits of each individual's authority and responsibility was clearly defined, and a body of elaborate rules which defined the roles and functions of everyone holding a position in the organization.

Many of the new rules that accompanied the growth of industrialism were degrading. In a Rochester, New York, carriage factory, each worker was known by his number. If he wanted a drink of water he had to get his foreman's permission. To make sure that he did so, the water faucets were locked up. In a Massachusetts tannery, guards patrolled the shop and reported any worker who talked during the day. Because of such draconian rules, workers began to complain that they were being treated like prisoners in a penitentiary. Instead of being responsible to a boss who knew their needs and with whom they were in daily contact, workingmen were now accountable to an impersonal foreman who usually did the hiring and firing. ". . . I never do my talking to the hands," said a New England mill owner, "I do all my talking to the overseers."[5] This new state of affairs was summarized in 1883 by a brass worker:

Well, I remember that fourteen years ago the workmen and the foremen and the boss were all as one happy family; it was just as easy and as free to speak to the boss as anyone else, but now the boss is superior, and the men all go to the foremen; but we would not think of looking the foremen in the face now any more than we would the boss.[6]

Unionization

Unionization was thus labor's response to the problems of technology and large-scale organization, just as trustification was the response of business. Actually, unions of workingmen were very old—we can trace them back to colonial times. But they were mainly unions of craftsmen—skilled workers who joined together to form local mutual-benefit associations and to bargain with employers over wages and working conditions. Indeed, as late as 1860 only 0.1 percent of the labor force was organized.

The idea of a nationwide labor union was slower in coming. In 1866 the so-called National Labor Union was formed in Baltimore. It was an amorphous body, composed of sovereign constituent units and embracing at its height somewhere between 200,000 and 400,000 members. Its financial strength, however, lagged far behind its numerical strength. In 1870, the union's best fiscal year, its expenses were nearly double its receipts. The primary objective of the National Labor Union was to abolish the wage system and to inaugurate worker-owned cooperatives. "By cooperation," said William Sylvis, the union's first president, "we will become a nation of employers—the employers of our own labor. The wealth of the land will pass into the hands of those who produce it."[7] The National Labor Union was short-lived—little wonder, with such ambitious plans and such weak finances.

The Knights of Labor and the AFL

Of longer duration were the Knights of Labor, founded in Philadelphia in 1869. Originally a secret organization with an elaborate ritual, the Knights tried to organize—with the exception of liquor dealers, gamblers, bankers, and lawyers—into one "great brotherhood." Under the leadership of Uriah Stephens, a garment-cutter who had once studied for the ministry, the Knights were an idealistic organization, more interested in the "rights of man" than in the dollar-and-cents concerns of the wage-earner.

By 1879 the Knights claimed some 9,000 members. In that same year the Knights were taken over by Terence V. Powderly, a Pennsylvania machinist and one-time mayor of Scranton, Pennsylvania. While Powderly was in office the Knights abandoned secrecy and opened their ranks to women, blacks, immigrants, and unskilled workers—a radical step in a period when most craft unions would admit none of them. In addition, the Knights came out in favor of the eight-hour workday at a time when ten hours was the norm. Curiously, Powderly matched his radical view of membership requirements with an extremely conservative view of his union's role. His principal objective was to organize society on a cooperative rather than a capitalistic basis. Because he believed so fervently in cooperation, Powderly refused to sanction strikes, engage in collective bargaining, or recognize any discernible difference between labor and management. Paradoxically, it was not until the Knights won several important strikes in the 1880s, despite Powderly's disapproval of them, that it became a significant organization. By 1886 some 700,000 workers belonged to the union. But this was far more than the central leadership could control. Hence its subsequent fall was as meteoric as its rise. The rank and file called strikes that failed. Workers became discouraged and dropped out of the union. Then the Knights were blamed, quite unfairly, for a bombing incident in Haymarket Square in Chicago in 1886. In the national hysteria that followed, the union dissolved.

With the collapse of the Knights, the craft unions took hold. To strengthen themselves, these unions of skilled workers founded the American Federation of Labor (AFL) in 1886. The AFL was led by Samuel Gompers, a cigar maker. Much more practical-minded than Powderly, Gompers concentrated his energies on "bread and butter" issues—higher wages, shorter hours, better working conditions—rather than on vague plans for social change. Samuel Gompers was once asked what was the philosophy of the AFL; he answered succinctly: "More." The way to obtain more, Gompers and other leaders of the AFL insisted, was to bargain collectively with employers and to be ready to strike to enforce union demands.

THE WORKER'S STANDARD OF LIVING

Did the union actually win "more" for its members? In a few pages we shall trace its efforts to do so at Homestead. But we can readily see that as a force for raising wages on a national scale unions could not have been very important. Despite the growing class consciousness among workers, trade unions were still in their embryonic stage, and much too small to be of any significance. In 1870 membership in trade unions was approximately 300,000, and, although the labor force more than doubled by 1890, trade unions could boast of only 370,000 members at that time. In his important work *Wages and Earnings in the United States: 1860–1900,* Clarence D. Long states that "it is highly questionable whether, up to at least 1880, most firms in manufacturing were either touched directly by unions, or obliged in setting wage rates to take the threat of unionization very strongly into account."

Had unions alone been responsible for wage levels there would have been no noticeable improvement in worker's incomes during this period. But unions were not alone responsible. The pace of growth, under the stimulus of industrialization, provided a steady increase in the demand for labor—enough to bring about a very considerable rise in wages. If we compare industrial wages in 1880 with those of thirty years before, allowing for price declines during the period, we find that real wages rose by 40 percent. As an overall generalization, it is probably true that the standard of living of the American worker was higher than that of any country in the world at that time.

Hidden Hardships

But this general truth conceals as much as it reveals. For one thing, the upward trend in purchasing power ignores the "panic and pain" with which working men and women also had to deal during the depression phases of the business cycle. The business collapse of 1873, for instance, took a terrible toll. "Probably never in the history of this country has there been a time," reported the Pennsylvania Bureau of Labor Statistics at the end of 1873, "when so many of the working classes, skilled and unskilled, have been moving from place to place seeking employment. . . ."[8] In its annual report of 1874, for example, the American Iron and Steel Institute said that as of November 1874 "at least a million" workers across the nation were unemployed. The actual figure was probably double that, or more.

Meanwhile, workingmen who were lucky enough to maintain their jobs were forced to accept wage cuts and longer hours of work during periods of depression. Between 1873 and 1879 the McCormick Harvester Company in Chicago cut salaries on five separate occasions; in 1875 the Whitin Machine Works in Massachusetts instituted the first pay cut in its history. Unskilled laborers who were averaging about $1.81 a day in 1873 were getting $1.29 in 1879. Artisans in the New York City building trades who were making from $2.50 to $3.00 for an eight-hour day in 1872 were receiving $1.50 to $2.00 for a *ten-hour day* in 1875.

We could repeat these statistics of unemployment and wage cuts for the depressions of 1882–1885 and 1893–1897. But the point is clear. The rough waves of the business cycle affected labor just as painfully as they affected business. The overall climb in labor's earnings masked a great deal of hardship and uncertainty. When a man enjoys an increase in pay for, say, nine years, but is unemployed for the tenth, it is hard to say that his standard of living has risen.

Moreover, even at their best, the wages paid industrial workers were barely enough to sustain a family. The Homestead laborers, as we have said, earned a modest living wage. Elsewhere in the nation, wages were often not up to subsistence for the family. In Massachusetts, for example, studies show that living costs for a worker's family exceeded the earnings of the head of the family by almost a third. The difference had to be earned by other household members, taking part-time work.* In the coal mines, Robert Layton of the Knights of Labor said that "absolute necessity compels the father in many instances to take the child into the mine with him to assist in winning bread for the family."[9] In the South, particularly, children were sent to work at tender ages under the duress of need: in the nation as a whole in 1880 approximately 6 percent of the children between the ages of ten and fifteen were employed in some kind of industrial work.

---

*One of the most important and sophisticated inquiries into the financial and social condition of the workingman and his family was conducted by the Illinois Bureau of Labor Statistics in 1884. This study covered over 2,000 families living throughout the state. The families interviewed represented sixteen different nationalities and 163 occupations. In this respect alone, the Illinois report dwarfed all previous investigations. Breaking down their findings, the Bureau noted that almost one fourth of the households in Illinois failed to make a living and that an equal percentage had to rely on more than one member of the family for supplementary income. Examining the nation as a whole, another contemporary study indicated that there was an increasing inequality in the distribution of wealth in these years. In 1890, for example, the wealthiest 1 percent of families owned 51 percent of the nation's real and personal property; the 44 percent of families at the bottom of the economic ladder owned only 12 percent of all the property. See Charles B. Spahr, *An Essay on the Present Distribution of Wealth in the United States* (1896).

Women at Work

An increasing fraction of the country's women were also working for wages. In 1870 only about 15 percent of all women aged sixteen or over were at work, and a much smaller percentage of white women. By 1929 over a quarter of the nation's women were working.

Of course women were at work in the 1830s and 1840s. But in those days it was held that there were only seven occupations open to women—teaching, needlework, working as domestics, keeping boarders, setting type, and working in bookbinding and cotton factories. By the census of 1890, of the 369 listed occupations, at least some women were engaged in all but nine. Mainly, as we might expect, women entered fields with which they had some familiarity. The factories they entered were extensions of the work they did at home: clothes-making, textile and millinery work, and food-processing.

Women enter the labor force

Industrialization thus provided new avenues of opportunity for women, for many of the jobs they entered were directly created by the new technology of industry. Between 1870 and 1900 the number of women working in offices increased 2700 percent, from 19,000 to 503,000. (Many of these women served as "typewriters.") By 1920 they made up more than half of the clerical workers in the nation. Moreover, it was no longer unusual for women to think in terms of entering business. The heroine of Sinclair Lewis' novel, *Main Street,* published in 1920, has no hesitation about discussing her business aspirations upon graduating from college. And in Booth Tarkington's *Alice Adams,* published in 1921, a middle-class daughter goes into clerical work because of the failure of the family business.

The entrance of women into the labor market had an effect on men as well. As women proved they were capable of doing many kinds of work, they began to displace men. Salesmen gave way to salesladies, as the number of saleswomen jumped from 7,462 in 1880 to 142,265 by 1900. This figure doubled by 1920, due to the expansion of department and franchise stores. Male telephone operators disappeared and telephone girls became a national stereotype of female employment. In 1870 only 350 women worked in telegraphy (the telephone was not invented until 1876), but by 1907, of roughly 80,000 telegraph operators in the country, only 3500 were male. Yet another area that opened up for women in these years was government employment. Women first entered government service during the Civil War, working for the Treasury Department. By 1900 about one-third of all federal employees were women.

With few exceptions, women earned much less than men for the same work. At the turn of the century men in manufacturing industries averaged about 75 percent more than women. Black women earned only about half the wages of white women. At James Buchanan Duke's factory in Durham, North Carolina, for example, the black women who prepared the tobacco leaves for the machines in the factory's segregated leaf department earned half the wages that white women earned on the so-called cigarette side, even though their work was more difficult and less pleasant. (To keep themselves from inhaling the dust and fumes, they worked with handkerchiefs tied over their noses.) Black men, too, it should be added, received less than half the pay of white men. The day of economic equality was—and still is—in the future. Indeed it was not until 1920 that women gained political equality with the passage of the Nineteenth Amendment to the Constitution.

The Overall Change

Our glance at the changing market for labor makes it clear that it is not easy to generalize about the well-being of the working family. Perhaps it is not even wise to do so. As the nation moved off the farm and into the city, as family size gradually diminished, as new patterns of consumption created new demands for income, as the hours worked per week slowly fell, the meaning of a given dollar income changed. We are probably correct in envisaging a considerable general improvement in the economic situation of most working-class families during our sixty-year period, but we are wise to remember that that impression ignores the periods of severe hardship and the plight of backwater areas or trades. Not least, it overlooks the growing strains and strife of industrial work.

The Strike at Homestead

We will get a glimpse of that strife if we return to the Carnegie mill at Homestead, Pennsylvania, where the AFL had a strong local union of 800 men. Those men were part of the Amalgamated Association of Iron and Steel Workers. With 24,000 dues-paying members and 300 sub-lodges, located mainly in western Pennsylvania, this was one of the largest unions within the AFL, which by then had a quarter of a million members. We focus on 1892 because that was the year of the terrible Homestead struggle. Meeting with the management in a year of adverse business conditions, the Amalgamated was faced with a demand for a *reduction* of wages of about 18 percent. Negotiations were in vain; in desperation the union struck. In retaliation, Henry Clay Frick, Carnegie's partner (with full support from Carnegie, who was enjoying life in his castle in Scotland), closed the plant and announced that he would hire a new labor force. Frick secretly hired the Pinkerton Detective Agency, an organization whose activities included labor espionage and strike-breaking, to send an armed force of 300 men to seize the Homestead plant from the striking workmen who were picketing it.

What happened thereafter was a miniature war. The Pinkertons approached the works by barge along the Monongahela under cover of night, but the landing went astray. To their dismay, the Pinkertons found themselves surrounded, rounded up, and marched as a body of captives toward the main gate. All might have ended without further incident, but along the march someone's anger snapped and the crowd of workmen fell upon the Pinkertons, savagely beating them. When the melee was over, seven Pinkertons and nine workmen were dead.

The victory of the workmen proved short-lived, however. The governor of the state sent in the National Guard; arrests followed; and within a few months the strike was hopelessly lost. Henry Clay Frick had the vindictive pleasure of watching his men file back into the plants on his terms. Of 3,800 strikers, only 1,300 went back on the payrolls—none of them Amalgamated men. The few gains the Amalgamated had won were washed away. The twelve-hour day was imposed on almost all workers. Grievance committees were abolished. Extra pay for Sunday ceased. Labor espionage became an established practice. Wages were reduced not by 18 percent but by approximately 50 percent.

Labor versus Capital

Homestead interests us because it tells us something about the attitudes against which workers had to struggle, as well as about the physical conditions they faced. Frick's hostility toward unions was by no means unusual in that period. Historian John A. Garraty has assembled a collection of views typical of the times:

> *John H. Devereux, railroad general manager:* I would proceed to discharge every man . . . who continued to foment, and cause a disturbance. . . . It would be a sad thing for some of the old white-haired Engineers to be thrown out of work, but I told the Committee I should strike with an unsparing hand.

> *N. F. Thompson, secretary, Southern Industrial Convention:* Labor organizations are today the greatest menace to this Government that exists . . . [A] law should be passed that would make it justifiable homicide for any killing that occurred in defense of any lawful occupation.

> *A Massachusetts textile manufacturer:* As far as [collective bargaining] is concerned, we will not agree to that. Our money built these mills, and we propose to secure whatever benefits may be derived from the business.[10]

Not all manufacturers were so adamantly opposed to unions. Despite his support of Frick's policy at Homestead, Carnegie had written with sympathy about the plight of the workers and had gone so far as to endorse the eight-hour day—as a long-term goal. But even Carnegie could not bring himself to see that the new conditions of industrial labor made his words often seem unrealistic: "The lot of the skilled workman," he had written, "is far better than that of the heir to an hereditary title, who is likely to lead an unhappy, wicked life."[11] We read the words and smile. But then, Carnegie's sentiment aside, what about the *unskilled* workman? What about the immigrants falling into the pits? What about the vast numbers of Homestead employees who were losing their skills because of industrialization itself? There was a side to the industrial expansion of America that Carnegie did not clearly see. Let us take a look at it.

THE WORSENING OF WORK

If we survey the era of industrialization with regard to its impact on labor, it is not the change in the living standards of workers that impresses us. It is the change in the nature of the work itself. For one element that Carnegie either did not see or did not understand was the significance of a process to which he himself was surely a major contributor. This was the increasing division of labor, far and away the most significant effect that industrial growth exerted on the life of the worker.

The Industrial Division of Labor

We are all familiar with the idea of the division of labor. But now we must distinguish between a division that allows workers to specialize in a single craft and one that breaks down that craft into specialized tasks that are performed by several people. In the 1770s, Adam Smith noticed that this second kind of division of labor was taking place in England and wrote about it in a passage that has been famous ever since:

> To take an example . . . from a very trifling manufacture . . . , the trade of the pin-maker. [A] workman not educated to this business . . . , nor acquainted with the use of the machinery employed in it . . . could scarce, perhaps, with his utmost energy make one pin a day, and could

certainly not make twenty. But in the way in which the business is now carried on . . . one man draws out a wire, another straights it, a third cuts it, a fourth points it, a fifth grinds it at the top for receiving the head, to make a head requires two or three distinct operations; to put it on is a peculiar business; to whiten the pins is another; it is even a trade by itself to put them into paper. [T]he important business of making a pin is, in this manner, divided into about eighteen distinct operations. . . .[12]

Why should labor be divided into these "distinct" operations, instead of having each person make pins from start to finish? Smith provided an answer: "I have seen a small manufactory of this kind where only ten men were employed. . . . When they exerted themselves [they could make among them about twelve pounds of pins in a day. There are in a pound upwards of four thousand pins of a middling size. These ten persons, therefore, could make among them upwards of forty-eight thousand pins in a day. . . . But if they had all wrought separately and independently . . . , they certainly could not have each of them made twenty, perhaps not one pin in a day."

The fragmentation of labor, in other words, enormously increases the productive power of human energy—a crucial fact for the phenomenon of growth itself. We will come back to it shortly. But here we want to note two other aspects of the industrial division of labor. First, as Adam Smith makes clear, it requires machinery if it is to be effective (and there would be no point in seeking a division of labor if it were not). Thus the ability to set up a small "manufactory" of ten men, grinding out pins, requires that machinery exist to enable each workman to accomplish his specialized job much more rapidly than he could do it unassisted.

Second, the industrial division of labor requires organization. The flow of work must be studied; the object, the task itself, must be scrutinized as if it were strange and unfamiliar. The product called a "pin" has to be examined very carefully. What does it consist of? How many different activities need one person undertake to make a pin? Can these activities be established as independent tasks, accelerated with machinery, and linked with the activities of other persons working on other aspects of that peculiar object, a pin?

Homestead was a pin factory on a giant scale. For what the Bessemer converter and rolling mill, the giant presses and the railroad cars filled with ore represented was a realization of the principle of the division of labor to a far greater extent than was attainable in Adam Smith's day. Here not ten men, but 3,800 men, were coordinated into a single work team. Not all of them did different tasks, of course; but the plant as a whole divided the complex task of making steel into the much simpler tasks of loading furnaces, cleaning out ovens, guiding machinery, picking up and moving ingots, shoveling fuel. If you had stopped a workman at Homestead and asked him what he did, he would have had to answer that he ran a hoist, or handled billets, or stacked bars, or scrubbed floors. None of them could have answered "I make steel," because no one person did make steel.

The division of labor, as Adam Smith's pin factory reveals, is much older than the era of rapid industrialization. Frederick Olmstead, the architect who designed New York's Central Park, visited Cincinnati in 1850 and described how rows of men transformed a carcass, traveling before them on an overhead conveyor, from hog to pork in a matter of minutes: "No iron cogs could work with a more regular motion," he wrote of their steady chop, chop, chop.[13]

What industrialization did was to give an enormous impetus to the process by which labor could be subdivided and given the strength, speed, and steadiness of machines to augment its human exercise. But industrialization also brought a renewed effort to organize the flow of work in a new manner. Not only machines but method were the secret of the Carnegie plants, and of successful industrial operations everywhere.

Taylorism

One of the most far-reaching suggestions for the reorganization of work was the product of a strange man named Frederick Winslow Taylor. The scion of a well-to-do Philadelphia family, Taylor gave up the study of law at Harvard and decided to work his way up from the bottom in a steel plant. Beginning as an apprentice in 1874, he used his intelligence, diligence, and sheer drive to rise to the position of "gang boss" of the lathe department in the Midvale Steel Works.

By temperament Taylor had been a curious personality since boyhood, given to splitting the world into its smallest parts. He counted his steps when he walked to learn the most efficient stride, calculated the angles of his shots at croquet, and chafed at anything that displayed less than the efficiency of a finely planned machine. The most irritating thing to Taylor was the extreme "inefficiency" with which most men worked. As gang boss he told his men that he intended to get much more work out of them—and he did, by alternately bullying and persuading them to work quicker, more accurately, harder.

But Taylor was not content merely to be a driver of men. He began to see that much more work could be performed if men would break their accustomed habits and perform their tasks in a "scientifically" planned way. Early in his career, he studied a seemingly simple task— the loading of ninety-two–pound "pigs" of iron into freight cars. Picking up his ninety-two–pound pig, walking up an inclined plank to the top of a freight car, and dropping his load into the car, an average worker loaded some 12½ tons of iron a day. Taylor watched each motion, each step; and then he taught his first subject exactly what to do. As he explained it later to a congressional committee in 1912:

> Schmidt started to work, and all day long, and at regular intervals, he was told by the men who stood over him with a watch, 'Now pick up a pig and walk. Now sit down and rest. Now walk—now rest.' etc. He worked when he was told to work and he rested when he was told to rest, and at half past five in the afternoon has . . . 47½ tons loaded on the car.[14]

Taylor's method was to search for the tool or the technique that would be exactly suited to a given purpose. "When we went to the Bethlehem Steel Works," he told the committee, "and observed the shovelers . . . , we found that each of the good shovelers . . . , owned his own shovel. There was a larger tonnage of ore shoveled in that works than of any other material, and rice coal came next in tonnage. We would see a first-class shoveler go from shoveling rice coal with a load of 3½ pounds to the shovel, to handling ore from the Massaba Range, with thirty-eight pounds to the shovel. Now, is 3½ pounds the proper shovel load or is thirty-eight pounds the proper shovel load? They cannot both be right. Under scientific management the answer to this question is not anyone's opinion: It is a question for accurate, careful, scientific investigation."

The "Homogenization" of Labor

Although Taylorism was much talked about in industrial circles, few plants seem to have instituted the system as a whole. What became known as Taylorism more often than not consisted of tighter managerial control of various sorts. Perhaps the most important of these was the gradual elimination of the practice of having gang bosses or foremen hire and fire their own labor crews on a kind of subcontracting basis. More and more, management took the hiring of labor into its own hands. The foreman now became a representative of management rather than a petty boss on his own.

In effect, the new system spelled the end of an era in which the organization of industrial labor still reflected its craft origins, and the establishment of a new era in which labor skills were "homogenized," to use the expression of labor economists David Gordon, Michael Reich, and Richard C. Edwards.[15] Homogenization meant that the making of commodities was more and more entrusted to the direction of management engineers, and less and less to the hand-me-down skills of craftsmen and artisans. In turn, the gradual elimination of skilled labor and its replacement by semiskilled labor—labor that could be trained for its tasks in a matter of a week or two—gave rise to a new, disciplined organization of the work process under the eye of foremen backed by time-and-motion engineers, a system that Gordon and his associates call "the drive system."

The Assembly Line

Machines and method came together most dramatically not in steel but in automobiles, in the famous "assembly line" technique developed by Henry Ford during the first decade of this century. Allan Nevins, the biographer of Ford and his company, has described the process as it existed in 1914:

> Four great principles [were] applied throughout: the use of the latest machinery of original design; the placing of men and machines in operation sequence; the employment of work slides and moving assembly lines; and the installation of overhead carriers to bring up materials. The period for assembling a motor, which only the previous fall had been about 600 minutes of one man's time, had been lowered to 226 minutes. The period for assembling a chassis had been reduced from twelve hours twenty-eight minutes . . . to one hour and thirty-three minutes. . . .
> . . . [Y]ou see men whose function is to join parts together and insert a bolt; others who put nuts on bolts; others who tighten the bolts and insert cotter pins; one who uses a hand lever . . . press to impose the

inside ball-bearing cone upon the stub-axle; another who applies a more complicated machine to bring steering arms and stub axles into combination.[16]

Without machines and method, the mass-produced, cheap car would have been impossible, just as without machines and method the production of cheap steel would never have been achieved. But here we want to summarize the effects of Taylorism on the worker who was exposed to it.

Two consequences stand out. First, *the pace of work was deliberately speeded up*. In 1890, Samuel Gompers was quizzed by a special Commission on Capital and Labor:

Samuel Gompers (1850–1924)

Q. Would you say that the new machinery, bringing in more rapid processes of production, has lightened the toil of the operatives?

A. No. . . . As a matter of fact, the velocity with which machinery is now run calls forth the expenditure of nearly all the physical and mental force which the wage-earner can give to industry. . . .

I can say . . . that in every mechanical trade, when European workmen come over to this country and stand beside their American fellow workingmen, it simply dazes them—the velocity of motion, the deftness, the quickness, the constant strain.[17]

Second, *the character of work was changed.* In place of the variety of tasks demanded of a farmer, a fisherman, a potter, a carpenter, or even an old-fashioned "mechanic," work was now more and more patterned after the impersonal repetition of machinery itself. A Massachusetts Bureau of Labor Statistics publication stated in 1872: "Skill, once the strong defense of the artisan, is now trembling . . . before the advance of machinery. In fact it is about conquered." Many years later, an operative in an automobile factory was to tell a visiting researcher:

I work on a small conveyor which goes around in a circle. We call it a "merry-go-round." I make up zigzag springs for front seats. Every couple of feet on the conveyor there is a form for the pieces that make up the seat springs. As that form goes by me, I clip several pieces together, using a clip gun. I then put the pieces back on the form, and it goes around to where other men clip more pieces together. By the time the form has gone around the whole line, the pieces are ready to be set in a frame, where they are made into a complete spring seat. That's further down the main seat cushion line. The only operation I do is work the clip gun. It takes just a couple of seconds to shoot six or eight clips into the spring, and I do it as I walk a few steps. Then I start right over again.[18]

PRODUCTIVITY

Taylorism and the homogenization of labor raises a question of great importance. For in the dehumanization of factory work, we sense the seeds of an immense latent conflict. The struggle between those who "owned" the jobs and those who performed them—between capital and labor—had long provided a major theme for history, a theme that Karl Marx had elevated to the main process of historical change when he wrote in the *Communist Manifesto* that "the history of all hitherto existing society is the history of class struggles."

The Missing Class Struggle

In Europe there was indeed a brooding revolutionary spirit. Though it was mainly muted, it broke into violent expression in 1848, again in Paris in 1870, in Russia in 1917, and in Germany after the First World War. In America, however, a revolutionary temper had never been an integral part of the labor movement. Some labor leaders did, of course, weave Marxian references into their speeches to summon up class consciousness, but these ideas never took hold among American working men and women. As late as 1872, the Marxist First International had only about 5,000 members and virtually no trade union support. As we have seen, labor unions—especially the successful ones— were concerned with defending and trying to better the lot of the worker under the existing scheme of things rather than striking out against the whole framework of capitalist society.* Perhaps this pragmatic, nonrevolutionary turn of mind reflected the pervasive air of American democracy, so markedly different from the European feeling of inherent class differences. Perhaps it was the consequence of the extraordinary openness of the vast American continent with its beckoning, if often delusive, opportunities for the "common" man. Perhaps it was simply the result of the economic improvement that proceeded so much more rapidly in America than abroad.

Whatever the reasons, the idea of a self-conscious, revolutionary working class never made much headway in nineteenth-century America. But with the advent of the de-skilling of labor, the stage seemed set for a decisive change in sentiments. The progressive reduction of the working person within the factory to a mere robot, a pair of hands whose very movements were no longer determined by their possessor,

---

*Let us raise in a footnote a question of deep importance. Lenin believed that trade unions and socialism were incompatible. Unions, he wrote, would produce class consciousness, but not revolutionary resolve—indeed, by obtaining material benefits for their memberships, unions would serve to undermine revolutionary sentiment. In the bitter opposition by the Communist Party of Poland to the Polish union Solidarity, this Leninist belief had been tragically acted out in the early 1980s. How it will finally end, now that the Soviet Union and the Communist Party are no more, we cannot tell.

seemed likely to sharpen the sense of class solidarity among working people and to rouse a feeling of class antagonism against the system that had so diminished their status.

Yet it did not. Why not? The history of the American labor movement is complex, and the reasons for its divergence from the more revolutionary European example are many. But one central part of the answer interests us, because it is intimately connected with the very process of industrialization that degraded the labor process.

This antirevolutionary effect of industrialization lay in the immense impulse that industrialization gave to *labor productivity*. Behind this surge in productivity were many factors with which we are now familiar. There had been an enormous accumulation of capital in the form of machines, buildings, railroads, and highways. There had been dazzling advances in technology. Although we have not heretofore called attention to it, human effort was itself becoming more adept and skillful as the consequence of education. In 1870 only 57 percent of the population between the ages of five and seventeen was in school; by 1929 the percentage had grown to eighty. And not least there had also been the "militarization" of labor—its reduction to the robotized, army-like functions that Taylorism so avidly promoted. Together, all these causes accounted for the stunning increase in productivity that tripled the tonnage of steel produced per man in the thirty years between 1870 and 1900 and that would triple it again in the years between 1900 and 1929.

To be sure, the total output of the nation did not grow at anything like the explosive rates of its most advanced industrial salients, but overall output increased mightily in the period from 1865 to 1929. In round numbers a person living in 1929 produced about four times as much as his father or grandfather living in 1865.

The Effects of Productivity

This increase in productivity meant, of course, that the amount of goods and services available per capita in the nation was steadily growing. And in turn this meant that the standard of living of most working people—with all the exceptions and irregularities that we have pointed out—was gradually increasing. Thus one reason why the harsh process of labor discipline did not give rise to a revolutionary labor movement was that it was tempered by a feeling of slowly improving conditions.

But this was not the only, and perhaps not the most important, reason. For despite the growth in income, had the industrialization process subjected ever more people to the rigors of factory life, the course of American (and, indeed, European) labor history might have taken a different course. But that is not the way industrialization worked. We would think, for example, that the rise of industrial technology meant that vastly larger numbers of men and women worked in factories and manufacturing establishments in 1929 than in 1865. In fact, the actual numbers did increase sharply, from 2.3 million to 10.9 million. But if we look at the *percentage* of the labor force in manufacturing we find an unexpected result. In 1865 about 18 percent of all workers were employed in "manufacturing and hand trades," to use the classification of official government statistics. In 1929 this percentage had indeed grown—but only to 22.5 percent, hardly a dramatic change.

This gives us a new insight into the economic transformation of the country. The rise of a highly mechanized industrial sector, marked by tremendous productive powers, did not mean that a rapidly growing portion of the American working force was subjected to the harsh discipline of the assembly line. On the contrary, it made it possible for more and more labor to be switched from onerous tasks whose output was enormously leveraged by industrialization into other, less physically demanding tasks.

The Reallocation of Labor

This release of labor did not mainly occur within the industrial sector where, after the 1890s, the proportion of the work force remained approximately constant. The main impact of the industrialization process was in another area—agriculture. In 1870 one worker out of every two was employed in agriculture. If there had not been a steady growth of the use of machines on the farm—such as the reaper, the combine, the tractor—Americans would have had to use half of the work force in 1929 just to feed the nation. That would have made it impossible to man the factories, the offices, the stores, the public services that they enjoyed in 1929. It also meant that the United States would have remained a nation of farm workers.

In fact, however, industrialization made labor much more productive in agriculture. From 1870 to 1929 the value of farm tools and equipment increased from $271 million to over $3 billion. Better machinery lowered the number of man-hours required to tend an acre of wheat from twenty to less than twelve. Thus, even though the actual output of all crops tripled from 1865 to 1929, the proportion of the labor force on the farm dropped from one worker out of every two to one worker out of every five. Instead of only half the labor energies of the nation being available for nonagricultural work, four-fifths were available. Today, less than 3 percent of our labor force works on the farm.*

The Rise of the Service Sector

Still more significant, from our point of view, the industrialization process allowed large numbers of the working force to be employed in the growing array of white-collar "service" jobs. In 1865, only 12 percent of the work force was employed in education, professional and personal services, trade, and government. In 1929, these white-collar tasks absorbed almost double that proportion of the labor force. By the middle of the twentieth century, over two-thirds of the working population had moved into service occupations.

Many of these service tasks were as routine as those on the assembly line, but they were typically located in offices and stores and not in factories or farms, they were performed by men and women in street clothes and not in overalls, and they carried with them the feeling that one belonged to a middle-class not a working-class way of life.

Thus economic growth defused the revolutionary potential inherent in factory life by using the productivity of the machine to support the rise of nonfactory occupations. Technology made America a "middle-class" nation. This process was not, of course, the outcome of anyone's decision. Like much of the economic history we have traced, it followed from the blind workings of the market mechanism. But the changing shape, as well as the changing content, of the labor requirements of industrial America helps us understand something more of the dynamics of the economic transformation itself—a process that

---

*We ought to note, however, that many tasks, once considered to be agricultural—such as canning or preserving food—are now done in factories, where it counts as "industrial" production. How much labor is actually connected with food production would be difficult to compute, but it is surely much more than 3 percent of the labor force.

brings change, often difficult to measure in terms of better and worse, along with mere expansion. The radical alteration of the labor process, both within the factory and in the society at large, is perhaps the most dramatic instance of this, but it is not the only one. In our next chapter we will see similar effects of growth and industrialization, for better and worse, in other areas of our national life.

Notes

[1]"Homestead and Its Perilous Trades," *McClure's Magazine* (June 1894), 3:3, 5.

[2]Quoted in R. G. McCloskey, *American Conservatism in the Age of Enterprise* (1951), p. 145.

[3]Leon Wolff, *Lockout* (1965), p. 37.

[4]Quoted in John A. Garraty, *The New Commonwealth* (1968), p. 142.

[5]United States Senate, Committee on Education and Labor, *Report on the Relations Between Labor and Capital* (1885), 3:38.

[6]U. S. Senate, *Report on the Relations Between Labor and Capital,* 1:473.

[7]Quoted in Samuel P. Hays, *The Response to Industrialism* (1957), p. 33.

[8]*Second Annual Report,* 1873–74, p. 433.

[9]U. S. Senate, *Report on the Relations Between Labor and Capital,* 1:19.

[10]*The New Commonwealth,* pp. 144–45.

[11]Quoted in McCloskey, *American Conservatism in the Age of Enterprise,* p. 145.

[12]*The Wealth of Nations* (Modern Library ed., 1937), pp. 4–5.

[13]Quoted in S. Giedion, *Mechanization Takes Command* (1948), pp. 217–18.

[14]Frederick Winslow Taylor, *Scientific Management* (1947), p. 106.

[15]*Segmented Work, Divided Workers* (1982).

[16]Allan Nevins and F. E. Hill, *Ford* (1954), 1:504–05.

[17]*Report of the United States Industrial Commission on Capital and Labor* (1901), 8:606ff.

[18]Quoted in Charles R. Walker and Robert H. Guest, *The Man on the Assembly Line* (1956), p. 46.

Henderson, Texas, c. 1920

Chapter 6

INDUSTRIALIZATION RUBS OFF ON LIFE

So far we have observed the impact of industrialization on the structure of business enterprise, on government, and on work. Yet if we could somehow manage to look simultaneously at the whole range of everyday life in 1865 and 1929, it would probably not be those economic aspects of industrialization that would first engage our attention. Rather, we would be struck by a series of other changes, also connected with the process of industrial growth, that would account for the wholly different "look" of the country at those two times.

URBANIZATION

The first of these changes would surely be the sharp contrast in the habitat of Americans. "The United States," writes Richard Hofstadter, "was born in the country and has moved to the city."[1] The growth of cities after the Civil War was both rapid and widespread. In 1860 Chicago had a population of 109,000 people; by 1900 it had 1.7 million. During the same period the population of Minneapolis grew from 2,500 to 200,000, that of Pittsburgh from 67,000 to 450,000. In 1865 no city had yet reached a million inhabitants; in 1929 there were five such cities. Even more striking, in 1865 only fourteen cities had populations over 100,000. By 1929, there were ninety-three such cities. Half the population was now classified as "urban"—that is, living in towns of 8,000 or more. Equally telling, between 1860 and 1920, for every urban dweller who moved to a farm, twenty farmers moved to a city.

From Farm to City

Who were these migrants? Small-town laborers in search of better jobs; farmers who were unable to secure a good piece of land or make their farms pay; rural dwellers who were tired of the narrow scope and isolation of rustic life; young Dick Whittingtons who believed that the streets of the cities were paved with gold.

Above all, however, it was the pressure of the economic transformation that served as the catalyst for urbanization. People came to cities to find work. The farm lands were booming in terms of output but not as places of employment. As we have seen, the new industrial machinery of agriculture steadily lessened the need for labor to bring in the crops. As the reapers and combines and tractors arrived in the fields, they displaced the farm hands who had previously done the reaping and binding and hoeing and plowing. It took twenty man-hours to bring in an acre of wheat in 1880; less than ten by 1930. As a result, the proportion of the total work force needed on the farm dropped from over half in the 1860s to less than a quarter in the 1920s.

Simultaneously, the expansion of industrial output steadily created new opportunities for employment in the urban areas. New York's sweatshops produced the blouses and skirts and shirts worn by Americans who never came within a thousand miles of the metropolis. Pittsburgh produced steel for the entire continent. Chicago slaughtered and packed the country's bacon and beef. And the cities were, par excellence, the locus of the burgeoning service tasks of trade, finance, government.

Urbanization changed not alone the distribution of our population but the quality of its life. America became a nation of city dwellers, enjoying the excitement of city life, suffering the evils of urban sprawl. For just as no one planned the overall economic expansion of the nation, so no one planned the expansion of the cities. As with industrialization, it was the lure of profit and the counterforce of competition that mainly directed the process of urbanization, with results that mixed gains and losses in often unexpected ways. Let us examine some of them.

The Tenement

One of the losses was the deterioration of the city, symbolized by the rise of the tenement. Because of steady population growth, urban real

Slum life, New York City, 1888

estate steadily rose in price. In Washington, D.C., for example, land that went for eight cents a square foot in 1882 was selling for forty-eight cents in 1887. In their quest for profits landlords subdivided and partitioned apartments, converted private residences into rooming houses, and built new tenement apartments to accommodate as many people as possible in the smallest amount of space.

In 1869 New York City had 14,872 tenements housing a population of 468,492; in 1890 there were 37,316 tenements with 1,250,000 dwellers; in 1900, 42,700 tenements contained 1,585,000 people. In some New York tenements as many as twelve families lived on one floor, in rooms that often had no direct ventilation. In 1867 the New York State Legislature passed "An Act for the Regulation of Tenement & Lodging Houses in the Cities of New York & Brooklyn," whose requirements tell us much about prevailing conditions. The law demanded that stairs have banisters, that roofs be kept in repair, that proper ventilation be provided, and that cellars could not be used as dwellings unless the ceiling was one foot above street level. In addition, the act stipulated that there must be one toilet for every twenty-one inhabitants, although it permitted the toilet to be located in the back yard.

In 1879, Henry C. Meyer, editor of the trade journal *Plumber and Sanitary Engineer,* sought to alleviate the tenement problem by announcing a prize for the design of an apartment building on a 25 × 100-foot lot that would best combine safety and convenience for the tenant and maximum profits for the investor. Of the 204 plans submitted, James E. Ware's design for the so-called dumbbell tenement was awarded first prize. This was a five- or six-story building, with front and rear rooms connected by a hall. Each floor had space for four families living in fourteen rooms—seven on either side, going back in a straight line—with two toilets (opposite the stairs) on each floor. The largest rooms in these tenements were $10\frac{1}{2}$ × 11 feet. Ventilation was provided by a narrow, enclosed, twenty-eight-inch indentation on the side of the building.

Yet even these reforms were inadequate. The air shafts formed by the indented flanks of the adjacent dumbbells failed to provide adequate ventilation. Moreover, they served as ducts to convey flames from one story to the next, and as garbage chutes that created a fetid odor.

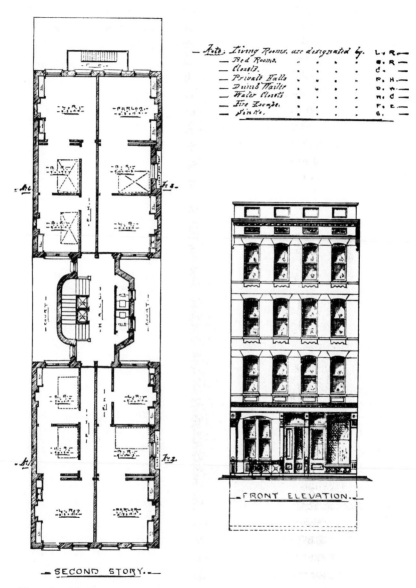

The "dumbbell" tenement

Playgrounds and open spaces were virtually nonexistent in most cities. Police and fire protection was inadequate. Garbage collection was haphazard, at best. City water was often impure. Sewers were smelly and often clogged. Disease could spread quickly under such conditions. In 1882, half the children in Chicago died before reaching the age of five. In one New York tenement area the annual death rate per 1,000 for the years 1883, 1884, 1885, and the first three-quarters of 1886 came to roughly 42 percent, as compared with roughly 26 percent for the city as a whole; nearly 62 percent of the deaths were children under five years of age, while in the city as a whole the percentage was just above 42. Like most cities, New York had become a city of extremes and contradictions, where the best and the worst, the highest and the lowest, existed side by side in sunshine and shadow, in splendor and squalor. The mansions of millionaire industrialists stood only a few blocks from ugly, unhealthy slum districts that housed the poor families who labored in their factories. Seeing the way people lived in these cities, southern visitors to New York once suggested that antebellum slaves on plantations lived more comfortably. Visiting Pittsburgh, Herbert Spencer, the English prophet of Social Darwinism, commented: "Six Months residence here would justify suicide."*

The Company Town

One person who believed that good housing and a healthy environment were essential to people's well-being was George M. Pullman of Chicago, the sleeping car king who had created the greatest railroad car–building organization in the world.

In 1880, Pullman decided to concentrate his operations outside of Chicago, where he would build a model city, named for himself, that

---

*We should note in passing that the conditions of tenement life were a stimulus to American reform movements. In Chicago Jane Addams founded the most famous settlement house in America, Hull House, providing services that ranged from day care for children to English classes for immigrants. Addams and her sister workers were also responsible for the passage of laws limiting female hours of work (an Oregon statute in 1908 set a limit of sixty hours per week), and for other kinds of factory legislation. In 1911 a fire broke out in the Triangle Shirtwaist Company in a New York tenement building. One hundred and forty-eight women perished in the blaze. Thereafter New York State passed thirty-five new factory inspection laws, and shortly other states began to require that manufacturers take out insurance against industrial accidents, so that injured workers could file claims for compensation.

would provide employee happiness, social progress, and employer profit. Accordingly, Pullman purchased over 4,000 acres of land in the Calumet region of Chicago (about eight miles south of the city) and engaged an architect and landscape designer to create a model work-home integration that would be both aesthetically pleasing and functional.

The typical cottage in Pullman was a two-story, five-room structure with a sink, water tap, gas fixtures for lighting and cooking, toilet facilities, and sufficient closet and pantry space. Although the rents for a comparably sized apartment were higher than in Chicago, the accommodations and surrounding environment were far superior.

But as mentioned, Pullman was also intended to serve as a profit-making enterprise. Pullman gave his workers expensive homes and libraries which he hoped would refine and uplift his workers' character and performance, but he expected a 6 percent profit on the capital he invested. As one student of his experiment points out, "Pullman was expected to show that man could be improved by proper surroundings and that American Industry could provide this without sacrificing profits."[2] But Pullman categorically refused to allow workers to own their own homes or to "sell an acre under any circumstances." Everything was rented, including the church. Moreover, Pullman permitted no saloons and insisted that his town manager visit workers' homes to enforce his forty-two page manual of tenants' regulations.

Virtually all Americans who were familiar with urban and industrial conditions were optimistic about Pullman, believing that it would usher in a new era in labor-management relations and urban planning. But although Pullman was a unique venture, it too contained a great deal of the residue of earlier company towns. "It was virtually impossible to come there without constant reminder that this was a company town," writes historian Stanley Buder, "and if the casual visitor was highly conscious of this fact, one can imagine the residents' awareness." Hence although the company's influence could not be measured, it could certainly be sensed.

Nor did Pullman pursue an enlightened attitude when dealing with its workers. In hard times, the company laid off workers and reduced wages while keeping rents constant; refused to accept any responsibility for industrial accidents; and employed such infamous tactics as blacklists and company spies. Surely such practices would one day reap the whirlwind, no matter how placid the town appeared. And in

1894, Pullman's workers struck to protest wage cuts he had ordered after the onset of the depression. The resulting strike spread to and included the American Railway Union, which supported the strikers by refusing to operate any trains that carried a Pullman car. In the end, President Grover Cleveland, arguing that the U.S. mails had to be delivered, ordered federal troops to Chicago to crush the strike.

Clearly many of Pullman's employees would have preferred the "free air" of the city to the iron-fisted authority of the company.

The Model Tenement

In sharp contrast to Pullman were the motives behind the worker-housing projects sponsored by a number of individual philanthropists and housing reformers. Their objective was to show that efforts to improve the living conditions of workers could be combined with "limited dividends," that is, profits of 5 percent annually. Among these model housing projects were Alfred T. White's Home Building development in Brooklyn, New York (1877) and Edward Waller's Francisco Terrace in Chicago (1895), which was designed by Frank Lloyd Wright.

Generally, these apartment buildings were constructed around a courtyard, thus providing playground space, and they usually offered communal facilities such as reading rooms and baths. The buildings were safe, clean, and well-ventilated, the apartments adequate for a working man and his family.

Reformers believed that the model dwellings would set a standard that other landlords would be forced to meet, partly because of public pressure, but mostly because of the workings of competition. Unfortunately, this solution to the housing problem did not take hold, even though most of the experiments succeeded in achieving their goal of philanthrophy plus a 5 percent profit. The great mass of urban workers, as well as newcomers in search of employment, were crowded into privately owned tenements that operated solely for profit.

The Ghetto

Among those who gravitated to the cities in search of jobs and housing were many blacks. With their arrival we witness the appearance of ghettos and the special problems that come in their wake.

Of all the nation's ghettos, probably the best known is Harlem, a thousand acres of concentrated misery that begins north of an ill-defined frontier across Manhattan Island and disappears in the dreary stretches of the Bronx. Few people realize that this was once one of the choicest neighborhoods in New York. Indeed, if we look at Harlem's housing we see that many of the decrepit brownstones and run-down apartment houses are the remains of what were once elegant town houses and expensive apartment dwellings built during the late 1800s.

What happened to Harlem? A building boom, fueled by extravagant and unrealistic expectations, played itself out in 1904. Vacancies began to appear, first scattered, then wholesale. As the neighborhood began to deteriorate, whites moved out and blacks were able to locate good housing at low prices. By 1914 some 50,000 blacks were in Harlem, many of them enjoying very good, low-priced housing. But this very good fortune served as a magnet to attract other, less well-housed, black families. Soon Harlem was overcrowded: by 1929 its population doubled, mainly by in-migration from out of state. Three-quarters of New York's blacks were now crowded into those 1,000 acres. Harlem was becoming a city within a city.

As population rose, so did rents, for landlords were quick to charge what the traffic would bear. Rents doubled between 1921 and 1927, and many black families—most of whom earned low wages—were forced to subdivide their apartments or to take in boarders. The ghetto syndrome began to appear: high rents, high density, low amenities. "The state would not allow cows to live in some of these apartments used by colored people," said the chairman of the city's Housing Reform Committee in 1927.[3] Overcrowding and unsanitary conditions soon took their toll. Between 1923 and 1927 the death rate in Harlem was 42 percent higher than anywhere else in New York.

Urbanization and Industrialization

The point, however, is not to lament the appearance of the ghetto, but to relate it to the larger development of industrial growth. The connection is not difficult to make. The rise of industrial employment and the decline of rural employment together served as a powerful stimulus to uproot blacks from their rural habitat. Bad as the city was, it was better than the rural slum; and as the nation's economy grew, it pulled the black population cityward. Between 1865 and 1929, millions of blacks left the South, most of them for city life in New York or elsewhere. During the 1920s alone, 600,000 blacks moved north, many of them to Harlem.

In the cities, the blacks provided an underlayer of cheap labor that served the economic needs of the growing industrial metropolis. Black males became the city's day laborers, its casual dockhands, its dish-washers, hallmen, bellboys. The black female workers became its ser-vants, laundresses, cleaning women. The presence of the low-paid, easily abused black labor force provided a lubricant for the growing economy. The last to be hired and the first to be fired, the black worker served as a buffer for the white worker, absorbing much more than his or her share of unemployment when times were bad, yet not competing strongly enough to prevent the rise of white wages when times were good.

But there is a lesson to be learned from the rise of the great city, with its ghettos and slums. The big city also testified to the growing interdependence of economic life in an industrial society. In the 1860s many city dwellers still had their tiny truck gardens; in Homestead, a worker could still have one foot in the factory and one on the farm. By the 1920s the link between rural and urban life had been largely severed. The city dweller was now almost entirely dependent on the network of rails and roads that brought his food from a countryside hundreds of miles distant. The citizens of New York and Chicago ate wheat grown in Kansas and meat raised in Texas and lived in houses built of Vermont stone and Pittsburgh iron and steel. Without the intri-cate web of transportation that bound together a thousand trades and localities, the city could not have existed for a week.

Industrialization is inextricably bound up with this kind of interde-pendence. Yet the effects of urbanization extended far beyond even this deep-reaching change, touching life in innumerable ways: techni-cal, cultural, political. Urban agglomerations that had grown up with-out plan or foresight had to find means of disposing of garbage and sewage on a mass scale. The city had to provide transportation from one area to another. It offered a new market for mass entertainment. It brought into being a class of office workers who sought to imitate their "betters" in stylish dress. It jostled races and cultures together: it was the city, not the country, that was the "melting pot." It was also the scene of loneliness and isolation for the newcomer: suicide rates rose from 3.18 per 100,000 in 1860 to 11.9 in 1922.

Residential street in a small town in Illinois, c. 1900

None of these problems was new, of course. Cities have always had their special attributes. But the extent and ubiquity of these urban traits were new. In 1860 cities were few in the United States and their excitement and despair were the exception in a land where rural placidity was the rule. By the first quarter of the twentieth century the city, with its strains and its vitality, had become the norm. It was a long while before the political structures and the prevailing beliefs and self-images of the nation caught up with the realities of its urbanized life: To some degree they have still not embraced the importance of the city. This lag is itself one reason why the city has remained a "problem." We continue to see our urban ills as intrusions upon, rather than as embodiments of, our economic evolution.

MACHINERY AND MATERIAL LIFE

A second change brought about by industrialization affected both city and country. It was the enormous acceleration of a trend whose beginnings we saw before the Civil War—the introduction of machinery into everyday material life. This change was so pervasive, so all-embracing, that it is impossible to itemize its particulars. Let us simply consider some of the differences that it brought.

Mobility

The first difference we notice is in mobility. In the 1860s the basic means of local transportation was the horse. But the horse was ill-suited to an urbanized nation: Where could a million New Yorkers or Chicagoans stable their steeds? Urban life became constricted, limited to journeys on foot or to occasional ventures on trains or steamboats.

But the constriction was not long-lasting. The first breakthrough was the development of the horse-pulled streetcar—the first urban mass transit. By 1895 the electrically powered trolley was running over 10,000 miles of track in the cities; indeed, by changing from one streetcar line to another you could even journey from New York to Boston.

Residential street in Chicago, c. 1906

Traffic jam, Chicago, c. 1910

Even more pervasive was the influence of the bicycle. It is hard to realize today how vast a change the bicycle ushered in. Small enough to be parked in a hallway, inexpensive enough to be bought by a working-class family, simple to maintain, the bicycle reopened the country to the city dweller. First introduced into the country in 1878, in less than two decades bicycle-manufacture had become a major industry. By 1900 the industry was turning out over a million vehicles, and an estimated four million people could be seen riding a strange assortment of high-wheelers, low-wheelers, bicycles built for two, bicycles with sidecars. The mass use of the bicycle also brought pressure on Congress to improve the road system of the country: the League of American Wheelmen was a kind of precursor of the American Automobile Association in the campaign for good public roads. As the census report for 1900 states, "It is safe to say that few articles ever used by man have created so great a revolution in social conditions as the bicycle."

Then, of course, there was the automobile. The first gas-powered auto appeared in the nation in 1892; in 1896 its inventors, the Duryea brothers, actually sold thirteen cars. That was the year in which a thirty-two-year-old mechanic named Henry Ford sold his first "quadricycle." In 1909, with the advent of the Model T, he sold 10,660 cars. By 1929 there were twenty-three million cars on the road—one for every five Americans.

The rise of the automobile industry affected economic growth in a number of ways. It was the prime center for the application of the mass-production techniques whose impact on labor we witnessed in our previous chapter. It was a stupendous source of employment—indeed, soon the largest employer in the country. It was the biggest customer for steel, rubber, sheet steel, lead, leather. It became the origin of one-sixth of all the patents issued in the country. With 2,471 plants in 1923, the automobile industry was the largest in the nation.

But we are interested in the automobile as a concrete manifestation of growth that changed material life. To the average American family it became the most prized (and most expensive) of all its possessions, save only its home. It was the means for cheap and easy travel that made Americans, always a restless people, into a nation of motorized vagabonds. It changed the location of industry and of workers' housing, for it was no longer necessary to live within walking distance of work or near a trolley route. It altered urban configurations: the move to the suburbs was made on rubber tires and would have been impossible without them. (Later, during the Great Depression, Will Rogers would claim that America went to the poorhouse in its automobiles.) It changed social habits. Vacationing became a national passion. Sex mores were radically affected by the car. The city stretched beyond its capacity by the vehicles that jammed its streets. Highways greatly increased in mileage: during the decade of the 1920s federal, state, and city authorities spent roughly $1 billion per year on highways and $400 million on city streets. The nation's police force had to be expanded to cope with a new major source of accidents, of theft, of exasperation. Not least, the car provided the greatest joy ride in the nation's history.

Power in the Home

Next to mobility, the most visible change in daily life was the increased use of energy. In 1860 the total amount of energy delivered by all "prime movers," such as steam engines, water wheels, windmills, and farm animals, totaled thirteen million horsepower. By 1930 the amount of energy used by the nation was 1.6 *billion* horsepower. Of this total, 1.4 billion was provided by that extraordinary power source, the automobile. But the power delivered by stationary motors of all kinds was also some twenty times as much as in 1860.

A great deal of this increased power was used by the factories of the nation, now mechanized to a degree unimaginable in 1860. But we are interested in the direct use of power by the average family as it ran the machines that were more and more part of the normal household's equipment. Here we have but to trace the growth of the use of electricity following Edison's installation of the first power-generating plant in New York in 1882. By 1907 only 8 percent of all homes had access to electricity, mainly because the problem of sending current over cables for long distances had not yet been solved. But by 1929, 85 percent of all nonfarm residences had wall receptacles that enabled them to "plug in" to this new source of energy. The residential use of electricity grew from next to nothing in the 1890s to nine billion kilowatt hours in 1929. In that latter year about 70 percent of the nation's industry was electrified. By 1930 the United States was using more electricity than the rest of the world combined.

Electricity brought power into the home. Perhaps the least revolutionary of its effects was the electric light, for candles or gas burners had provided reasonably good illumination before Edison perfected the carbon-filament lamp in 1887. The real change was the possibility of using machines in domestic life in a manner impossible before this extraordinary source of invisible, easily conducted energy became available. The washing machine and the refrigerator, the vacuum cleaner and the electric iron were the creations of electric power. Their effect on household life was dramatic. The availability of mechanical servants made it possible for the housewife to venture into the labor market and still to maintain her traditional role of "home-maker." Thus the advent of the working woman was intimately connected with the mechanization of household work.

Leisure habits were changed, too. As electric lights illuminated the night (and streetcars crisscrossed city streets), people were able to go to theatres, vaudeville houses, or just out for an evening stroll. Meanwhile, electricity also vastly increased the ability of households to communicate with one another. In 1887 there were 170,000 subscribers to the new telephone service; in 1917 nearly twelve million phones were in use. "What startles and frightens backward Europeans," said a visiting English author, "is the efficiency and fearful universality of the telephone."

Machines such as the electric washer had a dramatic effect on household life

The phone, and then the radio, served to open the ordinary household to events far beyond its previous ken. Together with the movies, those devices were probably more important than the schools as a force for social education and for the spread of sophistication. The jazzy, freewheeling spirit of the twenties would have been unthinkable without the electrical technology of communication. How few people had ever actually heard or seen Abraham Lincoln or Mark Twain! How few had not seen or heard Herbert Hoover or Al Jolson!

THE TRIUMPH OF INDUSTRIALIZATION

New household appliances were not the only changes in material life that the industrial era brought to the United States. There were also, for example, advances in medicine associated with the increased interest in and application of science. Life expectancy between 1865 and 1929 rose from just under forty years to just over sixty, mainly through the conquest of childhood diseases. The death rate from typhoid fell by 95 percent; from measles, by 75 percent.

Second, our overview has by-passed an important change in the tempo of life that also arose from the increased productivity of the age. This was the gradual decline in working hours from over sixty per week in 1865 to about forty-two in 1930. In 1923, after protesting for years that it could not be done, the U.S. Steel Works at Gary, Indiana, went from two grueling twelve-hour stints to three eight-hour shifts. In 1926 Henry Ford, who had already astonished the business world by instituting a five-dollar workday in 1914, announced that henceforth his plants would work on a five-day week. The International Harvester Company started another trend by granting its workers a two-week vacation with pay. Meanwhile, Ford reduced the price of his cars. When he introduced the Model T in 1908, it cost about $850. By 1925, a Model T cost $290, roughly the equivalent of three months' wages for factory workers.

Still another change was a greatly lengthened attendance at school. In 1929 30 percent of the seventeen-year-old population was in high school. This may not seem like a very high figure—today about 80 percent of this age group is in school—but in 1865 the percentage of seventeen-year-olds in school was two.

Not less significant, although less apparent on the surface, was the change in America's position in the world. Alone among the participants in the First World War, the United States emerged stronger than when it entered. Formerly a debtor to Europe—it entered the war with $3.5 billion in debts—it now became the great lender to Europe, with credits of $12.5 billion. By 1929 almost half of the world's industrial production was located in the United States. Meanwhile, the international thrust of business continued apace: Exports rose by a third between 1913 and 1929, and United States investment abroad in factories, mines and plantations rose from the $635 million we saw in 1897 to $7.5 billion.

In 1919, looking ahead to the postwar era, Woodrow Wilson had said: "The financial leadership will be ours. The industrial primacy will be ours. The commercial advantage will be ours."[4] He was right.

The National Feeling

All these new ways, and others that we have not included, constituted the reality of a vast economic transformation. Not all of it by any means was benign, as we have seen from our view of the ghetto, and its outcome would be anything but happy, as the impending—and wholly unsuspected—Depression would prove. Yet there can be no doubt that a general consciousness of prosperity was widely felt and much celebrated.

Americans were convinced they were on the threshold of a new era, a time of peace and prosperity. Given the economic statistics, it would have been difficult to cast cold water on this belief. National income rose from $63.1 billion to $87.8 billion between 1922 and 1929. Per capita income had jumped from $517 for the period 1909 to 1918 to $612 for the period of the 1920s. Despite generally shorter working hours, output per worker was up by 30 percent. Industrial production as a whole nearly doubled between 1921 and 1929. Two of today's most vexing problems, inflation and unemployment, were virtually nonexistent. The average annual rate of increase in prices between 1923 and 1929 was less than 1 percent and unemployment averaged only 3.7 percent of the labor force.

Another cause for the prevailing sense of well-being was the unusually friendly attitude of government toward big business. The tensions of the age of trust-busting were over. In their place was a strongly pro-business attitude, summed up in the words of President Calvin Coolidge that "the chief business of the American people is business." Secretary of Commerce Herbert Hoover virtually put his department at the disposal of big business, encouraging businesses in the same field to form trade associations to share information, and to act as a clearing-house for information on business opportunities abroad. Meanwhile, Secretary of the Treasury Andrew Mellon, one of the richest men in America, successfully urged that taxes on high incomes be lowered. Under Mellon's Revenue Act of 1926, a person with an annual income of $1 million had his or her taxes lowered from more than $600,000 to less than $200,000. This friendly attitude of government encouraged businesses to make new investments and this, in turn, stimulated economic growth.

"No Congress of the United States ever assembled," said President Calvin Coolidge in 1928 surveying the state of the Union, "has met with a more pleasing prospect." Coolidge was a very conservative man who believed that "The man who builds a factory builds a temple." His contemporary, Lincoln Steffens, was not. Once a famous muckraking reporter for *McClure's* magazine, he had reported with enthusiasm on the early days of the Soviet Union: "I have been over into the future, and it works." Now Steffens was himself saying, "Big business in America is producing what the socialists held up as their goal: food, shelter, and clothing for all."[5]

Certainly Coolidge's successor, Herbert Hoover, regarded the prospect as bright:

> We in America [he said to a Stanford University audience in 1928] today are nearer to the final triumph over poverty than ever before in the history of any land. The poorhouse is vanishing among us. We have not yet reached the goal, but, given a chance to go forward with the policies of the last eight years, we shall soon with the help of God be in sight of the day when poverty will be banished from this nation.

The Nation in 1929

It was assuredly a time of prosperity for the rich: the number of millionaires, which reached 4,000 in 1914, had almost trebled by 1926, and the stock market was making new ones every year. But it was not only the rich who basked in the warmth of the late twenties. The Niagara of production testified to an unprecedented degree of national well-being, although—as we shall see in our next chapter—it was a well-being by no means enjoyed by everyone. In turn, the Niagara promoted that "democracy of things" we first noted in the mid-1850s. Fresh vegetables were now widely available, thanks to new techniques of storage and transport. The consumption of ice cream soared—up 45 percent just from 1919 to 1926. Automobiles, now colored in Versailles Violet and Florentine Cream rather than just funereal black, were owned by two households out of three. Rich and not-so-rich alike shaved with the Gillette Safety Razor, snapped pictures with their Kodaks, went to the movies (in December 1923 the movie attendance in Muncie, Indiana, was almost four-and-a-half times the population of the town), and shopped at Macy's, where "Goods suitable for millionaires" were available "at prices in reach of millions."[6]

Thus, if the technical achievement of the age of industrialization was hugely to augment the volume and to alter the composition of the nation's output, its social achievement was to bring about an era of self-conscious prosperity unlike any the country had known before. Especially among those who fared well, there was an acute sense of the American economy as a triumph of enterprise. There was only one problem: Although the national edifice of prosperity appeared to be built of granite, it turned out to be built on sand.

Notes

[1] *The Age of Reform* (1955), p. 23.

[2] Stanley Buder, *Pullman: An Experiment in Industrial Order and Community Planning, 1880–1930* (1967), pp. 52–3.

[3] Quoted in Gilbert Osofsky, *Harlem: The Making of a Ghetto* (1965), pp. 135–36.

[4] Ray S. Baker and William E. Dodd (eds.), *The Public Papers of Woodrow Wilson* (1925), 1:640.

[5] Quoted in William Leuchtenburg, *The Perils of Prosperity* (1958), p. 202.

[6] From an 1887 Macy's advertisement, as quoted in Daniel Boorstin, *The Americans: The Democratic Experience* (1973), p. 113.

Migrant farm workers in the 1930s

Chapter 7

THE GREAT DEPRESSION

We turn now to a new aspect of the economic transformation of America. Up to now our narrative has mainly focused on two aspects of our principal theme. One has been the progressive development of material life—the life of work, of consumption, of command over the environment. Here the general thread has been the extraordinary alteration and enlargement that industrialization has brought about within daily life.

A second pattern of study has been concerned with the extension of what Fernand Braudel has called our economic life, the life that binds us into a working economic society. Here the main theme has been the widening and deepening of our connection with the market, the increasing complexity of our economic interdependency, and the growth of the business institutions that have shaped and channeled so many of our economic ties with society.

In all this overview, however, we have hardly mentioned Braudel's third great theme—the development of capitalism itself. That is, we have rarely stepped back to comment on the unfolding of that embracing web of institutions and relationships we call capitalism, with its central drive for the accumulation of capital, its division of society into a public and private realm, and its reliance on the guiding functions of the market mechanism.

Now, however, things change. With the advent of the Great Depression we encounter a phenomenon that cannot be grasped in terms of the routines and techniques of material life or through the pressures and pulls of the marketplace. To understand the Great Depression we must speak about capitalism as a *system* with tendencies and developmental characteristics of its own.

THE STOCK MARKET BOOM

This requires that we take a short lesson in economics—a lesson that will explain something about how capitalism works. It will also lead us to reflect on the momentum of growth that has played so central a role in our narrative. Thus our chapter will take us into realms of theory and speculation quite different from those that we have previously visited. We will, so to speak, mount to Olympian heights to look down on capitalism from the perspective of a historian of the future.

But we will begin far below these heights. The best way to learn about the advent of the Depression is to watch the spectacle that attracted the gaze of millions of Americans in the late 1920s—the stock market boom. In *Only Yesterday* social historian Frederick Lewis Allen has given us a vivid, if somewhat overdrawn, account of what we would have seen:

> The rich man's chauffeur drove with his ears laid back to catch the news of an impending move in Bethlehem Steel: he held fifty shares himself on a twenty point margin.* The window cleaner at the broker's office paused to watch the ticker, for he was thinking of converting his laboriously accumulated savings into a few shares of Simmonds. [One reporter] told of a broker's valet who made nearly a quarter of a million in the market, of a trained nurse who cleaned up thirty thousand following the tips given her by grateful patients; and of a Wyoming cattleman, thirty miles from the nearest railroad, who bought or sold a thousand shares a day.[1]

Behind the Boom

The market value of shares listed on the New York Stock Exchange soared from $4 billion in 1923 to $67 billion at the beginning of 1929. Stocks were going up for many reasons. One was that the profits of most corporations were rising. Between 1916 and 1925 the profits of large manufacturing companies totaled $730 million in an average year. From 1926 through 1929, their annual total profits jumped to an average of about $1,400 million. In 1929 profits were actually triple

---

*A "margin" means that stock has been bought by borrowing from the bank or from the brokerage firm to cover the difference between the value of the shares and the amount of the down payment.

those of 1920. Hence one reason for buying stocks was the expectation that dividends would rise. And they did. From 1920 to 1929, dividends almost tripled.

A second reason was that banks and brokerage firms were encouraging people to buy stocks by lending vast sums to potential buyers. Loans from brokers to enable individuals to buy stocks—loans that were often equal to half the value of the purchase—soared from just over $1 billion in 1920 to $6 billion in 1928. Who could resist the chance to become as rich as Croesus when you could buy $1,000 worth of stock by putting up only $500 of your own, borrowing the rest from a brokerage firm or a bank? Hundreds of thousands of people *didn't* resist. A million and a half people were stockholders, a far larger number than ever before and the number of shares traded on the New York Stock Exchange rose from 236 million in 1923 to 1.1 *billion* in 1928. In 1900 roughly 15 percent of all families owned some stock; in 1929, about 28 percent.

Finally, there was the allure of a seemingly foolproof method of getting rich. Many Americans were encouraged to join in the great stock market boom because they listened to the advice of trusted men. In 1928 John J. Raskob, a director of General Motors and chairman of the Democratic Party, projected the recent rise in stock prices into the future and predicted that riches could be within the reach of anyone who saved money. In an article for the *Ladies Home Journal* entitled "Everybody Ought to Be Rich," he said: "If a man saves fifteen dollars a week and invests in common stocks, at the end of twenty years he will have at least $80,000 and an income from investments of around $400 a month. He will be rich." In New York City a big electric sign over Columbus Circle blinked out the message: "You should have $10,000 at the age of thirty; $25,000 at the age of forty; $50,000 at fifty."

THE CRASH

Thus the growth in incomes that we traced in our earlier chapters was paralleled during the 1920s by a spectacular growth in wealth—alas, paper wealth. For on October 24, 1929, without any prior warning, the bottom suddenly dropped out of the market. The headlines in the *New York Times* for October 25 read:

Worst Stock Crash Stemmed by Banks; 12,894,650-Share Day Swamps Market; Leaders Confer, Find Conditions Sound

What was meant by the "crash" was that investors all over the country decided that the market was "too high" and placed orders to sell. But no one can sell a security—or any other item—at whatever price he or she wishes. The seller has to find a buyer. And if the buyers are nervous and pessimistic, the price at which they will agree to buy the stock may be much lower than the sellers expected.

What happened on the morning of October 24 was that buyers were only willing to buy stocks at prices far below the prices of the preceding day. Montgomery Ward, a favorite, had "opened" at a price of eighty-three, that is, the first transaction was a sale at eighty-three dollars per share. By mid-morning, it was being traded at fifty. Goldman Sachs Trading Corporation, a speculative favorite, opened at eighty-one and dropped to sixty-five. General Electric slid from 315 to 283. Some stocks could not be sold at all—there were simply no buyers to take them at any price.

By noon the roar of voices on the stock exchange floor had reached panic proportions, and a group of bankers met to issue reassuring statements that "conditions were sound." On Saturday, October 26, President Herbert Hoover echoed this optimism by insisting that "the fundamental business of the country—that is, production and distribution of commodities—is on a sound and prosperous basis." For a week the market rallied as buyers lifted up their courage and sellers lost their terrified impulse to sell. Then on October 29 came an even more devastating day. As the *New York Times* wrote about it the next morning:

Stocks Collapse in 16,410,030-Share Day

Stock prices virtually collapsed today, swept downward with gigantic trading losses in the most disastrous trading day in the stock market's history. Millions of dollars in open market values were wiped out as prices crumbled under the pressure of liquidation of securities that had to be sold at any price. . . .

Efforts to estimate yesterday's market losses in dollars are futile because of the vast number of securities . . . on which no calculations are possible. However, it was estimated that 880 issues, on the New York Stock Exchange, lost between $8,000,000,000 and $9,000,000,000 yesterday.

And October 29 was not the end. In 1932 Frank Vanderlip, former president of the National City Bank of New York, a leading financial institution, surveyed the wreckage in an article in the *Saturday Evening Post:*

. . . The quoted value of all stocks listed on the New York Stock Exchange was, on September 1, 1929, $89,668,276,854. By July 1, 1932 the quoted value of all stocks had fallen to $15,633,479,577.

Stockholders had lost $74,000,000,000. The figure is so large that not many minds can grasp it. It is $616 for every one of us in America. It is, roughly, three times what we spent fighting the World War. . . . In the bursting of the New York Stock Exchange bubble, the value of all stocks fell to 17 percent of their September 1, 1929 price. . . . Never before, in this country or anywhere else, has there been such a general loss in "security" values.[2]

In 1932 the United States Senate held a hearing on the fate of some of those stocks:

SENATOR COUZENS: Did Goldman Sachs and Company organize the Goldman Sachs Trading Company?
MR. SACHS: Yes, sir.
SENATOR COUZENS: And it sold its stock to the public?
MR. SACHS: A portion of it. The firm invested originally in 10 percent of the entire issue for the sum of $10,000,000.
SENATOR COUZENS: And the other 90 percent was sold to the public?
MR. SACHS: Yes, sir.
SENATOR COUZENS: At what price?
MR. SACHS: At 104 . . .
SENATOR COUZENS: And what is the price of the stock now?
MR. SACHS: Approximately $1\frac{3}{4}$.[3]

Behind the Crash

What caused the crash? To this day we do not know what item of news, what rumor, what particular event may have started the collapse. Clearly there must have been an underlying nervousness among hundreds of

A run on a bank

thousands of stockholders, for the fall in prices soon fed upon itself. In addition, the collapse worsened because holders of stocks on margin—that is, on borrowed money—were forced to sell their securities to pay off their loans. Perhaps in the end we can only classify the Great Crash with other speculative busts that had happened elsewhere in history—land booms that came to nothing, crazes such as the tulip bulb speculative mania in seventeenth-century Holland, prior stock booms like the famous English South Sea "Bubble" of 1720.

What interests us is the impact of the crash on the economy. For as everyone knows, the Great Crash ushered in something worse—the Great Depression.

THE DEPRESSION OF THE 1930S

It was an oddly invisible phenomenon, this Great Depression [wrote Frederick Lewis Allen]. If one observed closely, one might note that there were fewer people on the streets than in former years, that there were many untenanted shops, that beggars and panhandlers were much in evidence; one might see breadlines here and there, and 'Hoovervilles' in vacant lots at the edge of town (groups of tarpaper shacks inhabited by homeless people); railroad trains were shorter, with fewer Pullmans; and there were many factory chimneys out of which no smoke was coming. But otherwise there was little to see. Great numbers of people were sitting at home, trying to keep warm.[4]

LABOR FORCE AND UNEMPLOYMENT, 1929–41
(NUMBERS IN MILLIONS)

Year	Labor Force	Unemployment Number	Unemployment % of Labor Force
1929	49.2	1.6	3.2
1930	49.8	4.3	8.7
1931	50.4	8.0	15.9
1932	51.0	12.1	23.6
1933	51.6	12.8	24.9
1934	52.2	11.3	21.7
1935	52.9	10.6	20.1
1936	53.4	9.0	16.9
1937	54.0	7.7	14.3
1938	54.6	10.4	19.0
1939	55.2	9.5	17.2
1940	55.6	8.1	14.6
1941	55.9	5.6	9.9

SOURCE: United States Department of Commerce, *Historical Statistics of the United States* (1960), p. 70.

However hard it was to see, the Great Depression was a vivid reality to virtually everyone. To begin with, unemployment soared beyond any previous experience. All through the long period of industrialization, recurrent periods of unemployment had plagued the economy, sometimes reaching as high as 10 percent of the work force. But those times of trial had always been brief and had always been followed by a resumption of growth, which brought with it job opportunities for almost everyone who wanted work.

The depression was different. The table on page 281 reveals its severity.

Nothing like this had ever happened before. For it was not only unemployment that the depression brought, but a total cessation of growth. In the nation as a whole, home-building came almost to a standstill—residential construction fell by 90 percent. Eighty-five thousand businesses failed, and production in those that survived was often reduced to half the volume of the 1920s. Wages reached levels that made sheer survival a problem: in Pennsylvania men were paid five cents an hour in sawmills; $7^1/_2$ cents in general contracting. In Ohio the earnings of office workers were cut by a third, those of store clerks by nearly half. Considering the nation as a whole, national income fell from over $80 billion in 1929 to under $50 billion in 1932. Thus, while the Great Crash had dashed American illusions about instant riches, the Great Depression threatened something much more fundamental. It brought into question the faith of Americans in the economic system itself. The system simply did not work.

Political Paralysis

At first no one believed that. "We have now passed the worst," said President Hoover in May 1930. One year later he declared the depression to be "over." Meanwhile business spokesmen continued to assert that things were "fundamentally sound":

> Charles Schwab, Chairman of Bethlehem Steel, December 10, 1929: "Never before has American business been as firmly entrenched for prosperity as it is today."
>
> John Edgerton, President, National Association of Manufacturers, December 1929: "I can observe little on the horizon today to give us undue or great concern."
>
> James Farrell, President, United States Steel, January 1931: "The peak of the depression passed thirty days ago."[5]

But as the situation stubbornly refused to mend itself, sentiment began to change. Among the unemployed an ugly mood of frustration and anger was surfacing. In 1932 a small "army" of unemployed veterans converged on Washington to demand payment of a bonus promised them for their service in the First World War. Hoover refused to meet with them. Instead, the veterans were attacked with bayonets and tear gas, to the shock and dismay of the nation. In the farm states, representatives of banks who arrived to take possession of farms that could not keep up their mortgage payments were met by groups of unsmiling men carrying clubs. Representatives of farm groups warned the Hoover administration that the countryside was ripe for revolution.

Worst of all, however, was the inability of the business leaders to provide a recipe for renewed prosperity, save for "prudence" on the part of government. A Senate committee in 1932 spent two weeks listening to businessmen give the following advice:

> Bernard Baruch, financier and advisor to many presidents: "Balance budgets. Sacrifice for frugality and revenue. Tax—tax everybody for everything."
> Jackson Reynolds, First National Bank: "I have [no remedy] and I do not believe anyone else has."
> Nicholas Murray Butler, President of Columbia University: "Government economy and balanced budgets."[6]

Heeding the counsel of business leaders and the philosophy of laissez faire, the government under President Hoover believed that the economy would restore itself if it were left alone. Although his administration did more than any previous administration to revive the economy, Hoover felt that no radical steps were called for. His administration bought some agricultural surpluses to help bring farm prices up, and it began a modest program of public works, including the building of Boulder Dam (later renamed Hoover Dam) on the Colorado. Mainly, however, it tried to persuade business to maintain wages, prices, and employment—that is, to conduct business as usual. In 1932 Hoover asked Congress to establish the Reconstruction Finance Corporation (RFC), which lent government money to banks, life insurance companies, railroads, and mortgage associations. The theory behind the RFC was that it would lend funds to large businesses at the top of the economic structure, and benefits would filter down to the people at the bottom through a sort of trickle-down effect. Later that year the Home Loan Bank Act further aided financial institutions in danger of bankruptcy. With more money available, these institutions could extend credit to mortgage holders and meet their depositors' needs for cash. This, it was hoped, would make it possible for more people to buy homes, which, in turn, would give a boost to the construction industry.

The Sins of Omission and Commission

All this did help somewhat. But what was striking was the administration's unwillingness to help the neediest—the unemployed. Before 1932 the federal government provided *no* funds for direct relief to the unemployed. Finally, in July of that year, the federal government began allocating relief money in the form of *loans* to the states. But by the end of 1932 the national government had released only $30 million for relief. Partly this was due to Hoover's belief that charity was the work of voluntary groups and institutions, not of the federal government. In 1930, for example, Hoover endorsed a $45 million appropriation to feed the livestock of Arkansas farmers during a drought, but he rejected a grant of $25 million for food for the farmers and their families. Partly it was due to the fact that the president could not bring himself to believe in the severity, or even the reality, of the plight of the unemployed. "No one is actually starving," he told reporters. "The hoboes, for example, are better fed than they have ever been. One hobo in New York got ten meals in one day."[7] Later, the president was actually to write about the many unemployed who eked out a living by selling apples on street corners: "Many persons left their jobs for the more profitable one of selling apples."

Inaction was the government's worst moral sin, but perhaps its greatest economic sin was in taking actions that unwittingly exacerbated the situation. Believing that the American business system was inherently sound and that the depression was a European import, Hoover signed the Smoot-Hawley Tariff Act of 1930, which raised tariff rates on imports to the highest levels in the country's history. This action had profound repercussions. By making it very difficult for foreign countries to sell their products to America, the tariff deprived European nations of a major source of revenue that would have

Louisville flood victims, 1937

enabled them to buy American goods (especially farm output) and to repay their war debts to the United States.

Nor did the government exercise its taxing and spending or monetary powers prudently. Arguing that a balanced budget was one of the major requirements for a nation's economic health, the government, in 1932, decreased its expenditures and actually enacted the largest tax *increase* up to that point in American history! Even more serious were the Federal Reserve Board's actions. During the speculative mania of the twenties, the monetary authorities could not bring themselves to check the unwise expansion of bank loans by raising the discount rate (the interest rate at which member banks can borrow from the Federal Reserve) or by taking other measures. But when the depression came and the crying need was for banks to encourage business by lending them money for expansion, the Federal Reserve Board suddenly tightened the monetary screws, *raising* interest rates and generally discouraging the financial community from helping its customers.

Yet, before we blame the Hoover administration out of hand for its undoubted mistakes, we must realize that most people did not understand how the depression could be cured—or why it did not cure itself. As time went on and the economy failed to recover, economists as well as businessmen felt baffled by events. The most frightening thing about the depression was that the nation was not only bankrupt in its affairs but bankrupt in its ideas.

Behind the Collapse

What *was* the cause of the Great Depression? The question leads us toward that lesson in economics mentioned at the outset of this chapter. But at least some of the reasons for the collapse do not require any special knowledge at all. Let us examine three of them before we turn to an analysis of the depression itself.

Apple seller, New York City, 1932

1. *The economy was extremely vulnerable to a crash.*

The get-rich-quick philosophy of the 1920s was not limited only to the public. It also infected the business community. An orgy of financial manipulation, wild speculative ventures, and reckless practices made the decade of the 1920s reminiscent of the period of the robber barons.

More to the point, these practices resulted in pyramids of corporations, each holding the stock of others. The pyramids were very profitable as long as the corporations on the bottom stood firm. But when one of them slipped—when one company in a pyramid failed— it often brought down the heap with it. For example, the structure of a giant utility company controlled by a Chicago financier named Samuel Insull was so complex that it was said, in all seriousness, that no one, including Insull himself, could understand it. (Insull held sixty-five chairmanships, eighty-five directorships, and seven presidencies of corporations.) One small part of the structure, Georgia Power & Light, was controlled by Seaboard Public Service Corporation, which was controlled by National Service Corporation, which was controlled by Middle West Utilities Corporation, which was controlled by Insull Utility Investments, which was controlled by Corporation Securities Company, which in turn was controlled by Insull Utility Investments. . . .

Thus despite endless assurances by businessmen that things were fundamentally sound, things were *not* fundamentally sound. Nowhere was this more true than in the banking industry. Banks were up to their ears in the very unsound business of lending money for security purchases; and when the market fell, the lending banks were grievously stricken. In addition, banks not only foisted all manner of unsound securities on the public but became convinced of the value of those very same investments and bought them themselves. Nor did the Federal Reserve Board use any direct controls,* such as raising the discount rate to check the speculative mania of the times. And not least, the acquisitive mania of the twenties tempted banks into practices that hardly squared with "soundness." For instance, the First National Bank (one of the leading New York banks) paid $450,000 to the son of the president of Peru for his services in connection with a

---

*It should be noted that the Federal Reserve Board did not have control over margin requirements until 1934.

$50 million Peruvian loan the bank was about to make at a considerable profit. The services of the president's son, it should be added, consisted entirely of his agreement not to block the deal.

Hence one terrible consequence of the crash was that it toppled many banks whose failure in turn toppled other businesses. In the first six months of 1929, 346 banks failed. By 1932, 4,835 banks had closed their doors. When they did so, it meant that depositors or businesses could not redeem their savings or checking accounts. In the years from 1929 to 1933 over nine million savings accounts were lost and countless businesses went bankrupt because they could not get their money out of the banks.

2. *There was trouble on the farms.*

The crash brought down the fragile banking structure, but even without the stock market there was trouble brewing during the 1920s. The trouble was not in the cities or the big corporations, or among the suburbanites who danced the Charleston, but in rural America. Here lived seven million of America's thirty million families. They did not dance the Charleston because they had no radios on which to hear the music—less than 10 percent of America's farms had electricity. This meant that over 90 percent of the farms were entirely excluded from the market for refrigerators and electric appliances and even electric light.

Moreover, the average farm household was not only poor but was growing relatively poorer. In 1910 an average farmer's income had been about 40 percent of an average urban worker's income. By 1930 it had fallen to less than 30 percent. More telling still, in 1919 farmers had received 16 percent of the national income; in 1929 the figure was 9 percent. Moreover, each year more and more farm families lost their ability to maintain their own farms. Unable to meet the mortgage payments on their properties, they went into sharecropping or tenantry: By 1929 four out of every ten farmers were tenant farmers.

Perhaps what was most ironic in this rural tragedy was that it was caused in substantial part by the very success of the industrial portion of the nation. One of the results of industrialization, as we have already seen, was that farm tasks were increasingly mechanized. This gave rise to a flood of output from the farms—a flood that resulted in a drop in farm prices every bit as painful, though not quite so dramatic, as the drop in stock prices. For example, wheat sold for $1.45 a bushel in 1925 and slid to $1.03 in 1929 (it would go to forty cents in 1931); cotton fell from thirty-four cents a pound to sixteen cents. At those prices farmers could not make ends meet, especially when their shipping costs and local taxes were rising.* A witness described the rural scene before a congressional committee in 1932:

> The roads of the West and the Southwest teem with hungry hitchhikers. The campfires of the homeless are seen along every railroad track. I saw men, women, and children walking over the hard roads. Most of them were tenant farmers who had lost their all in the late slump in wheat and cotton. Between Clarksville and Russellville, Arkansas, I picked up a family. The woman was hugging a dead chicken under a ragged coat. . . . She told me she had found it dead on the road, and then added in grim humor, 'They promised me a chicken in the pot, and now I got mine.'[8]

3. *There was a serious maldistribution of income.*

Last, there was a weakness in the very heartland of prosperity—not in finance or farming, but in industry. This was the problem of wages and profits.

As we have seen, all through the 1920s output per worker had been rising in the manufacturing sector. A steady flow of technological improvements kept raising output even though employment was stationary or even falling in some industries. This obviously made it possible to pay higher wages to workers. Yet their earnings did not keep pace with their rising productivity. In mining, for example, where output per man rose by 43 percent between 1920 and 1929, yearly earnings *fell* from $1,700 to $1,481. In transportation and manufacturing, yearly earnings dropped from 1920 to 1922 and did not regain their

---

*Another cause of the farm sector's problems was the great drop in foreign demand for agricultural foodstuffs. By 1920 the European nations were beginning to recover from the devastation wrought by World War I. Thus their imports of foodstuffs from the United States drastically declined. In 1919 agricultural exports to Europe were valued at $2.6 billion; in 1923 they slipped to under $1 billion. Between 1926 and 1930 they averaged $756 million.

1920 level until 1929, although output per worker was up 50 percent over the period.*

What happened to the gains from higher productivity? They showed up mainly as higher corporate profits—those booming profits that helped cause the stock market boom. Between 1923 and 1929, corporate profits rose 62 percent. Now we can see, however, that the boom in profits not only sparked the stock market rise but seriously undermined the prosperity of the country. For the profit boom signaled the fact that the achievements of the economy were very unevenly enjoyed.

At the top of the income pyramid, the boom created enormous prosperity, as the table below shows.

Notice that the share of total income received by the richest families in the nation grew steadily larger as the twenties went on. And the not-so-rich? It follows that their share must have declined. According to a study made by the Brookings Institution, a leading research organization, an income of $2,000 would buy a family "basic necessities" in 1929. Yet that same study showed that in 1929 almost 60 percent of all American families received less than $2,000. Hence the contrast between the top and the bottom was extreme. In 1929, 15,000 families with incomes of $100,000 or more actually received as much income as 5 to 6 million families at the bottom.

PERCENTAGE OF TOTAL INCOME RECEIVED BY TOP GROUPS

	Top 1 Percent	Top 5 Percent
1919	12.2	24.3
1923	13.8	27.1
1929	18.9	33.5

SOURCE: *Historical Statistics,* Bureau of the Census (1975), Tables G–341, G–342.

---

*In addition, workers in "sick" industries like coal and textiles enjoyed little of the prosperity of the 1920s. Over 1,000 coal mines were shut down in the 1920s and nearly 200,000 miners lost their jobs. Textile manufacturers were receiving stiff competition from the new synthetic fabrics industry. Thus they had to lower their prices, cut back on output, and lay off workers.

Other statistics show that between 1920 and 1929 per capita disposable income for all Americans rose by 9 percent, but the top 1 percent of income recipients enjoyed an explosive 75 percent increase in disposable income. The share of disposable income going to the top 1 percent rose by almost 60 percent in 1929.

One further statistical breakdown is necessary to round out the picture: In 1929 approximately 80 percent of the nation's families—roughly 21.5 million households—had no savings whatsoever. The 24,000 families at the top—0.1 percent—held 34 percent of all savings. The 2.3 percent of families with incomes of more than $10,000 controlled two-thirds of the nation's savings.

The consequence was not just a matter for tongue-clucking. Income was being diverted away from ordinary families, who would have spent it for the products of mass industry, into the hands of the rich, who spent it for luxuries or who did not spend it at all.

In other words, the prosperity of the 1920s was a good deal less substantial than it appeared on the surface. A rickety financial structure brought havoc when the stock market collapsed. A declining farm sector created an undertow of falling incomes in the agricultural areas where a fourth of the nation lived. The boom in profits and the swelling of topmost incomes came at the expense of a much-needed encouragement to mass buying power. Thus the economy operated very unevenly, bringing real riches to a few but a false sense of widely shared well-being to the nation at large. It was a prosperity based largely on speculation, easy credit, and foolish spending.

THE ANATOMY OF DEPRESSION

All these reasons help explain why the depression was so deep, so hard, so long. But they do not quite enlighten us as to the main question—namely, why an economy in full growth should suddenly go into a kind of paralysis. For that we need to take a brief lesson in economics.

Much of our understanding about the nature of depressions derives from a book published in the midst of the period, *The General Theory of Employment, Interest, and Money,* written by the English economist, John Maynard Keynes. Controversial at the time, Keynes's basic theories have by now become accepted by economists and governments all over the world. And like so many new theories that seem extraordinarily difficult at the time they are first pronounced, Keynes's essential ideas now appear very simple.

At the heart of Keynes's explanation of depression is a fundamental fact about a market economy: *the source of all its employment is spending.* Unless money is spent, money will not be received. Unless dollars are spent, neither businesses nor employees will get paid. Spending—*expenditure* is the more formal term—is the key to the generation of employment and income.

Who Does the Nation's Spending?

Keynes divides spenders into two groups: households and business firms. Households spend money for the goods and services they consume—consumer goods. These include food and clothing and automobiles and doctors' services and similar items. But consumers are not the only spenders in the economy. Business also spends money, not merely to keep its operations going, but to add to its plant and equipment, its capital wealth. We call this second kind of spending *investment.* A business invests when it is building a new factory, adding a wing to an existing establishment, piling up larger inventories to service its customers.

All that was familiar enough, even in the 1930s. But Keynes emphasizes a very important distinction between consumer spending and business spending. Consumer spending, he explains, is not usually marked by rapid changes (upward or downward), *unless consumers' incomes have previously changed upward or downward.* That is, households tend to spend a fairly steady proportion of their incomes. When their incomes fall—as in a depression—naturally they spend less. When their incomes rise, they spend more.

But it is different with business spending for investment. A business firm does not decide to build a new plant or to buy new equipment only because its *current* income is high. Indeed, we recall that Andrew Carnegie launched the great Thomson Steel Works even though there was a severe depression in 1873. Business spending for investment depends on businessmen's expectations of *future* sales. If a business firm expects to be able to sell more goods, it might spend money to enlarge its factory even though its current income is low. Vice versa, even if a business is highly prosperous, it might cut its investment spending if it feels that the future is not likely to continue as favorably as the past.

The Crucial Role of Investment

This gives us a first clue to the real meaning of the depression. *All depressions, or "recessions," or business slumps are brought about because the economy is not spending enough to create high levels of employment or income.*

That is exactly what caused the Great Depression. In 1929 the gross national product—the value of total final output—was $104 billion.* In 1932 the gross national product (GNP) had fallen to $56 billion. What caused the terrific collapse? The main reason is that the Great Crash, added to all the weaknesses that we have seen, sent a wave of pessimism through business. Businessmen simply cancelled their plans for business expansion in the face of deep and growing concern about the future.

---

*What is gross national product? *It is the market value of all the final goods and services produced by the economy in a year.* The word "final" means that the statisticians who compute GNP add up the value of all the "last" goods we produce but do not include the value of output that *goes into* those goods. Example: the statisticians count in GNP the market value of all the automobiles that are made, but not the value of the rubber, the steel, the paint, and the cotton cloth that various companies sell to the auto-makers. The reason is that the value of these goods is *included* in the value of the finished car. In the same way, GNP includes the value of the clothes that are made, but not the value of the cloth, the thread, and the buttons that are included in the selling price of the finished garment.

What are "final" goods? There are four kinds. First, there are all the domestically made *consumption goods* or services that households buy, such as autos and clothes. Second are the domestically produced *investment goods* that business buys, such as new buildings, machines, and additions to inventories. Third are the domestic goods or services that *government buys*—roads, public education, police, arms, and so forth. And fourth is the value of all *foreign goods* and services of all kinds bought by the nation, minus the value of all domestic production sold abroad. To recapitulate, then, *GNP is the total market value of the annual output of all domestic consumer output, all domestic investment output, all domestic public output, and all output sold abroad less foreign output imported into the country.*

Recently our national output has been calculated as GDP, not GNP—D standing for domestic instead of national. The change affects the way we treat the earnings of U.S. corporations abroad, and foreign corporations operating within the U.S. In dollars, the difference between GNP and GDP is small.

We can see the collapse in investment spending in the figures below:

INVESTMENT SPENDING (BILLIONS OF $)		
Housing	**Other Construction**	**Plant & Equipment**
1929 4.0	5.0	5.6
1932 1.7	1.2	1.5

SOURCE: *Historical Statistics,* Bureau of the Census, 1975, Tables F57, F55, F56.

The Multiplier Effect

Between 1929 and 1933, investment spending of all kinds shrank by 88 percent! One-third of all unemployment was directly generated by the shrinkage in output of industries that supplied capital goods. Unemployment then spread throughout the economy as a consequence of the cutback in investment spending. As workers were fired and lower incomes were paid out by construction firms and steel plants and other businesses making capital goods, employees were forced to cut back their spending for consumer goods. In turn, because they bought fewer consumer goods, firms that sold clothing, food, housewares, and so forth began to fire some of their workers, or to lower their wages. Thus the sharp drop in investment spending spread throughout the economy, creating a "multiplier" effect as it went.

Indefinite Depression

Keynes's explanation of the mechanism of depression was very clear, and not too controversial. But buried in his analysis was a deeper implication. It was that there was no *automatic* cure for a depression. Only a resumption of spending—investment spending—could move an economy off dead center. But there was no mechanism that would bring this about from the normal workings of the system. An economy could remain in a stagnant condition indefinitely. A depression could go on forever.

It was this last part of Keynes's analysis that was most disturbing. For economists had always maintained that depressions would ultimately cure themselves, not merely because businessmen would recover their optimistic expectations and begin again to invest, but because the workings of the system would by themselves create the stimulus for reexpansion. As the economy contracted, economists argued, unused savings would pile up in the banks, forcing down the rate of interest to a point where businessmen would be irresistibly tempted to borrow and spend. After that, the upward march would resume.

Keynes's book dealt a disconcerting blow to that reassuring belief. For it pointed out that there would be no unused savings as a depression continued. Rather, savings would shrink along with investment as the economy ran downhill. Moreover, even if interest rates did fall, Keynes pointed out, businessmen would not invest if their expectations remained pessimistic. Hence the economy could go on in "equilibrium"—without any internally generated upward thrust—even though it was full of unemployed men and women and underutilized plants and equipment. That dead part of the economy might as well be on the moon, for all the positive effect it exerted on the business community.

Growth or Stagnation?

A full discussion of Keynesian economics is obviously far beyond the scope of this book. But we can see how Keynes's idea of a stagnant economy touches our own central theme. The economic transformation of America has been a narrative of capitalist growth. All through our historic journey, the theme of capitalist expansion—of a rising trajectory of output and income—has provided the setting in which occurred the changes in material and economic life to which we have paid heed. But now the Great Depression—the endless, endless depression—and the idea of an economy in stagnant equilibrium causes us to ask another question: Is growth the norm for capitalism? Is it a state of affairs to be taken for granted, with depressions viewed as temporary aberrations from the main path? Or is growth a prelude to something else, of which the Great Depression provided a frightening glimpse?

It may come as something of a surprise to learn that all the great economists have pictured capitalism as tending finally toward a kind of stagnant, stationary condition. Adam Smith, the first magisterial student of the system, believed that sooner or later a market society would accumulate all the capital it needed, after which it would begin to decline. David Ricardo and his disciple, John Stuart Mill, writing in the nineteenth century, also thought that capitalism would move toward a stationary condition—not because it had built all the capital it needed, but because profitable investment would become ever more difficult as wages and material costs rose as a consequence of expansion. Karl Marx also perceived the system as reaching a limit. Marx foresaw a series of "crises" generated by capitalism, each one resulting in a more concentrated structure of business and a more proletarianized lower class, until the tension within the system finally snapped, and capitalism came to an end.

Essentially then, almost all the great economists, Keynes among them, have expected that capitalism would eventually change so profoundly that it could no longer be called by its name. The main point of disagreement has been over the nature of the forces bringing about that change—Smith's exhaustion of investment opportunities, Ricardo's or Mill's squeeze on profits by rising costs, or Marx's complex dynamics of instability and concentration—and over the length of time the system could be expected to continue. In 1942, Joseph Schumpeter, perhaps the most distinguished conservative economist of the twentieth century, put the matter point blank. "Can capitalism survive?" he asked. "No," he answered. "I do not think it can."[9] However, Schumpeter hastened to add that it would take another fifty to 100 years before capitalism gave way before the advance of a kind of bureaucratic socialism.

The Social Structure of Accumulation

How does the Great Depression fit into these possible evolutionary tendencies of the system? An interesting answer has been proposed by economist David Gordon.[10] It focuses our attention on the milieu within which capitalism carries on its accumulative activity. This milieu begins in the workplace where capitalists must organize and oversee a work force to create a profitable flow of output, a relationship that sometimes works very well and sometimes very poorly. The milieu then extends into the interaction of business and government, where businessmen sometimes find their investment activities supported by public action, and sometimes find them blocked by it. It moves out still further into the realm of public opinion where businesses may encounter a favoring or hostile reception to their general aims. And it reaches out finally into the world economy within which each national economy must find its place.

Gordon calls this complex set of relationships and institutions *the social structure of accumulation*. It is in this social structure that he finds the crucial connection between growth and stagnation. For the network of relationships that supports capital accumulation in one period may become a hindrance in another. Thus we can distinguish between the normal business cycle, in which investment booms may be interrupted but quickly resume their course within a favoring milieu, from turning points, or crisis periods, in which investment comes to a halt because the milieu itself stands in the way of capital expansion. In these critical periods we need more than a recovery of business optimism. We need a social restructuring that will permit capital expansion once more to take place.

The Crisis of the 1870s

We have spent a good deal of time studying one such crisis period. This was the era of the Robber Barons, when capitalists struggled to cope with the disruptions of a new high speed, mass-volume technology. We watched as a framework of giant-business, created by vertical and horizontal integration, brought order into the chaos of cutthroat competition by replacing the unmanageable currents of the marketplace with the steadying guidance of management's visible hand.

The concept of a crisis period caused by an inadequate social structure of accumulation helps us put this period into a perspective of capitalist evolution. For we can see that the structure of the pre–Robber Baron period with its small-scale enterprises, its craft-organized labor force, and its nonregulative government, could not handle the economic pressures and strains caused by the technology of mass production. Indeed, in the milieu of the 1860s, the new technology did not produce growth but chaos and disorder. It required a wholly different social structure of giant organizations, "de-skilled" labor, and regulative government, before those technological forces could give rise to capital accumulation.

The 1930s as a Crisis Period

This brings us once again to the Great Depression. For now we can see that the era of the 1930s was also a time in which an older milieu was no longer able to provide the necessary support for the accumulation process. The difference was that the immediate problem of the 1930s was not technological. The big business system had more or less overcome that once formidable threat. But that selfsame system had brought into existence a new difficulty, previously absent. This was the tremendous downward momentum generated by the system when investment halted, for whatever reason. The economy of the 1930s was no longer an economic landscape of small enterprise with a few great enterprises towering over the whole. It was the great enterprises themselves that constituted the main elements of the system. In place of an economy that resembled a pile of sand, there had arisen an economy that resembled a great steel scaffolding. A pile of sand can withstand a heavy blow without losing its stability. A scaffolding whose main members are weakened comes toppling down with a crash.

Essentially the crisis of the 1930s was caused by the vulnerability of a structure of business that had become interlocked on a previously unknown scale. It was the collapse of the scaffolding that caused the extraordinary damage, the sense of an economy in ruins. Perhaps, as some business leaders affirmed, the system would in time recover its optimism and begin once again to grow. But it was time that was running out. The country was exhausted. There was no patience left.

But what was to be done? With the gift of hindsight we know the answer, as did Keynes and a few others at the time. In part it was to use government powers to restore order to shattered elements of the system, such as the banking structure. In part it was to use government to emplace a floor of security beneath the nation's households. And most important of all, it was to use government spending itself as a means of imparting momentum to the economy—a task that had formerly been solely entrusted to business investment spending. In a word, the overriding task was to rescue the capitalist economy by altering its social structure of accumulation in ways that would make the government vastly more responsible for the functioning of the economic mechanism.

None of that was very clearly seen by most of the nation's business leaders or its politicians. Indeed, the idea of creating such a new "socialistic" milieu was as foreign and as unwelcome to most leaders in the 1930s as was the idea of fostering an economy of "trusts" in the 1860s. Yet in one period of crisis as in the other, changes of vast extent were carried out, despite the absence of any clear blueprint for the future, and over the protests of those who felt that the changes were against their interests. And in one period as in the other, after the changes had been made, the new social structure of accumulation did generate a new era of growth, and the long upward trajectory of the system was renewed.

How did this far-reaching change come about? To find out we must pick up our narrative as a discredited and discouraged Republican administration leaves office in 1932 and a new Democratic president takes over, with very few convictions except that *something* had to be done.

Notes

[1] *Only Yesterday* (Bantam ed., 1946), p. 349.
[2] Nov. 5, 1932, pp. 3–4.
[3] Quoted in John Kenneth Galbraith, *The Great Crash* (1955), pp. 69–70.
[4] F. L. Allen, *The Big Change* (1952), p. 148.
[5] Arthur Schlesinger, Jr., *The Crisis of the Old Order* (1957), pp. 162–63, 177.
[6] Quoted in Schlesinger, *The Crisis of the Old Order,* pp. 457–58.
[7] Quoted in William Manchester, *The Glory and the Dream* (1974), p. 41.
[8] David Shannon (ed.), *The Great Depression* (1960), p. 27.
[9] *Capitalism, Socialism, and Democracy* (1942), p. 61.
[10] David Gordon, Michael Reich, and Richard C. Edwards, *Segmented Work, Divided Workers* (1982), pp.9–10, 22–26.

National Industrial Recovery Act banners, 1933

Chapter 8

THE NEW DEAL

On election day, 1932, Franklin D. Roosevelt won an overwhelming victory over Herbert Hoover. The popular vote, 22,800,000 to 15,750,000, and the Electoral College vote, 472 to fifty-nine, tell only part of the story. In addition to carrying every state south and west of Pennsylvania, and capturing more counties than any previous candidate, the new president had taken from Hoover all but six of the forty states the ex-president had won in 1928. With the exception of the election of 1912, when the Republican Party was split between Taft and Theodore Roosevelt, no Republican presidential candidate had ever been defeated so soundly.

THE HUNDRED DAYS

The nation had unequivocally declared its need for a new policy to deal with the depression. In the four months before Roosevelt took office the depression deepened and worsened. When inauguration day finally came, on March 4, 1933, the country was glued to its radio receivers to hear what the new president would say. What they heard was this:

> First of all, let me assert my belief that the only thing we have to fear is fear itself—nameless, unreasoning, unjustified terror. . . . I shall not evade the clear course of duty that [confronts] me. I shall ask the Congress . . . for broad Executive power to wage war against the emergency, as great as the power that would be given to me if we were in fact invaded by a foreign foe. . . . I pledge you, I pledge myself to a new deal for the American people.[1]

Roosevelt's clarion call was magnetic. "America hasn't been as happy in three years as they are today," wrote Will Rogers the next day. "No money, no banks, no work, no nothing, but they know they got a man in there who is wise to Congress, wise to our so-called big men. The whole country is with him."[2] That weekend the new president received 450,000 messages confirming Rogers' opinion.

Financial Crisis

About few subjects have so many volumes been written as about the "New Deal"—those two words Roosevelt first uttered casually in his acceptance speech before the Democratic convention in Chicago in 1932. Not since Lincoln or Theodore Roosevelt had a personality so engaged the public. Millions of Americans hung pictures of Roosevelt in their living rooms and felt him to be a member of their families.

What the country desperately wanted from FDR was action—almost any action—rather than a continuation of Hoover's policy of waiting for the economy to cure itself. The public was not disappointed. The New Deal began with what historian Arthur Schlesinger, Jr., has called "a barrage of ideas and programs unlike anything known to American history." In the first dazzling "Hundred Days," March 9 to June 16, 1933, over fifteen major pieces of legislation were passed.

The most pressing problem that the president had to address himself to was the financial crisis, which had now reached a point of near panic, with more banks closing every day. Even before he convened Congress into emergency session, Roosevelt issued an executive order declaring a nationwide bank "holiday." Thereafter he instructed his first Secretary of the Treasury, William Woodin, to prepare an emergency banking bill within five days. When the special session of Congress convened on March 9, it gave its approval to actions Roosevelt had in fact already taken. The Emergency Banking Act gave the President unequivocal control over gold and currency movements, outlawed the hoarding of gold, sanctioned the issue of new Federal Reserve Bank notes, and established a procedure for reopening those banks that possessed liquid assets and for reorganizing those that did not.

The Emergency Banking Act represented a bold extension and assertion of government power. Curiously, the bill was written at lightning speed by conservative bankers and by Hoover's own Treasury officials and was then passed unanimously, *sight unseen,* by the

President Franklin D. Roosevelt

House of Representatives! A few days later, some sixty million Americans turned on their radios to hear the first of Roosevelt's "fireside chats." In informal, fatherly tones, the president's voice conveyed a spirit of national purpose and demonstrated one of his many charismatic qualities—the power to persuade. After describing the complex banking structure in simple terms, he told the country that the banks would be safely opening in the twelve Federal Reserve Bank cities the next morning. They opened safely, because people believed Roosevelt and did not rush to withdraw their deposits. Indeed, by the end of the month net inflows of currency into banks amounted to $1.25 billion. "Capitalism," a member of Roosevelt's advisory team (the so-called brain trust) later wrote, "was saved in eight days."[3]

Other Financial Legislation

Subsequent banking legislation established the Federal Deposit Insurance Corporation to guarantee bank deposits up to $5,000 ($100,000 today), divorced investment and commercial banking, and broadened the power of the Federal Reserve Board. These measures also had an immediate impact. People began to deposit rather than withdraw money, and bank failures were sharply reduced.

In retrospect, the "obscure, unpretentious, unwanted Federal Deposit Insurance Corporation" (as John Kenneth Galbraith has described the measure, which was opposed by the American Bankers Association* and endorsed only halfheartedly by the administration) may well have been the most important single piece of financial legislation passed by the Roosevelt administration. As Galbraith points out, for the first time an utterly reliable lender of last resort—the federal government itself—was squarely committed to the safety of bank accounts. No more powerful measure of financial or psychological endorsement was ever taken by the government.

Closely related to the reorganization of the banking structure was Roosevelt's determination to curb financial abuses, particularly in the securities market. Writing to Congress on March 29, 1933, he stated: "What we seek is a return to a clearer understanding of the ancient truth that those who manage banks, corporations, and other agencies handling or using other people's money are trustees acting for others."[4]

Within a year the country saw the birth of the Securities and Exchange Commission (the SEC) charged with broad powers to oversee the issuance of new securities, to insist on the divulgence of full information regarding new issues, and to establish an agency to maintain a watchful eye over the operation of that great gambling casino, the stock exchange. It would be too much to say that the Banking Act, the Federal Deposit Insurance Corporation, and the SEC cured American finance of all its problems or prevented financial misdeeds in the future. But with these acts, and the Public Utility Holding Company Act that prohibited the old pyramiding of utility companies, the New Deal effectively removed the worst elements of the financial crisis that was threatening to undermine the system itself.

---

*Big bankers opposed the act because they believed it would give unsound banks "a license for reckless behavior that the supervision authorized by the legislation could not hope to restrain." Hence the sound establishments would "have to accept responsibility for the recklessness of the worst." See Galbraith, *Money* (1975), p. 197.

Unemployment

The New Deal was not so successful in combating unemployment. For one thing, Roosevelt was himself a strong believer in balanced budgets for government,* and therefore he shrank from the full application of a Keynesian remedy of government spending, whatever the effect on the deficit. We will go into this in more detail later in this chapter. But despite the inhibitions imposed by a genuine desire to achieve budget economies, the New Deal did attack the problem of unemployment and human suffering far more vigorously than its predecessor.

On April 5, 1933, Roosevelt created the Civilian Conservation Corps to provide jobs in reforestation and conservation projects for young men between the ages of eighteen and twenty-five. Wearing their forest-green CCC uniforms, over $2^{1}/_{2}$ million youths planted 200 million trees, not only beautifying the land but establishing windbreaks to prevent the erosion that had devastated many farm lands.

Then, in May, Roosevelt signed into being the Federal Emergency Relief Administration, headed by Harry Hopkins, a confidant and trusted adviser. The FERA had $500 million to allocate to state and local relief agencies, but Hopkins was convinced that jobs, not money, were the prime requisite to restore confidence. Hopkins persuaded the president to sponsor the Civil Works Administration, a federally sponsored program to employ people in building roads, schools, playgrounds, airports, or to teach. Before Roosevelt finally disbanded the CWA because of its mounting costs, it had given work to over four million people and had channeled some $950 million into the economy. Then, in 1935, Hopkins was put in charge of another alphabet agency—the WPA (Works Progress Administration). By 1943 this agency had employed $8^{1}/_{2}$ million people and had spent a total of $11 billion.

In a nation that had not yet heard of Keynes and that was still wedded to the ideas of laissez faire, all this was a radical departure indeed.

---

*During his campaign for the presidency, Roosevelt had attacked the Hoover administration for "being the greatest spending Administration in peace times in all our history. . . . "Indeed, Roosevelt's second piece of Hundred Days legislation, the Economy Act, was an effort to honor his pledge to cut government spending. The purpose of the measure was to help balance the budget by slashing veterans' benefits and allowances by $400 million and by reducing by $100 million the pay of federal employees.

Yet few voices were raised in protest. For the country knew, as did Roosevelt, that the alternative to these experiments in government employment was the risk of an interminable depression with massive unemployment. No one dared run that risk.

Industry and Labor

One of Roosevelt's pet proposals for ending the demoralization of the economy was the National Industrial Recovery Act. The NIRA was a curious mixture of things, designed to please many constituencies. It contained the authorization, for example, for the Public Works Administration (with a budget of $3.3 billion), a works project that supplemented the WPA. It contained a clause specifically guaranteeing workers the right to unionize and to bargain collectively with their employers. It outlawed much child labor. It established a precedent for the government regulation of minimum wages and hours. Not least, it allowed business to do legally what it had sought in vain to do through pools, trusts, and collusion—namely, to establish industry-wide prices and codes of fair practice. The hope was that the act would turn the sluggish industrial economy around and, at the same time, usher in a new era in labor-management relations. Internecine warfare among firms in the same field would be avoided and the threat of strikes would be minimized.

The National Recovery Administration (NRA) did not achieve all its objectives by any means, and its use of government powers to protect labor on the one hand and to legalize "trusts" on the other offended many people. Though it was greeted with much initial enthusiasm, there was a general sigh of relief among several government offices when the act was finally declared unconstitutional by the Supreme Court in 1935.* But by then the NRA had served its purpose of restoring orderly markets in many areas, and its specific reforms were soon continued under new legislation (the Fair Labor Standards Act) aimed at establishing minimum wages and maximum hours in certain

---

*In the case of *Schechter v. United States*, the high court ruled unanimously that Congress had delegated too much of its law-making power to the boards that administrered the industrial codes established under the measure. Roosevelt, however, continued to believe in the NRA approach of government-business-labor cooperation and never abandoned the idea of trying to restore it.

Works Progress Administration workers

industries, at abolishing child labor, and most important, at protecting the rights of labor. According to James MacGregor Burns, the passage of the Wagner Act in 1935, which once again assured the right of unions to organize and to bargain collectively, was "the most radical legislation passed during the New Deal" because it helped to create "powerful unions that . . . would furnish votes, money, and organization to future liberal coalitions." Under the auspices of the Wagner Act, and the National Labor Relations Board which it created to run union elections and settle disputes, union membership jumped from 3.2 million in 1932 to 8.3 million in 1938.[5]

Agriculture

The NRA had something for business and something for labor. But the Roosevelt program for farm relief was incorporated in another major piece of legislation. This was the AAA—the Agricultural Adjustment Act of 1933. The AAA went much further than Hoover's efforts to help the farmer through the government purchase of some surplus crops. It aimed to break the vicious circle of farm poverty by making it possible for farmers to do collectively what they could not do individually—to limit their production so that the price of their products would rise.

The program was intended to work through compulsory restrictions on the production of designated crops, together with government subsidies for staple commodities such as wheat, cotton, and pork. However, since crops were already growing when the law was enacted, Secretary of Agriculture Henry A. Wallace felt it necessary to tell farmers to destroy their produce in the field. Thus, while millions of Americans were still hungry, cotton planters received $100 million for plowing under ten million acres of growing crops, and farmers were paid to kill six million baby pigs and 200,000 pregnant sows! Yet, if the program revealed an appalling insensitivity, it did succeed in its overall objectives. More than 30 million acres were taken out of cultivation, and farm prices rose from depression lows to more normal levels. By 1936 the farm sector had doubled its income, and there was no more talk of revolution brewing in Ohio.

Soon thereafter a much more imaginative program made up for the government's failure to deal more sensibly with the problem of farm surpluses. This was its effort to bring economic growth to a backwater region through the establishment of a federal power-generating system, the Tennessee Valley Authority. During the First World War the government had built a hydroelectric plant at Muscle Shoals, Alabama, to provide power for the manufacture of synthetic nitrate explosives. Although farmers and other interest groups succeeded after the war in warding off plans to hand these facilities over to private enterprise, they failed in their efforts to have the site come under federal control. Now Roosevelt hoped to turn one of the country's most underdeveloped areas into an experimental laboratory for extensive social planning. The TVA constructed dams and powerhouses, established programs for flood control, soil conservation, and reforestation, and produced electricity and fertilizer. Moreover the TVA became a "yardstick" that enabled the government to measure the fairness of the rates charged by private power companies.

Together with the power generated by the TVA, one other New Deal action dramatically altered the course of the farmer's life—the Rural Electrification Administration of 1935. One statistic sums up its accomplishment. Before 1935, nine out of every ten farms had no electricity; by 1950, nine out of ten had electric light.

Social Security

We have not yet discussed what is perhaps the most important single measure that the New Deal passed: Social Security. After signing the measure on August 15, 1935, Roosevelt remarked: "If the Senate and the House of Representatives in this long and arduous session had done nothing more than pass this bill, the session would be regarded as historic for all time."[6]

Essentially, the Social Security Act established a national system of old-age insurance. Once workers reached the age of sixty-five they would receive retirement benefits paid for by taxes on their wages and their employers' payrolls. Payment would, up to a point, vary with the amount each individual earned. The act also created a federal-state system of unemployment insurance and provided for federal-state joint assistance to the destitute, to the handicapped, and to dependent mothers and children.

Not all Americans approved of this unparalleled legislation. "Never in the history of the world," said conservative Congressman John Taber, "has any measure been brought in here so insidiously designed as to prevent business recovery, to enslave workers, and to prevent any possibility of the employers providing work for the people." Congressman Daniel Reed agreed: "The lash of the dictator will be felt and twenty-five million free American citizens will for the first time submit themselves to the fingerprint test."[7]

These were not isolated criticisms, nor did they match the more strident invective that was hurled at Roosevelt. Many businessmen regarded the president, who came from a wealthy New York family, as a "traitor to his class," and the reforms of the New Deal, far from being welcomed by them, were bitterly resisted and interpreted as the entering wedge of socialism. In 1934 some of these arch-conservative businessmen formed the American Liberty League, around which anti–New Dealers from both parties coalesced.

The innovations of the New Deal were also regarded suspiciously by another conservative element in society—the nation's courts. One after another of the major New Deal efforts, such as the Agricultural Adjustment Act* and the National Industrial Recovery Act, were declared unconstitutional by a Supreme Court that viewed with alarm the efforts of the federal government to use the powers of the Constitution to regulate and restrain economic life. Even some of the most liberal justices felt that Roosevelt exceeded the proper bounds of executive power. Not until the Eisenhower years in the 1950s was the new role of the government finally accepted as a necessary element in a highly organized industrial system, rather than as a threat to that system.

THE NEW DEAL IN PERSPECTIVE

Can we sum up the economic accomplishments of the New Deal as a whole? Looking back on its array of accomplishments from the perspective of our last chapter, we can see that the New Deal can be regarded as an attempt—a quite unconscious attempt—to alter the social structure of accumulation in three ways.

First, *the New Deal was an effort to make the system work in certain areas in which it had failed.* The stock market crash, the farm disaster, the bank failures, massive unemployment—these were not merely localized or transient failures that could be safely left to the dynamic forces of the economy to cure. The public had waited too long to believe that things would straighten out by themselves. What was needed was a new assurance that serious problems affecting the livelihood and lives of millions of wage-earners would not be allowed to fester unheeded. If the economy did not function reliably by itself, the public wanted the government to make it work.

That is what the New Deal tried to do, though not always with success. For all the accusations of "socialism" that were hurled against it, the New Deal was essentially conservative in its intent. As evidenced

---

*The AAA was declared unconstitutional in the case of *United States v. Butler* (1936). In a six to three decision the Court held the AAA's processing tax—the means by which farm subsidies were financed—to be unconstitutional. According to Justice Owen Roberts, the tax expropriated "money from one group for the benefit of another."

by the authorship of the emergency banking legislation, it sought not to replace the business system with another totally different system but to amend the business system to make it succeed.

Second, *the New Deal was an effort to create a new relation between government and citizenry in economic life.* The belief that prevailed throughout the years of American economic growth had been that the best guardian for each able-bodied citizen was himself. This was indeed an integral part of the philosophy of laissez faire. When Herbert Hoover spoke of "the American system of rugged individualism" and deplored agencies for relief and for the provision of a retirement income, he was speaking not just as an individual whose view of the economy inclined him in a conservative direction, but as a true spokesman of a philosophy endorsed by large numbers of the business community.

What Hoover and the business community failed to realize was that the basis for a system of rugged individualism had been eroded by the very success of the industrial growth of the economy. In 1890, for example, twice as many Americans lived in rural areas as in urban ones. When growth slackened in the industrial centers and unemployment grew, at least some affected families could move in with their relatives on the farm. In the 1930s, as we have seen, the proportion of rural and urban dwellers had swung the other way. Almost 60 percent of the nation lived in urban areas; so it was no longer possible for a recession affecting large numbers of workers to be cushioned by a reliance on country cousins. The workable basis for rugged individualism had gone with the industrialization and urbanization of the country. The New Deal was not an effort to make people dependent on government for security in case of economic trouble. It was a response to a situation in which no other solution was possible.

Third, *the New Deal was an effort to renew growth, not merely by repairing the weaknesses of the nation's financial and farm sectors, but by using the government as a means of spending to supplement the laggard expenditure of private investment.* Certainly the idea was very far from Roosevelt's mind when he took office at the very bottom of the depression. Campaigning for the presidency, he urged "balanced budgets," just like everyone else, and the idea of a large and aggressive program of public spending as a way of swelling the nation's output was as foreign to him as it was to the most conservative of the nation's businessmen. What was different about Roosevelt and the New Deal, in its early days, was a sense of the human urgency of the situation. Herbert Hoover was able to speak of the unemployed shivering at wintry street corners with their little piles of apples for sale as having *chosen* their economic condition. In contrast, Roosevelt and his advisers saw the unemployed as the victims of an economic disaster for which they were not responsible and over which they had no control. Hence they responded to the immediate situation by hastily throwing together the collection of emergency programs that we have seen.

Of course this necessitated the spending of money by the government. Federal Emergency Relief increased from $6 million in 1933 to $115 million in 1935. Expenditures by the Civilian Conservation Corps began in 1933 at $141 million and grew to $332 million in two years. The Civil Works Administration spent $215 million in the first year of Roosevelt's term and more than double that the next year. These are all very small numbers to us, who are used to billions and tens of billions rather than mere millions, but they were very large numbers in a day when the total military expenditures of the government were less than $700 million in a normal year. Do not forget, either, that in the 1930s gross national product was less than $100 billion, whereas today it is over $6 trillion.

As a result of these emergency measures, total government spending rose. In 1932, the last year of the Hoover administration, the federal government spent $4.6 billion for all purposes—education, highways, national defense, postal services, relief, and so forth. By 1935 the total was up to $6.5 billion; by 1936, $8.4 billion—an unprecedented sum. Helped along by this "pump-priming," business began to spend more too—spending for business investment rose from $0.9 billion in 1932 to $11 billion in 1937. Consumer spending rose as well, supported by the new dollars flowing into households: consumers spent $46 billion in 1933 and $67 billion in 1937.

Disappointing Results

On the face of it, then, it would seem that the effort to restore growth was a success. Real gross national product had fallen to a low of $74 billion in 1933—off by one-fourth from the high of 1929. By 1937 it was back to $109 billion. Unemployment, which had reached the dreadful total of almost thirteen million men and women in 1933, was down to 7.7 million by 1937.

Yet it is clear, at second look, that the program was at best only a partial success. For despite the recovery under the impetus of federal spending, gross national product in 1937 was still only 5 percent above its peak in 1929—instead of really growing, the economy was only catching up (and was far below the trend of the past). And although 7.7 million unemployed was a good deal less serious than thirteen million, it still meant that 14 percent of the labor force was unable to find work, compared with only 3 percent in 1929.

Chart 1 shows us what was happening with government spending and GNP. Notice how government spending rose, helping to push up GNP but hardly bringing it above the level of 1929 prosperity.

Chart 2 shows the problem even more clearly, for now we place the New Deal period in a longer-range historical context. The second chart shows the long, irregular upward slope of growth prior to the Great Depression, the subsequent collapse, and then the recovery following on the New Deal. Note that by 1937 the economy had not yet reached the "trend line" established by the pre–New Deal period.

The Doldrums

Why was the economy in 1937 barely above the level of 1929? Why had not the bold new program of the New Deal quickly brought the country back onto the long "growth path" of the past?

If we had been able to visit Washington or the main industrial centers of the country in 1937, the answer we would have heard was that the government was doing "too much." James Farley, chairman of the Democratic Party, warned Roosevelt: "The one criticism which is being constantly hammered home and which seems to be having the most effect is the charge that the President and his Administration are carrying on an orgy of public spending. . . . "[8]

Farley's opinion was widely held. After resigning as Roosevelt's director of the budget because he believed that the president was spending too much, Lewis Douglas wrote the president: "I hope, and hope most fervently, that you will evidence a real determination to bring the budget into actual balance, for upon this, I think, hangs not only your place in history but conceivably the immediate fate of western civilization."[9] Ironically, Roosevelt himself worried that he was spending too much money. In 1937, when the economy seemed on the way toward a modest recovery (as we can see from Chart 2), he

CHART 1
Pre-New Deal and New Deal Periods

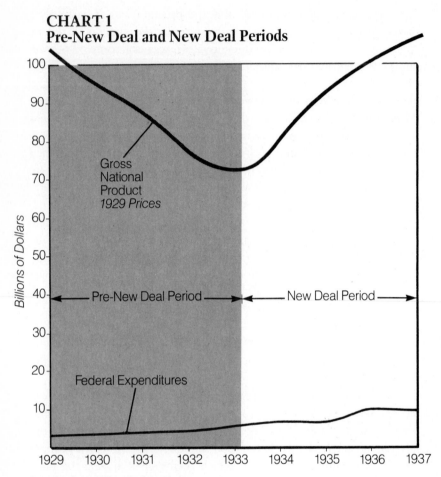

Source: from *Historical Statistics.*

slashed spending, sharply cut the rolls of the WPA, and turned off the "pump-priming" expenditures of the PWA.

The result was disconcerting. Government expenditures fell by a billion dollars—but gross national product fell by $5 billion! Out of the blue, another selling wave hit the stock market, which dropped a staggering 40 percent. Worst of all, unemployment jumped from 7.7 million to over ten million.

The severity of the collapse of October 1937 actually exceeded that which followed the Crash of '29. During the next nine months,

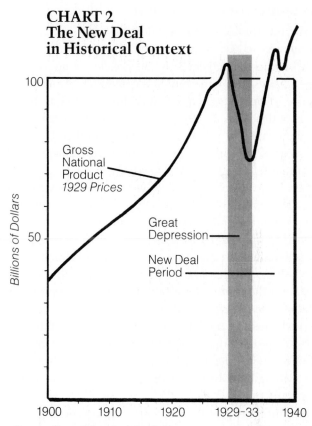

CHART 2
The New Deal
in Historical Context

Billions of Dollars

100

Gross
National
Product
1929 Prices

Great
Depression

50

New Deal
Period

1900   1910   1920   1929-33   1940

Source: from *Historical Statistics.*

national income fell 13 percent, industrial production by 33 percent, employment in manufacturing industries by almost 25 percent, and payrolls in general by 35 percent.

There was very little choice as to what to do next. The PWA was hurriedly given additional funds; government spending increased by over $1 billion; unemployment slowly fell to 9.4 million in 1939, then to eight million in 1940. The country resumed its sluggish recovery. In 1939, gross national product went up to $111 billion—just above the 1937 level—and finally, in 1940, it climbed to $121 billion, surpassing by a mere 16 percent the level of 1929.

The Dilemma of Government

What *was* the trouble? Looking back, we can see that much of the stagnation was in fact caused by the *belief* that the New Deal was doing "too much." Frightened by the policies of an activist, anti–laissez-faire administration, the business community never gained enough confidence to bring its own spending for investment purposes up to the levels of the 1920s. In 1929, businesses had poured $16 billion into new equipment, new plants, and home and office building. In 1937, the best year of the early New Deal, private investment was only $11.7 billion (and it fell to half that the following year).

Thus the critics were not entirely wrong when they blamed the doldrums on the policies of the New Deal, with its "dangerous" spending proclivities. But the critics were right only because the business community was so alarmed by New Deal spending that business spending for investment never regained its pre–1929 momentum.

Indeed, from our present-day perspective, we can see a quite different reason for the failure of the New Deal spending program. *The New Deal did not spend nearly enough!* Precisely because business did not spend predepression amounts for investment, the full-scale applications of Keynesian policies would have meant that the government should have spent twice or even three times as much as it did, financing its spending by borrowing money from the public in exchange for government bonds.

But that truly bold policy was quite impossible in a period when even the modest measures of the New Deal were enough to inspire fears of "socialism" and when government borrowing was not seen as an alternative to private investment borrowing but as a reckless and dangerous policy. Thus the New Dealers were caught in a trap. They were unable to spend enough to restore the full momentum of growth, but they were also unable to cut back their spending programs without sending the economy into a tailspin.

The War

No one knows how this dilemma of policy might have eventually been resolved, for suddenly events took a dramatic change that provided a decisive demonstration of the power of government spending. In 1939 war broke out in Europe; in December 1941 the Japanese bombed Pearl Harbor. Suddenly the nation found itself in a position of peril before which all quarrels about economic policy seemed trivial. The clear necessity, to which all agreed, was to mount a gigantic war effort—to build an armada for the sea, and another for the air, and simultaneously to equip a vast army for the land. All this required the expenditure of stupendous sums, and no one worried about the fact that only government could raise those sums by taxing and borrowing. Again Keynes was correct, for in 1940 he wrote: "It seems politically impossible for a capitalistic democracy to organize expenditure on the scale necessary to make the grand experiment that would prove my case—except in war conditions."[10]

Thus government spending skyrocketed—in the first six months of 1942 the government placed over $100 billion in contracts. GNP boomed. And unemployment quickly fell almost to zero:

	Federal Purchases ($ billions)	**GNP ($ billions)**	**Unemployment (millions)**
	THE EFFECTS OF WAR SPENDING (CURRENT PRICES)		
1940	6.0	99.7	8.1
1941	16.9	124.5	5.6
1942	51.9	157.9	2.7
1943	81.1	191.6	1.1
1944	89.0	210.1	.7
1945	74.8	211.9	1.0

SOURCE: *Historical Statistics,* Series F67, F47, D85.

To be sure, with the outpouring of military spending there was some inflation—consumer prices were about 28 percent higher in 1945 than they had been in 1940. Price ceilings imposed by the government helped prevent much greater wartime inflation. But even if we adjust the GNP figures for this inflationary influence, there is no doubt that growth was fully resumed. Chart 3 shows us the dip caused by the cutback in spending in 1937, and then the great surge that followed with the onset of spending during the war.

Many volumes have been written about the Second World War. Most of us study the war as a heroic chapter in the defense of democracy, or as a great contest between rival political systems. Yet history can be "read" from many angles, bringing into focus themes that give it special meaning for different purposes.

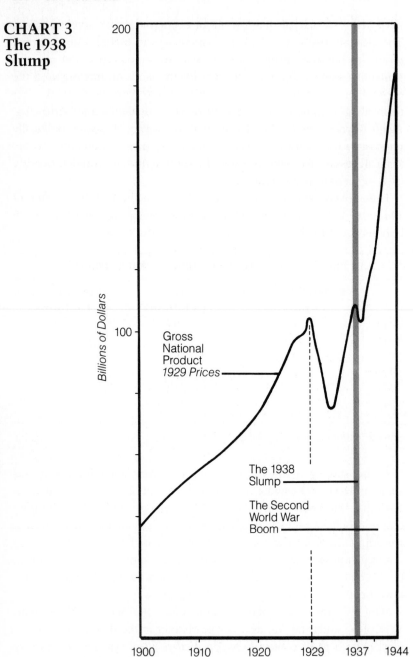

**CHART 3
The 1938
Slump**

200

Billions of Dollars

100

Gross
National
Product
1929 Prices

The 1938
Slump

The Second
World War
Boom

1900   1910   1920   1929   1937   1944

Source: from *Historical Statistics.*

As students of economic history, we "read" the chapter of the Second World War in an unusual light, just as we read the history of the Civil War in an unaccustomed way. From our perspective, it is the burst of economic growth brought about by war spending that provides the main lesson. It shows that government spending can indeed play a decisive role in creating economic expansion, just as private investment spending did in the past. To put it differently, we can see that a new social structure of accumulation in which government spending could play a decisive role in providing the forward thrust of the system was indeed possible.

The new structure of accumulation was, however, put into place under special circumstances. The imperatives of war provided a rationale that overrode all kinds of objections that would otherwise have impeded government spending at anything approaching wartime magnitudes. Thus the great question to be answered was whether growth could continue after the war, when government spending would necessarily be pulled back to a much more modest place. As we shall see, that question continues to be asked—and answered in different ways—down to our present day.

Notes

[1] *The Public Papers and Addresses of Franklin D. Roosevelt* (1938), 2: 11ff.
[2] *How We Elect Our Presidents* (1952), p. 141.
[3] Raymond Moley, *After Seven Years* (1939), p. 155.
[4] *Public Papers and Addresses,* 2: 93–94.
[5] *Roosevelt: The Lion and the Fox* (1956), pp. 218–19.
[6] *Public Papers and Addresses,* (1938), 4: 325.
[7] Quoted in Arthur Schlesinger, Jr., *The Coming of the New Deal* (1958), p. 311
[8] Quoted in Arthur Schlesinger, Jr., *The Politics of Upheaval* (1960), p. 621.
[9] Quoted in William Leuchtenburg, *Franklin D. Roosevelt and the New Deal* (1963), p. 91.
[10] Quoted in Richard Hofstadter, *The Age of Reform* (1955), p. 309.

Satisfied shoppers

Chapter 9

FROM POSTWAR BOOM TO POSTWAR INFLATION

The war was over in 1945, but the euphoria of victory was tempered by an undercurrent of anxiety. The Great Depression had left an invisible scar on the American character, and the end of the war signalled to many the reappearance of a time of economic troubles. Predictions of gloom and doom filled the air: it was darkly said that twelve million veterans, trained to fight, would not meekly submit to the mass unemployment that seemed an all too likely consequence of the decline in war spending.

The Fair Deal

The person charged with the responsibility of leading the nation through this time of worries was Harry S Truman, catapulted into the presidency after the death of Franklin Roosevelt on April 12, 1945. Truman found himself immediately on the horns of a dilemma. On the one hand, he wanted to remove as many wartime controls as possible to encourage a resumption of private spending. On the other hand, he feared that dismantling controls too rapidly would unleash a flood of pent-up spending that would bring inflation and inequity. Complicating his problem was the mood of the public, tired of a long period of belt-tightening and eager to spend its war-swollen savings. And most difficult of all was the disappearance of a national purpose. With peace at hand, every group thought first and foremost of its own interest. Thus labor demanded higher wages but insisted that price controls be retained; industrialists demanded higher prices, but asked that the government continue to control wages; farmers pressed for a retention of price supports for their crops but opposed any price controls on their output.

Truman tried valiantly to reconcile these diverse and contradictory interests, setting forth a program of domestic reforms that came to be called the Fair Deal. In many ways it was a continuation of the main lines of the New Deal–strengthening New Deal legislation on Social Security and minimum wages, extending New Deal price supports and public housing programs, and pioneering with legislation aimed at creating health insurance and a government commitment to full employment. Many of these objectives were gained. But in one critical area Truman failed. He could not convince Congress—or the public—of the need to continue wartime controls over prices.* Cautiously Truman responded to the general demand for a free economy. First he ended the wartime rationing of scarce goods like gasoline. Then he signed a bill cutting taxes by some $6 billion. Finally in June 1946 he lifted all price controls except those on rent.

The result was all too foreseeable. Prices skyrocketed as consumers scrambled for goods. Food prices rose by more than 25 percent between 1945 and 1947. The inflation rate for 1946 was a staggering 18.2 percent. Worse, the rise in prices predictably sparked a demand for higher wages. When management refused to meet these demands, a wave of strike activity coursed through the nation—in 1946 alone nearly 5,000 strikes affected 4.5 million workers. Recognizing that unions were well organized, management decided to negotiate settlements and to pass along the costs of the new contracts to their customers.** Thus began an upward spiral of wages and prices that has continued as a central inflationary mechanism to our own day.

---

*During the war the Office of Price Administration worked assiduously to control eight million commodities and services through both rationing and price controls. Its efforts were rewarded: Consumer prices rose only 30 percent over 1939 levels, whereas in World War I, with no rationing and price controls in place, prices had more than doubled.

**In 1947 a Republican-led Congress tried to undo what it regarded as a privileged position for labor under the Wagner Act. Led by Senator Robert A. Taft of Ohio, it passed the Taft-Hartley Act, outlawing the closed shop (an arrangement under which job applicants had to join a union before they could be hired). In addition, the Taft-Hartley Act gave the president the authority to obtain court injunctions forcing striking unions to call off their strike for an eighty-day "cooling off" period. Truman vetoed the bill, but Congress passed it over his veto.

POSTWAR GROWTH

For all these shaky beginnings, the American economy showed remarkable strength and resilience in weathering the reconversion period. Government spending did fall precipitously between 1945 and 1946, from $83 billion to $31 billion, but the rush of pent-up consumer and business spending was large enough to hold the fall in GNP to scarcely more than 1 percent. In addition, as the production process picked up speed and as industrialists switched back from war to peacetime outputs, supply soon caught up with demand, and the initial inflationary burst petered out. In fact, the increase in supply was so great that prices were effectively stabilized after 1948, until the Korean War broke out in 1950. Not least, to the nation's immense relief, the transfer from the military to the civilian work force was managed without the expected difficulties. The Office of Mobilization and Reconversion had predicted that eight million people were likely to be out of work by the spring of 1946, but in fact postwar unemployment never rose above 2.7 million.

The Great Boom

Thus contrary to all expectations, the economy found itself launched on a great boom, rather than headed toward a repetition of the Great Depression. And it *was* a great boom—the longest and most successful period of expansion in American history. Between 1945 and 1970, the nation's real output of goods and services—that is, its gross national product, corrected for inflation—doubled. The median real income of families rose almost as fast: There were a third more households in 1970 than there had been after the war, but the average household's consumption of goods and services was nevertheless almost twice as high as it had been in 1947. In current dollar figures, gross national product in 1970 was almost at the trillion-dollar mark, a hitherto unimaginable number that was becoming a TV newscast cliché, and the median family was enjoying an income of $10,000 a year, a number that seemed very large to most Americans. Meanwhile, real per capita income growth rose 5.9 percent between 1946 and 1950, another 15.2 percent in the 1950s, and an even more impressive 31.7 percent in the 1960s.

Affluent teenagers, c. 1965

It is not surprising, then, that the short-lived euphoria of the immediate postwar victory slowly became a long-lived euphoria of national prosperity. The words "economic growth," previously unknown to most economists much less to ordinary Americans, entered the national consciousness, as commentators and presidents alike projected the current trend into the future and painted a vision of an America that was now middle class in its income as well as in its aspirations.

Looking Back on the Boom

Two forces were responsible for the wonderful two and a half decades that followed the Second World War. One was the outpouring of dammed-up private expenditures, part household, part business, that had been held back for four years during the war. Thus the boom was in part simply the product of normal economic expansion, accelerated by the long-denied needs of a starved household and business community.

But the other stimulus was new, and very important. It was the boost given to production, both directly and indirectly, by government. As we have mentioned, federal expenditures fell sharply for two years when the war stopped. Here is where the rush of private spending headed off a major economic contraction. But very shortly thereafter, government spending began to rise again. In some degree it was buoyed by the needs of states and localities for schools, roads, hospitals, fire-fighting equipment—all deferred, like household or business spending, during the war. More important was the renewal of federal spending for arms. With the onset of the Cold War in general and the Korean War in particular, arms spending became a major economic stimulus. In 1947 the military budget was roughly $9 billion. By 1949, when the Defense Department was formed, outlays had climbed to $13 billion. Four years later they topped $50 billion. By 1970 they were $74 billion.

Arms expenditures were thus an indisputable source of the initial growth surge, but they were by no means the sole source of the long boom. Indeed, from the mid-1950s on, military expenditures were a steadily *declining* portion of gross national product. Now, however, came the last and perhaps most significant contribution of the government: the rise of welfare expenditures. In 1950 these expenditures amounted to about $23 billion, just short of 9 percent of GNP. By 1970 the total was $146 billion, 15 percent of GNP. Here was the propulsive stimulus that took over after the boost of war spending stopped.

The growth of welfare spending was by no means a return to New Deal "relief." Rather, it embraced a broad series of programs that aided many sectors and groups within the economy. An early instance was the GI Bill of Rights, which provided demobilized veterans with loans to start new businesses and subsidies to continue their educations. About one million veterans entered college under the Bill, and another million used the Bill to open their own business. By the time the Bill ended in 1956, it cost the government $14.5 billion. Another was the rapid increase in federal aid to education at every level from elementary through college. Still another was the slow growth of payments for health programs, culminating in the Medicare and Medicaid programs of the late 1960s. But most important by far was the widening and strengthening of the Social Security program. Under Truman, Social Security outlays had reached a level of $2 billion a year, but the number of individuals covered was not much larger than in the late 1930s. The leap occurred under Dwight D. Eisenhower, the conservatively inclined but pragmatic general who became the Republican successor to Truman. Eisenhower was responsible for a dramatic increase in the number of families covered by Social Security. Ten million households, previously uncovered, were brought under the Social Security umbrella, and expenditures rose from $2 billion to $11 billion.

A New Economic Structure

Taken together, the federal, state, and local expenditures within GNP—partly for arms, partly for welfare, partly for domestic improvements—provided an indispensable underpinning for the long boom.* In 1929 the contribution to GNP of all these streams of government spending had been less than 10 percent. The spending of the federal government alone, for both goods and services and welfare, had been less than 2.5 percent of GNP. By 1970 federal spending for "warfare and welfare" had risen to over 20 percent of GNP, and the spending of all levels of government, including states and localities, to almost a third of GNP. To put it differently, whereas private investment spending was (in round numbers) 50 percent more than all government spending in 1929, by the 1970s it was 50 percent less.

The direct economic stimulus of government was therefore a major element in the long boom. But it was not the only reason for the two and a half decades of almost uninterrupted growth. Along with the increase in expenditures had also come a change in the relationship of government and business—that is, a change in the social structure of accumulation. The change had two main aspects. *First, there was a general acknowledgment of the necessity for government to provide floors under the economy.* The floors ranged from agricultural subsidies of various kinds to minimum wages, which were raised under Eisenhower; from widened Social Security to lengthened and strengthened unemployment benefits; from federally assisted state welfare programs to federally run job-training programs. By making the government an active force for personal income security, the threat of a demoralized and disgruntled work force was avoided, and the groundwork laid for a stable political climate, a necessity for business investment.

---

*An important contribution was the Interstate Highway Act of 1956, which committed the federal government to pay 90 percent of the construction costs of interstate highways.

Second, the business community was gradually brought around to an acceptance of government as a guarantor of economic stability. As the prestigious Rockefeller Panel Reports stated in 1958, "Public expenditures in support of growth are an essential part of our economy. Far from being a hindrance to progress, they provide the environment within which our economy moves forward."[1]

THE CHANGING ROLE OF GOVERNMENT

To be sure, the idea of a mixed economy did not emerge overnight or without resistance. In retrospect we can see that it began with the passage of the Employment Act of 1946 under President Truman, committing the government to the promotion of "maximum" employment through fiscal (tax and budget) and monetary policies. The law also required the president to submit an annual economic report to Congress, and created the three-member Council of Economic Advisers to assist him.

The Employment Act marked a new stage in the evolution of government's role in the economy. In the first part of the nineteenth century, the government was a *promoter* of business, underwriting "internal improvements," granting land to railroads, and helping infant industries to take root. A second stage was the emergence of the government in the latter half of the century as a *regulator of the economy,* using its powers to assure the orderly workings of individual markets or industries—witness the emergence of the ICC and antitrust policies. With the Employment Act came a third stage. The government now took on the function of *guarantor,* taking as its prime objective the maintenance of socially acceptable rates of growth and levels of employment.

The transition of the national government from promoter, to regulator, to guarantor of economic growth gained further support under Eisenhower and a conservative Republican Congress. Eisenhower tried to steer a middle course between the conservative policies of the Republicans of the 1920s and the New Deal liberalism of the 1930s, but veered in the direction of the Old Guard. His plan was to turn over as many federal programs as possible to the states. Among the federal programs that Eisenhower wanted dismantled and restructured on the basis of private enterprise was the TVA, which the president saw as a symbol of "creeping socialism." "If I do anything,"

Eisenhower said after his first inaugural, "it's going to be less govern-ment and not more government."[2] Yet the exigencies of the time forced him to abandon many of his orthodox ideas and to extend many of the "welfare" provisions of the New Deal. In 1954, for exam-ple, Eisenhower signed bills extending Social Security benefits to more than seven million Americans, raising the minimum wage to one dollar an hour, and adding four million workers to those eligible for unem-ployment benefits. Another important piece of legislation, the Soil Bank Act of 1956, authorized payments to farmers who let portions of their land lie fallow in order to reduce production. As a result, one dollar of every six dollars that farmers and agricultural corporations earned at harvest time came not from sales but from government sub-sidies—for crops that were never planted.

After the start of the first of three recessions during his administra-tion (1953–54, 1957–58, and 1960–61), Eisenhower told his cabinet that the Republican Party must be prepared to use the full power of gov-ernment to prevent "another 1929." As a result, despite Eisenhower's deep desire to cut government spending, federal disbursements rose from $68 billion when he took office in 1952 to $92 billion when he left in 1960, and the federal government incurred the largest deficit in its peacetime history.

More Intervention

The idea of a mixed economy became still more explicit under John F. Kennedy, to whom it was a foregone conclusion that government intervention was a necessity. Under his presidency, the government entered into economic affairs much more freely than it had under Eisenhower. Wage "guidelines" were initiated to help dampen the wage–price spiral of inflation. Minimum wages were further increased and Social Security extended. Assistance was provided for regional development of the backwater areas of the country.

But Kennedy's greatest departure from traditional economic policy took place in January 1963. The economy was hesitating on the verge of what seemed to be a potentially serious recession, with rising unemployment levels. Urged on by his advisers, Kennedy proposed a bold step. He asked Congress to reduce taxes by $13.5 billion *without reducing government spending*. That is, he asked Congress deliber-ately to incur a government deficit, using the government's borrowing powers to finance its spending. The result, he explained, would be a stimulus to the economy, because consumers would have more money to spend. As GNP rose, government tax revenues would also rise, and in the end the budget would be balanced at a higher level of GNP than if there had been no tax cut to stimulate total output.*

Kennedy's proposal to incur a deliberate government deficit produced a furor, and the tax cut was not actually passed until Lyndon Johnson assumed the presidency after Kennedy's death. By that time the idea had begun to win the approval of much of the business community.** Meanwhile, Johnson extended the idea of the mixed economy in other directions. His program for a Great Society brought new departures for government, including direct aid to the nation's elementary and secondary public schools and a far-reaching program of Medicare for people over sixty-five. But Johnson's most ambitious program was the Economic Opportunity Act of 1964, which launched a frontal assault on poverty. The purpose of the law was to help poor people improve their ability to earn money. Thus it established a Head Start program to give extra help to disadvantaged children even before they entered school, a Job Corps to train school dropouts, and an adult education program. Between 1965 and 1970 nearly $10 billion was committed to Economic Opportunity Act programs.

Income Distribution

As a consequence of efforts made by the Eisenhower, Kennedy, and Johnson administrations, the distribution of income in the United States showed a considerable change compared with the distribution

---

*The question of government deficits is a complicated one, better covered in an economics course than in a survey of economic growth. A key aspect of the problem lies in the "internal" character of government debts. By internal, we mean that a government debt is usually held by its own citizens. Because government has the power to tax, it can always raise the necessary funds to pay off its bonds when they come due, or to pay interest on them. By way of contrast, a corporation, no matter how large, has no way of forcing people to buy its products so that it can pay back its debts. The power to tax is what makes government debts entirely different from private debts. That is why it is said, quite correctly, that a government debt, held by its own citizens, is a debt that a nation owes to itself.

**In *The Fiscal Revolution in America* (1969; p. 372), economist Herbert Stein referred to this tax cut as "the act, which more than any other came to symbolize the fiscal revolution."

before the war. The table below shows the shift in overall shares among the lower, middle, and top groups in the nation:

DISTRIBUTION OF FAMILY INCOME (BEFORE TAX)		
	Percent of all incomes	
	1929	**1971**
Lowest 40 percent of families	12.5	17.4
Next 40 percent	33.1	41.1
Top 20 percent	54.4	41.6
Top 5 percent	30.0	14.4

SOURCE: *from Historical Statistics;* 1929, series G319–324.

Much of this change was the direct consequence of the welfare programs undertaken during the long boom. Between 1959 and 1969, the number of persons whose incomes fell into the brackets officially classified as "poverty" or "near poverty" declined from thirty-nine million to twenty-four million, and the percentage of the population in these low income brackets fell from 22.4 to 12.1.* Poverty thereafter continued to decline slowly until the 1980s, when it took a sharp turn upward as a result of cutbacks in welfare programs under the Reagan administration.

FROM GROWTH TO INFLATION

Measured in terms of growth or distribution, then, the long boom was an unparalleled success. Why, then, did it come to an end?

The first answer is that it produced inflation. Already noticeable in the 1960s, inflation became a matter of growing national concern as

---

*Mention should here be made of a highly influential book, *The Other America*, published in 1962 by Michael Harrington. Harrington's study graphically brought to the attention of the American people the existence of poverty in the midst of prevailing affluence. In particular, he cast light on the culture of what he termed "the invisible poor," the roughly fifty million Americans who lived a hand-to-mouth existence, wrestling daily with physical disease, mental illness, and a pervasive feeling of hopelessness. Harrington's book was a call to arms to eradicate poverty, and struck a responsive chord with many Americans, including Presidents Kennedy and Johnson.

Inflation protest, Brooklyn, New York

the boom went on. From 1950 to 1960 the average rate of inflation in the United States was about 2 percent a year. During the last five years of the 1960s, the average inflation rate climbed to 4 percent. In the first five years of the 1970s it reached 6 percent. In the next five years it rose to 9 percent. After 1980 it moved into the double digit range, over 10 percent.

Why the rise in inflation? An enormous amount has been written on the subject, but no single explanation of inflation has been generally accepted comparable to Keynes's explanation of stagnation. Nevertheless, we understand a good deal about the process. In 1973 the Organization of Petroleum Exporting Countries (OPEC) took advantage of a tight market for oil, following the Arab–Israeli War, to boost the price of oil fourfold within a matter of a few months. The resulting "oil shock" hit all capitalist nations like a tidal wave, and was regarded by everyone as a tremendous impetus to inflation.

But why was the rise in oil prices *inflationary*? Suppose that the Pennsylvania coal mines had managed to form a cartel in 1873 and had quadrupled coal prices. Would that have produced inflation? Far more likely, it would have resulted in a sharp depression. Coal mines would have shut down, steel mines curtailed their operations, householders gone without coal. This imaginary but very persuasive "counterfactual" scenario causes us to ask an illuminating question: What happened between 1873 and 1973 so that the identical shock—a rise in energy prices—could give rise to such opposite results?

The question is not hard to answer. If coal prices had been boosted in 1873, there would have been no additional purchasing power to enable coal buyers to maintain their levels of coal consumption. Either coal miners or producers of some other goods would have been put out of work for sheer lack of demand. But in the 1970s no such constraints held back the system. On the contrary, when the price of oil rose, additional amounts of purchasing power were quickly created by government to assure that the needed dollars would be there. Householders, faced with higher costs of living, found that their pay checks were larger or their Social Security checks increased because wages and salaries were informally adjusted to changes in the cost of living, and Social Security checks were "indexed" by law to compensate for them. Industries, faced with higher costs of production, turned to banks for more credit, and the banks provided them with that credit with the blessings of government. Thus the increase in oil prices, far from constituting a drain on purchasing power, became a stimulus for the creation of additional purchasing power through the mechanisms of the mixed economy and the welfare state.

These mechanisms were certainly not the only reason for the onset or the persistence of inflation. Inflation received its disastrous first push from the Vietnam War. It was "exported" to Europe by the high-handed manner in which the United States conducted its international economic affairs. It was aggravated by the increasing concentration of business and labor power, and because industries in the vital manufacturing core of the system reached a tacit agreement with unions under which wages were steadily raised and the resulting higher costs passed along to consumers in higher prices.

Not least was a dangerous change in expectations shared by business and the public alike. In the unsupported economy of the 1920s the prevailing wisdom was that "What goes up must come down." Hence a certain wariness tempered the behavior of all but the most speculative-minded. But as prices began to move inexorably upward, a new conventional wisdom displaced the old: "What goes up today is likely to go up more tomorrow." Such inflationary expectations become powerful mechanisms for creating the very kind of behavior that itself accelerates inflation.

Thus there were many specific causes for inflation. Yet the imaginary comparison of OPEC and a coal cartel brings home a central point. It is that the structure of capitalism itself had become inflation-prone by virtue of the very institutional changes that had laid the basis for its postwar growth. Had the mixed economy and the welfare state been taken away from mid–twentieth century capitalism, its inflationary tendencies would almost certainly have disappeared as well. But so, too, would its remarkable prosperity.

The Effects of Inflation

It took some time before inflation became a central political issue. Eisenhower's administration was more concerned about preventing or cushioning the minor recessions that occurred during his term of office than with holding back the rise in prices. Kennedy and then Johnson were first absorbed in efforts to stimulate the economy—the Kennedy tax cut to which we have referred—and thereafter in trying to finance the unpopular Vietnam War without raising taxes. As a consequence, the inflation problem itself did not become a main focus of political concern until Richard Nixon's administration. From January 1969 to August 1971 the cost of living increased by 14.5 percent. In mid-August, 1971, Nixon announced a ninety-day price-wage freeze, to be followed in November by a system of wage and price controls.

The system of controls worked—for a while. But pressures were clearly building up behind it, like a river rising behind the frail bulwarks of a sandbag levee. When he was reelected in 1972 Nixon removed the controls, and with a rush the flood spread out across the countryside. From an inflation rate of 3.4 percent while the controls still held, the cost of living rose by 9 percent in 1973 and by nearly 12 percent in 1974.

Nixon's successor, Gerald Ford, was ideologically opposed to a reimposition of controls. Instead he sought to bring inflation under control by reducing federal spending and encouraging the Federal Reserve Board to tighten credit. Ford's hope was that a moderate rise

Urban unemployment office, 1983

in unemployment would hold back both labor and management from pursuing their wage–price spiral.* The result was the worst slump since the Roosevelt recession of 1937–38. Unemployment rose to nearly 9 percent of the work force by mid-1975. By the next year the inflation rate had been cut to less than 5 percent, but the rise in unemployment was more than Congress or the public were willing to tolerate. Ford was reluctantly persuaded to stimulate the system by cutting taxes. By early 1976 the economy had responded sufficiently well so that he could announce that the recession was over. Alas, so was the lull in inflation, which soon began its upward course again.

From Stop-Go to Full Stop

The dilemma of choosing between inflation and unemployment was not just an American problem. All through the Western world, the drift toward accelerating inflation was being met with similar policies—and similar failures. Efforts to arrest inflation by slowing the economy

---

*Ford suggested that patriotic citizens should wear WIN buttons (Whip Inflation Now) to evidence their support for his policies.

down through tight money policies that restricted the abilities of banks to make loans and through stringent fiscal measures soon resulted in unacceptable increases in unemployment. Thereafter the red light of restrictive policies was rapidly changed to a green light of expansive policies. As a result, all over the world capitalist economies displayed stop-go symptoms—first enjoying some respite from inflation only to encounter rising unemployment; then easing the unemployment situation only to come up against a renewed burst of inflation.

The dilemma came to a head in the United States under the administration of Jimmy Carter, a Democrat. Elected in 1976, Carter determined that inflation required a much more vigorous and tough-minded policy of monetary austerity, and he appointed Paul Volcker to be Chairman of the Federal Reserve System to bring the growth of the money supply under much tighter control. Volcker stepped harder on the monetary brakes than anyone had dared to up to that time. By refusing to allow bank reserves to expand as rapidly as in the past, he brought about a credit squeeze that pushed interest rates steadily higher. The prime rate—the interest rate charged by banks to their best commercial customers—rose from below 7 percent to over 12.5 percent. By 1980, the last year of the Carter presidency, the prime rate was an unprecedented 15 percent, and the Consumer Price Index was soaring at an annual rate of 18.2 percent, the highest in U.S. history.

Predictably, the consequences of tight money were painful. Businesses—especially small and medium sized firms—were unable to finance their inventories or their normal borrowings, and began to contract their activities. Unemployment grew from 5.8 percent of the work force in 1979 to 7.1 percent in 1980. Economic growth came to a total halt; corrected for inflation, the economy actually contracted in 1980, the first post–World War decade in which American purchasing power actually declined. In 1980 Americans earned 5 percent less in real income than in 1970. But even the growing disarray in the system could not stop the momentum of inflation, now mainly kept going by "indexing" Social Security payments and wage contracts—that is, adjusting them annually to stay abreast of inflation. In 1980 the inflation rate rose to 12.4 percent, despite the tightest money and the largest unemployment in the nation's postwar history.

Thus the great boom ended in the great inflation. This was not just an American dilemma. To a lesser degree, the same disappointing end to the great boom was experienced in other capitalist nations, especially in Europe. By the early 1980s, no way had been found to bring about sustained economic growth without suffering inflationary consequences. The stage was set for one of those pendulum swings that seems to affect American political history—and as a consequence, its economic history as well.*

Notes

[1] *Prospect for America*, p. 279
[2] Quoted in Herbert Parmet, *Eisenhower* [1972], p. 174.

*For a stimulating discussion of political cycles in American history, see Arthur Schlesinger, Jr., *The Cycles of American History* (1986).

President Reagan relaxing in California

Chapter 10
THE CONSERVATIVE ERA

The pendulum swing was ratified in the 1980 presidential election, when—in a mood of frustration—the public turned to Ronald Reagan, a conservative Republican. Reagan carried forty-four of the fifty states, and his party gained control of the Senate for the first time since 1954 and added thirty-three seats in the House. The Reagan juggernaut ushered in an era of conservative hegemony that would persist until President George Bush was defeated by Governor Bill Clinton of Arkansas in the election of 1992.

Those twelve years of conservative authority are the basis for the title of this chapter and the theme of its content. It is too early to attempt anything like a historian's perspective on the complex political and social currents and consequences of the Reagan–Bush years. But it is not too soon to attempt an appraisal of the problems that dominated them and the adequacy of the response that was forthcoming.

THE CONSERVATIVE BANNER

The regnant economic philosophy of those dozen years was clearly "conservative," a label worn by Presidents Reagan and Bush as proudly as Kennedy and Johnson had worn the badge of liberalism. Moreover, there was no mistaking conservatism's first and most important objective. It was to reduce the role of government in economic affairs. In his inaugural address Ronald Reagan said, "In this present crisis, government is not the solution to our problems; government is the problem. . . . "* According to historian Robert Dallek, "no president in American history entered the White House more determined to reduce the role and size of government than Ronald Reagan."[1] In one of his first acts as president, Reagan ordered the portrait of Thomas Jefferson removed from the East Wing of the White House, replacing it with that of Calvin Coolidge, whose pro-business philosophy of government is already familiar to us. Reagan hailed Coolidge for having cut taxes four times. "During the Coolidge years," he said, "we had probably the greatest growth in prosperity that we've ever known."[2]

Cutting Government

Reagan was determined to unleash energies that he believed had been dammed up by administrative regulation and anti-business legislation. Blaming this on Democratic "excesses," and sensing general dissatisfaction with—even a loss of confidence in—government policies of "tax and spend," Reagan undertook a large-scale trimming of welfare programs, a dismantling of government regulations, and a diminution of government in all areas except the military.

No sooner did Reagan enter office than he called on Congress to reduce by billions of dollars such well-established federal programs as Medicare, welfare subsidies for the working poor, urban aid, food stamps, and school lunch programs. In July 1981 Congress agreed to most of the president's demands, and Reagan followed up with a second round of domestic spending cuts in September of that year.

Another purpose of the spending cuts was to push forward Reagan's program to establish a "New Federalism" which would transfer over to the states many of the social services then under federal funding and supervision. According to Reagan, local governments were far better equipped to measure and to meet the needs of the citizenry than the far removed, bureaucracy-laden government in Washington.

Having lightened expenditure, the administration next advocated, and Congress passed, the largest tax cut in American history. The

---

*It is worthy of note that conservatism was gaining vitality as a rallying-ground throughout the world. In May 1979 Margaret Thatcher's Conservative Party came to power in England. After Reagan's election, conservative governments were placed in office in Canada, West Germany, and Italy. Voters were expressing their dissatisfaction with government-dominated solutions to economic problems, and increasingly calling on their governments to follow conservative policies to expand their economies.

Economic Recovery Act of 1981, as the law was called, reduced individual income tax rates by 25 percent over a period of three years, and lowered the top rate on unearned income from 70 to 50 percent. Other sections of the new measure provided an investment tax credit, and a system of depreciation allowances making it possible to recover capital costs more rapidly.

The conservative philosophy behind the act can be seen in its deliberate tilting of tax relief in favor of the rich. The 31.7 million tax-paying families earning $15,000 or less were to receive only 8.5 percent of the reduction, whereas the 12.6 million families earning $50,000 or more were to get 35 percent of the savings. The greatest gains by far were enjoyed by the topmost 1 percent. In 1977 this group paid 36 percent of its average income of $350,000 in income taxes. By 1983 the average income of the top 1 percent had risen to $400,000 but the average tax levy had dropped to 22 percent.[3]

Supply-Side Disappointments

Reagan's economists predicted that this measure would stimulate saving, investment and growth precisely *because* it was aimed at upper-income groups whose initiative was believed to be crucial in determining the pace of economic life. This philosophy was called "supply-side" economics, in contrast to the "demand side" that typically depended on government spending to increase output. According to supply-side thinking, well-to-do families would spend their tax savings on consumption, lifting the economy out of the doldrums, or would invest their tax savings in new ventures, providing an even more important stimulus for jobs and production. Thus additional income at the top would trickle down to those below, bringing new economic vitality as its dividend.

Fatal Contradictions

Would trickle-down economics have worked? We cannot really say, because the program was marked from the start by two glaring inconsistencies. The first was a failure to realize the spending cuts that had been so boldly announced. Spending for Medicare, for example, increased from $32 billion when Reagan was inaugurated, to $132 billion when his successor left office. Social Security expenditures rose from $118 billion to over $300 billion. And the largest peacetime build-up of military strength swelled the military budget from $130 billion to double that. In addition, although the tax burden of the rich was greatly reduced, that of the middle and working classes was greatly increased by higher payroll taxes. Between 1978 and 1990, for example, the Social Security payroll tax increased 30 percent.* In all, when Reagan entered office in 1981, total federal tax revenues were $599 billion. Twelve yars later, they were $1,091 billion. Thus the years saw neither a massive scaling back in total federal spending or in federal tax receipts. Supply-side was more of a slogan than a reality.

Second, Reagan's plan also banked heavily on squeezing inflation out of the system by continuing a policy of very tight money. This directly contradicted the desired effects of supply-side incentives. Supply-side policies were supposed to spur the economy on; tight money was supposed to hold it back. In this conflict of objectives, tight money won. Inflation fell from 12.4 percent in 1980 to less than 7 percent in 1982, and the discount rate—the rate at which the Federal Reserve loans money to member banks—fell from a record 21.5 percent in early 1981 to 10.5 percent in the summer of 1982.

But tight money also meant that loans were hard to get. As businesses desperately cut costs and unions agreed to cut wages, production and consumer spending came down along with prices. During the last three months of 1981 GNP fell by 5.3 percent and unemployment rose to a six-year high of 8 percent. At year's end one-third of the country's industrial capacity was idle; real take-home pay was below that of ten years earlier; agricultural income dropped precipitously, resulting in an increase in farm foreclosures, auctions, and bankruptcies; and the number of Americans living in poverty was 60 percent higher than in 1979. Supply-side hopes had become depression realities.

---

*Why does the Social Security payroll tax claim a higher portion of the earnings of the middle and working class than of the rich? In part it is because this tax has a ceiling above which no more payments need be made. As of January 1993 that ceiling was 7.65 percent of the first $57,600 in earnings and 1.45 percent of the next $77,400. In addition, the tax exempts investment income, such as interest and capital gains. Thus the payroll tax is like an income tax in reverse, exempting high rather than low incomes. As a result of this and other increases in state and local taxes, by the middle years of the 1980s, the middle-bracket taxpayer bore a heavier tax burden than the more well-to-do citizen.

A homeless person in Washington D.C.

A Rebound—and New Problems

Fortunately for Reagan, the economy rebounded dramatically just before the 1984 election. Gross national product rose 6.8 percent in 1984, the highest increase since 1951, and mid-year employment statistics seemed to indicate a complete turnaround: Unemployment fell to 7.1 percent, a four-year low, and inflation dropped to 4 percent, the lowest since 1967. Against these successes, the ever-popular president* soundly defeated his Democratic opponent, Walter Mondale, winning forty-nine of the fifty states.

Merger Mania

Meanwhile, however, a different problem was beginning to emerge in the corporate sector. We have seen how a great merger movement

---

*One of Reagan's much-noted skills was an ability to distance himself from bad news. Representative Patricia Schroeder of Colorado said that Reagan was "perfecting a Teflon-coated presidency. . . . He sees to it that nothing sticks to him."

brought about a concentration of industry in the late nineteenth century. Another such movement, not quite so dramatic, brought further concentration in the 1950s and 1960s. Thereafter the statistics of concentration seemed to stabilize, as we see in the table below.

Suddenly, beginning in the mid-1980s, this condition changed dramatically. A new merger wave broke out that dwarfed all earlier periods of corporate agglomeration. During the relatively stable years before this wave, the annual number of mergers among the largest corporations came to less than 100, and the total value of assets involved in all mergers amounted to only about $5 billion a year. When the merger mania began, those numbers changed out of all recognition. In 1984, 2,999 "big" mergers took place, involving $124 billion in total assets. The next year the number was even higher, and in that year at least five mergers involved sums larger than the total value of all mergers during the premerger decade.

Behind the Merger Wave

What was the cause of this frenzied acquisitiveness? Two factors seem of paramount importance. The first was the financial impetus that resulted from a combination of high interest rates and inflation. Together these depressed the price of corporate shares on the stock market to the point at which the cash value of the assets of many companies, such as the oil reserves of the petroleum group, were worth a good deal more than the market's valuation of the companies that owned them. This presented financiers and aggressive competitors with the chance to buy out undervalued corporations, and then to realize bonanza profits by selling off their assets for much more than the entire company had cost.

The second cause of the merger frenzy was a change in the attitude

Largest Manufacturers' Share of Assets						
	1948	**1960**	**1970**	**1981**	**1982**	**1983**
100 largest corporations	40.2	46.4	48.5	46.8	47.7	48.3
200 largest corporations	48.2	56.3	60.4	60.0	60.8	60.8

SOURCE: *Statistical Abstract of the United States*, Table #866.

Heavy trading on the New York Stock Exchange

of government. The much more benign attitude of the Justice Department toward mergers removed an obstacle that had formerly dampened the enthusiasm for merger. As a result, the drive to deregulate as many industries as possible set the stage for a general competitive consolidation within those industries. As the airlines, for example, were progressively released from the supervision of the Federal Aviation Authority, airlines began to gobble one another up, radically reducing the number of carriers, and changing the route and the rate structures of the industry.

Hostile Mergers

The merger wave also differed from earlier waves in another respect. Previous merger waves were largely the consequence of a widely shared desire to minimize competition. Hence all parties to the merger cooperated eagerly to bring it about. During the wave of the 1980s, "hostile" takeovers dominated the scene—purchases of one company by another, or by financial raiders interested only in making a killing for themselves, not in creating a more stable industrial pattern.

Two new developments accounted for this change. One was the anonymity of most corporate managements, whose names were unknown to their stockholders, unlike the days of owner-managers like Ford or Carnegie. As a result, when shareholders received offers for their stock from the raiders at a price far above the current market value, they paid little heed to the appeals of existing management to remain loyal to them. Similarly, large institutional investors, such as pension funds and life insurance companies, also looked kindly on hostile takeovers, since bidding wars for control of a company tended to boost share prices.

A second element was that hostile takeovers were often made possible because banks were willing to lend the raiders large amounts of money, often on frail security. The merger deals were then financed by using the bank's money to buy out stockholders, after which the raider typically unloaded his bank debt onto the company he had acquired, causing the company to issue high-interest, high-risk "junk bonds." These bonds, with their tempting coupons, were then sold to the public, thereby raising the money to reimburse the bank for its original loan. Later these free-and-easy financing methods were stopped by the Federal Reserve Board, but for a time they were a source of immense financial purchasing power that fueled the merger process.

Consequences of the Wave

The effects of the merger wave are not as clear-cut as its causes. For the wave has had supporters as well as opponents. Those who have looked favorably on it believed that the wave of takeovers was a bitter but necessary medicine for a slack and lazy business community. As a result of the merger wave, say its defenders, corporations are today lean and mean, as they must be if they are to hold their own in the increasingly rough competition of the global market. On the other side of the argument, opponents of the merger process point to the damage that has been done to many corporations by forcing them to exchange equity for debt—that is, to exchange shares of stock that carried no legal obligation to pay dividends, with bonds whose interest payments had to be met. In all, something like $200 billion of new debt has been added to U.S. corporations as a result of the merger wave. The obligation to "service" this debt—that is, to pay interest on it—saddles the corporate world with a huge expense that must be met before any profit can be had.

By and large, the conservative administrations saw the positive side of the merger movement. It will be some time, however, before we know which side of the argument has won the day. It is quite likely that surviving corporations will be leaner and meaner, and therefore better able to hold their own in the world's market. But there is no doubt that many companies will have dropped by the wayside because of their inability to handle their massive new debt load. In the end, the validity of the conservative view may perhaps be determined not by the winners, but by the ability of the losers to reenter the business scene. On the success of that largely overlooked aspect of the merger movement will depend the economic fate of hundreds of thousands, perhaps even millions, of workers and middle managers, displaced by no fault of their own.

The Reagan Finale

Although somewhat diminished by alleged scandals within his administration and by questionable uses of power in foreign affairs, Reagan's popularity was still powerful enough for him to turn over the presidency in 1988 to the Republican candidate, Vice-President George Bush. Bush easily defeated his Democratic rival, Governor Michael Dukakis of Massachusetts. Paradoxically, it was during Bush's administration that American capitalism won its greatest ideological victory abroad, but suffered a most telling defeat at home.

THE BUSH YEARS

The ideological triumph was the downfall of Communism, an event of momentous importance in world history. The fall occurred with lightning speed, as mass movements ousted Marxist–Leninist regimes throughout Eastern Europe. On November 9, 1989, the Berlin Wall, a symbol of Communist repression and the Cold War since 1961, was torn down. But the fatal blow was struck in August 1991, when the people of Moscow, led by the popularly elected president of Russia, Boris Yeltsin, heroically resisted a coup that tried to depose President Mikhail Gorbachev and to restore power to the old guard. The bloodless victory sealed the fate of the hardliners and opened the way for the democratic reorganization of the Soviet Union. That transformation is still far from complete, and may yet founder, but the very possibility would have been impossible to imagine in the opening days of the Bush presidency.

Americans greeted these events with great pride and high expectations, hoping not only for the dawn of an era of peace and order abroad, but for the possibility of a "peace dividend" at home, as military expenditures were diverted to much needed peacetime projects. They were soon disappointed on both counts. Events in Eastern Europe, Germany, Yugoslavia, and in the former Soviet territory made it plain that a peaceful and stable era was not yet at hand; and the rapid emergence of serious domestic economic problems made it equally evident that the end of the Cold War would not, in itself, bring about a resumption of strong economic growth for the United States. On the contrary, from the date of Bush's administration to that of his leaving office, there was essentially no real growth in average personal income. The last years of his administration were marked by another recession, almost as painful as that which tight money had brought on in the early 1980s.

The Neglect of Infrastructure

What was the cause of these economic difficulties? Many of them had their roots in earlier neglect. One of these, without question, was a crippling decline in the quantity and quality of the "infrastructure" of the economy. Infrastructure refers to the publicly owned productive capital of a nation—its roads and dams, harbors and airfields, public research facilities, educational institutions, and the like. This public capital does not normally *make* goods, which are usually produced in the private sector, but it determines to an important degree the efficiency with which private goods can be produced. Business clearly depends on good road, rail, and air transport, on water, power, and postal facilities, as well as on purely private physical capital. In this light, infrastructure can be likened to the roadbed that determines how fast a train can run.

During the years of the conservative era, the national infrastructure was allowed to deteriorate to an unprecedented degree. According to the figures of the Office of Management and Budget, federal investment in public capital was cut by a third from 1976 to 1990; education and training by almost 40 percent;* physical capital by almost 30 percent; research and development by the same. Economist David Alan Aschauer, to whose research we owe the first full-scale airing of the problem, has estimated that total nonmilitary public investment in the 1980s was only half that of the previous decade and only one-fourth the level of the 1950s and 1960s. In fact, public investment had been neglected to such an extent that, according to Aschauer's estimates, a dollar spent in the public sector raised GNP by considerably more than a dollar spent for private investment.[4]

The Role of the Public Sector

By the end of Bush's term the extent and consequences of the neglect of public capital had become obvious. But behind that neglect lay a view of the economy that placed private activity as the source of economic progress and well-being. That was not the view of Adam Smith, whose *Wealth of Nations* was often taken to be the blueprint for a capitalist system. There Smith wrote that government had three duties to its citizens. The first two were the provision of national defense, and the establishment of a framework of law and order—activities that coincided very well with the aims of conservative presidencies.

But the third duty spelled out by Smith was quite different: it was

> the duty of erecting and maintaining certain public works and certain public institutions, which it can never be for the interest of any individual, or group of individuals, to erect and maintain, because the profit could never repay the expense. . . , although it may frequently do much more than repay it to a great society.

---

*It has long been a fundamental American belief that education is the surest means of bettering society. Moreover, all through the nineteenth century that belief was manifested in public expenditures that made Americans the best-educated people in the world. During the conservative era, that trend came to an end. By the late 1980s, per-pupil expenditures were higher in Switzerland, Sweden, Norway, Japan, Denmark, Austria, West Germany, and Canada than in the U.S. At the same time, public funding for retraining workers dropped by more than 50 percent in the 1980s. The result was a shortage of skilled workers in America, quite unlike the case in Europe or Japan. In France, for example, companies are required either to allocate a percentage of their gross earnings to worker training or to pay a tax into a nationwide training fund.

Smith is making clear that government has a positive economic function to perform—namely, the provision of adequate public works, including, by Smith's explicit mention, public education. That is a view of the economy that the conservative era forgot. During the Reagan and Bush administrations several aides used to sport neckties with Smith's profile on them, but the policies of those years give no reason to believe that the aides had read his great work.

The S&L Disaster

The infrastructure problem festered silently until it was suddenly "discovered" in the late 1980s, several years after motorists had discovered the problem for themselves along the nation's decaying highways. A second issue burst into prominence in a much more dramatic fashion. It was a financial crisis of a kind that the country had not experienced since the 1930s, when there was a nationwide failure of the banking system.

This time the disaster was limited to savings and loan institutions (S&Ls), principally based in the Southwest. By the late 1980s, S&Ls were collapsing with alarming regularity and mounting consequence. As with the infrastructure problem, however, the seeds of the disaster were sown during the Reagan years.

Traditionally, S&Ls were engaged in the narrow business of taking small deposits and providing mortgage loans. They were non-profit mutual associations owned by their depositors, and had limits on the interest they could pay those depositors. During the deregulation-minded Reagan administration, the S&Ls successfully lobbied Congress to expand their operations. Soon they were converted to for-profit, stockholder institutions that could compete for depositors by bidding up interest rates, and for borrowers by making loans on virtually everything. Because Reagan was opposed to any regulation that might affect business profits adversely (he actually appointed opponents of regulation to enforce its rules!), his administration trusted that banks, as well as other businesses, would police themselves. Congress was also at fault. It happened that S&Ls were significant contributors to election campaigns, and Congress failed to make adequate provision for the monitoring of their business practices. As a result, billions of dollars disappeared in the form of unsound bank loans—usually for highly speculative projects utterly unsuited for banking investment, and sometimes in shady dealings that echoed the manipulations and reckless practices of the 1920s.

So widespread was the S&L debacle that it soon affected major banks of hitherto substantial standing. Fortunately, the government repaid depositors for their federally insured accounts. But that "bailout" was very expensive. It appears that the total cost of the S&L failure will eventually exceed $500 billion over a thirty-year period.

Behind the S&L Crisis

Once more, we stop to ask whether there was greater significance in this debacle than sheer mismanagement or skullduggery. Here the issue seems to be the criteria that are applied to the question of regulation itself. On the one side is efficiency. This is the side from which a

Depositors in Randallstown, Maryland wait to withdraw their money

conservative philosophy principally draws its strength. The wastefulness of many government procedures make them a natural target. The cost overruns of public undertakings, the endless delays in approving new processes and products, the avalanche of paperwork, the layers of bureaucratic self-protection of government-in-general are its anathema. And there is reason for this anti-government orientation. Left to themselves, the costs of government can be fatal to the vitality of any society, as exemplified in the progressive decline of the Soviet economy, leading to its collapse.

There is, however, another criterion. It is self-protection. The conservative view, which seeks its justification in a desire to maximize the energies latent in a capitalist system, tends to overlook the damage that can be inflicted by those selfsame energies. The excesses of the S&L disaster testify to the harm that can ensue when private energy is allowed to overstep the boundaries dictated by social prudence. The precept to be borne in mind is that all private economic activity has public consequences, just as all public economic activity has private consequences. The conservative era tended to emphasize the second injunction and to ignore the first.

Fiscal Difficulties

A third major issue can likewise be traced to President Reagan's term in office, although it did not become acute until his successor took charge. It was the problem of a federal deficit that had apparently become uncontrollable.

The federal deficit refers to the amount that the national government borrows from the public by issuing Treasury bills and notes and bonds.* When Reagan came into office in 1981, the deficit was $74 billion, or less than three percent of GNP. By 1992, as Bush left office, the deficit had grown to $340 billion, or 5.7 percent of GNP. Over the same years the gross national debt, which is the sum of all outstanding government borrowings, had grown from $629 billion to over $4 trillion, or from a sum equal to 23 percent of GNP to one equal to 68 percent of GNP.

---

*A Treasury bill has a short maturity, usually thirty, sixty, or ninety days; a note comes due in a year; and a bond over a longer period, up to thirty years.

Expenditure Profligacy

What accounted for this alarming increase? Two elements can be clearly identified. One was the failure of the two administrations to put a cap on expenditures. We have already noted that Reagan's enthusiasm for cutting government back did not extend to the military budget, or to the two rapidly growing areas of social expenditure, Medicare and Social Security. President Bush, likewise, could not effectively deal with the military build-up or the tremendous growth in medical costs. Nor was Congress willing or able to check the rising tide of spending.

In turn, expenditure profligacy can be attributed to two factors. Military spending was supported partly because of the severe employment costs that cutbacks would impose on many states and localities, and partly because both Congress and the president were unwilling to relinquish America's place as a super power—a role dramatically realized in January 1991 when the Gulf War prevented Iraq's conquest of Kuwait and blocked its threat to Saudi Arabia.

The rise in social expenditure must be explained differently, in the presence of very large needs for which there existed no alternative to federal programs of support. By way of example, roughly thirty-five million Americans had no health care benefits, another fifteen million were underinsured, and another ten million were covered only by an inadequate Medicaid system. The paradox was that U.S. medical costs were at an all-time high. In 1992, the nation's total expenditures on health care was $838.5 billion, or approximately 14 percent of GNP. This was the highest percentage of any nation in the world. Certainly there were no easy solutions to America's health care crisis, but equally clearly, the stage was set for government to take the lead in developing a comprehensive program to provide all Americans with an affordable health care umbrella. But that brings us beyond the reach of this chapter.

Tax Phobia

But the problem of growing deficits must be attributed as well to a quite different source. Americans consider themselves to be a very heavily taxed people, and punish representatives who dare to vote for tax increases. In fact, Americans are almost the lowest taxed of any industrial nation. The Organization of Economic Cooperation and Development (OECD), representing the chief industrial nations in the world, has pointed out that American tax revenues, as a percentage of GNP, are the second lowest among their twenty-four member states, exceeded only by Turkey. German tax revenues, for instance, equal some 38 percent of its GNP, France's revenues are equal to not quite 44 percent, those of the Netherlands or Belgium are close to 50 percent. Our ratio of tax revenues to GNP is 28 percent.

Thus, if we were willing to tax ourselves in the same proportion as do our OECD counterparts, there would be a much smaller deficit. Raising our tax collection ratio to that of Germany would have increased our intake in 1992 by about $130 billion, or more than a quarter of that year's deficit. Raising it to the level of France would have brought in an additional $150 billion, enough to cut the deficit by over 40 percent.

Why are we such inefficient tax collectors? One part of the answer is probably that we rely on much more strongly disliked tax measures than do our fellow industrial nations. We raise about 36 percent of our tax revenues through the income tax, compared with less than 30 percent for Germany and just under 12 percent for France. To many economists, the income tax is the fairest of all taxes, insofar as it is usually proportional to one's income, but that is not the way it is regarded by those who pay it. Rightly or wrongly, households feel that the government is trespassing when it levies a tax on the incomes they have earned, whereas taxes on gasoline or goods in general may be resented but are not regarded in such a politically charged fashion.

If we were to adopt a gasoline tax or a value-added tax—a kind of national sales tax—our tax revenues would certainly rise, our deficit fall, and our tax tempers cool.*

A Question of National Character?

In such a fiscal program there is nothing inherently incompatible with a conservative economic philosophy, as witness its application by many conservative governments overseas. Perhaps the difficulty lies at

---

*An interesting analysis of the American tax phobia will be found in *No Pain, No Gain*, by Louis A. Ferleger and Jay R. Mandle (1992).

a deeper level. The sociologist Seymour Martin Lipset has called to our attention two countries that shared a very similar experience but reacted very differently to it. The countries are the United States and Canada, and the shared experience was the taming of a wilderness to their west. From this common experience, however, the two nations spontaneously chose two strikingly different culture heroes. The Canadians chose the scarlet-coated Northwest Mounted Police, the symbol of law and order. The Americans chose the cowboy.[5] A nation that admires the values of cowboy life—and they are not inconsiderable— is not likely to welcome a larger government role, no matter what the means of financing may be.

The Concentration of Wealth

This view reflects not merely a conservative view, but a peculiarly American brand of conservatism, one that celebrates and rewards business success more lavishly than other capitalist nations. The table below lists executive compensation in the biggest firms in the United States compared with other nations:

AVERAGE CORPORATE EXECUTIVE COMPENSATION*		
	Top 30 firms	**All firms**
United States	3,200,000	747,000
Britain	1,100,000	399,600
France	800,000	448,500
Germany	800,000	364,500
Japan	500,000	371,800

*Includes bonuses and stock options.
SOURCE: *New York Times,* Jan. 10, 1992.

More specifically, in 1990, chief executive officers (CEOs) of American companies earned 119 times as much as their average workers, whereas CEOs of Japanese companies earned only eighteen times as much. Moral questions aside, a nation whose economy is built on mass production runs an economic risk from a highly unequal income distribution.

Although conservatives may argue that this structure may generate more savings from its prosperous upper class, the economy as a whole is likely to suffer from the diminished purchasing power of its middle and lower classes. This is precisely what occurred during the conservative years. Despite economic expansion, income became concentrated in fewer and fewer hands. Looking at the nation as a whole, during the 1980s the income of the top 20 percent of U.S. families went up 19 percent, while the poorest 20 percent lost 9 percent of their income. Over the same period, the share of national income received by the wealthiest 20 percent climbed from 41.6 percent to 44 percent, while the 60 percent in the middle ranks experienced a slight decrease in income. Put simply, the rich got richer and the poor poorer. This concentration of wealth reversed three decades of growing equality, and marked the 1980s as the first decade since the 1930s in which large numbers of Americans actually suffered a serious decline in living standards. According to economist Paul Krugman, "The growing gap between rich and poor was arguably the central fact about economic life in America in the 1980s."[6] This bears not only on the question of the American tax phobia, but on the forces that may have been responsible for turning an era of high economic hopes into one of disappointing attainments.

Deficit Fears

One last aspect of the fiscal problem deserves mention. It is the extraordinary degree of alarm that has been generated by the term "deficit." Let us remember that deficits mean borrowing, and that with government, as with corporations and households, there is borrowing for good purposes as well as bad. A government that borrows to pay interest on its own debt or to pay the salaries of its regular employees is misusing its borrowing powers as badly as a corporation or a household that borrows for the same purposes. But a government that borrows to finance infrastructure is pursuing a course that is in no wise less prudent than a company that borrowed to finance a new productive venture or a household that borrows to send its children to college.

The difference is that it is very easy to tell from the public or the private records of companies and households what they borrow for, and thereby to judge whether their debts will become a burden or a source of growth. That is not the case with the way the United States keeps its national accounts. We count as revenues only our tax income, but measure our expenditures by adding both normal expenses and our public capital expenditures. Every company and household, and every industrial country other than our own, separates the two accounts so that one can tell at a glance whether the borrowing is for a good purpose or a bad one. Proper accounting may well reveal that our deficit is too large. But we cannot ascertain *how* large until we have sorted out those expenditures that should certainly be paid for by taxes (such as interest on the national debt) from expenditures such as infrastructure that have a prima-facie claim to be financed by borrowing.

Adopting a "capital budget" would not ensure that our government will use intelligence and responsibility to determine how much to borrow and for what purposes to use it. But it would at least give us an indication whether the government is in fact profligate or stingy, thoughtful about tomorrow's needs or neglectful of them.

America and the World Economy: The Making of a Debtor Nation

One further problem deserves our notice: This was a dramatic reversal of America's position in the world of international economic affairs. With few exceptions, the United States had enjoyed a substantial advantage as a world producer, starting well before World War I and mounting to a seemingly impregnable superiority after World War II. The superiority was not only the consequence of our safe distance from the world's battlefields, but also the result of our vaunted technological and organizational edge in industrial production. Thus, a quarter of a century after the end of World War II, the United States was exporting, on average, something like $10 billion a year more than it imported. Our position as an international producer seemed assured.

It was not. Beginning in the 1980s, our long-standing favorable balance began to turn negative. In 1982 our balance on goods and services was a *negative* $20.6 billion—that is, we bought that much more goods and services from the world than we sold in return. The next year that negative balance more than doubled. In 1984 it doubled again, to reach the total of $102.7 billion. Three years later the adverse balance had become an astounding $143.1 billion. We had moved from a trade creditor—that is, a trader who regularly sold more than we bought—to a world debtor on current account.

By 1988 the tide in trade again turned, and our balance on current account began to decline. By 1991 our adverse balance was down to $21.8 billion, and the worst of the crisis seemed over, although we continued to run uncomfortably large adverse balances.

Behind the Trade Problem

What lay behind this disconcerting change? Two explanations can be put forward. One is historical. Scarcely had World War II ended than the United States realized that the devastation wrought by the conflict seriously threatened its own domestic economy and international well-being. Europe had lost some thirty million people in the war; Japan, about two million. Entire cities were levelled or damaged; factories were destroyed; infrastructure was demolished; farm lands charred and ravaged. This was not a world in which capitalism and democracy could thrive. On the contrary, it was a world open to political turmoil, poverty, revolution, and, worse still, to Communist takeover. To promote international stability, and to maintain an "open door" world for American commerce, the United States took the lead in rehabilitating war-torn Europe and Japan. The cornerstone of this program was the Marshall Plan (1947), which ultimately channeled $13 billion into European restoration.

As the currents of international trade and finance were re-established, Europe and Japan quickly recovered from World War II, and America—the world's leading exporter and producer of manufactured products—prospered accordingly. By the 1980s the international economy was in the midst of its fourth postwar decade of growth. In the 1970s alone, world trade increased sevenfold, growing much faster than world GNP.

Although the United States remained the largest and richest economy in the world, it was inevitable that sooner or later its overwhelming pre-eminence would ebb. Products that foreigners could once purchase only in America became available elsewhere. Improvements in agriculture abroad reduced the world's dependency on American farm exports. Meanwhile, Americans "discovered" a wide variety of new, well-made, well-priced products manufactured abroad. As a result, from 1960 to 1983 U.S. merchandise exports expanded tenfold, but U.S. merchandise imports expanded twenty-five-fold. Hence, part of the changing balance of trade can be traced quite simply to the reemergence of Europe and Japan, as the disasters of World War II were gradually repaired.*

The Dollar Soars

The other explanation is more complex, and we shall only sketch it briefly here. It involves not merely the changing strength of the U.S. economy versus its competitors, but the entrance of new, special forces that affected our place in the world economy. These forces originated with the decision of the Reagan administration (and before that, of the Carter administration) to look to the Europeans—and later to the Japanese—as a promising source of dollars to help finance the deficit. This policy had two effects. First, it raised the value of the dollar on the foreign exchange market because Europeans rushed to invest the proceeds earned from their flourishing trade with the U.S. in the high-interest bonds of the Treasury. As a consequence, foreign goods became dirt cheap as the rising dollar bought more and more yen or francs or marks. One of these basement bargains was the cost of living abroad, which led, in turn, to a boom in foreign travel— tourism actually became the largest single industry in the world!

. . . and Then Plummets

At the time, of course, as the high dollar made foreign goods cheap to Americans, it made American goods expensive for foreigners. American exports suffered as a consequence, and pressure rose within the United States to "devalue" the dollar—that is, to take measures to lower its price in terms of other currencies. This became official policy in 1985, and within two years the dollar had fallen almost 50 percent against the Japanese yen and the German mark. Now America became the bargain basement of the world.

Thus foreign exchange fluctuations help explain the downs and ups of American fortunes in the world trade market. But they also had another, quite unexpected result. As the dollar took a precipitous fall, it brought a demand not just for U.S. exports but for American capital

---

*There is also a second reason. Europe and Japan not only regained their strength but began to forge ahead of the United States in the management of their national economies. This is a question to which we will turn in our next chapter.

assets—stocks and bonds, real estate, entire corporations. In 1980 only 3 percent of America's manufacturing assets were foreign-owned; by 1988, 12 percent were owned by overseas investors—German, Swiss, Japanese, French, and others.

This was a new and unsettling experience. We had ourselves long been major holders of foreign corporations, and never thought about it when General Motors or IBM or General Electric picked up a company here and there; but we did not like it when "American" firms such as the record division of RCA or Purina Mills or Firestone were bought, respectively, by a German conglomerate (Bertelsmann), a British oil company (British Petroleum), and a Japanese corporation (Bridgestone).

Thus the vicissitudes of the American trade balance and the American dollar are important not merely for the immediate problems they brought, and will continue to bring, but because they announce that the 1970s, 1980s, and 1990s have ushered in a sea change for America. The sea change is the immersion of American economic life into world economic life; or to depict the same phenomenon from a different perspective, the advent of a truly global economy in which America plays only one part.

U.S. arrival of foreign-made cars

The End of an Era

That is a change of huge significance for the future, and it will play its part in the chapter to come that looks toward that future. But first we must conclude this chapter. We left our survey of the period with the advent of the Bush presidency, and an account of some of the major problems it faced. Other problems also began to assume national importance, not least of them social pathologies of a kind that the country had not witnessed since the depression years. As many as a million Americans were homeless—begging on city streets and huddled on sidewalks at night. A nationwide drug epidemic became a matter of universal concern. Crime assumed greater importance than ever before. By the end of the president's term, these problems had brought the country to a standstill. A serious recession began in 1990—unemployment resumed its upward march, real output in the nation declined, and a growing sense of unease was almost palpable, with one important exception: The White House continued to declare that the economy was fundamentally sound and would soon recover.

Although Bush had replaced Calvin Coolidge's portrait with that of Theodore Roosevelt's, he did not use the presidency as a "bully pulpit" to initiate economic reforms or inspire the citizenry. The fundamental policies of the Reagan years continued. This provided the Democrats with a central issue on which to fight the election campaign of 1992. In Governor Bill Clinton of Arkansas they found a candidate who understood the political appeal and the economic importance of promising to break the stalemate in Washington, and to replace an apparently indifferent and passive administration with an engaged and concerned one.

Clinton's election was more than just a sign that the president had badly misjudged the economic situation. It was evidence of the end of an era in which government was automatically regarded as the problem, and the inauguration of an era in which government would be regarded as a means to deal with many problems. Whether or not the Clinton presidency will succeed to grappling with the vast issues of the times cannot be foretold; but it may be that the pendulum of American political and economic sentiment had again swung, as has been the case so often in the past.

Notes

[1] *Ronald Reagan: The Politics of Symbolism* (1984), p. 63.
[2] Robert McElvaine, *The Great Depression* (1984), p. 14.
[3] Robert S. McIntyre, *Challenge* (Nov./Dec. 1991), p. 28, fig. 5.
[4] David Alan Aschauer, *Public Investment and Private Sector Growth* (1990).
[5] Seymour Martin Lipset, *The First New Nation: The United States in Historical and Comparative Perspective* (1963), p. 251.
[6] *The Age of Diminished Expectations* (1992 pb. ed.), p. 25.

Bill Clinton on the campaign trail

Chapter 11

AMERICAN CAPITALISM: RETROSPECT AND PROSPECT

Our discussion has taken us to the very edge of the present, with its uncertain and unwritten future. This now seems a good place to halt our journey and to look back over the terrain we have traversed, before venturing a glance—of necessity speculative and hazardous—into the possible shapes of things to come.

We have traced the main lines of the economic transformation of the United States. Can we find large-scale patterns in that transformation? Are there lessons to be drawn from the past? Clarifications that can be applied to the present? The questions suggest that we must find a frame of reference other than the chronology of events that have provided our thread for the last several chapters. Let us therefore return to the organizing principle of our initial chapter—an organizing principle that we have always kept in sight, but that can now once again be placed at the center of our inquiry. Let us look back over the past and reflect on what has happened to material life, to economic life, and to capitalism itself in America.

MATERIAL LIFE

Material life, Fernand Braudel tells us, is the foundation on which all else is raised. It comprises the work we do, the products we create, the forces of nature that we capture within our tools and machines, the techniques and learning we invent and retain. Nothing has changed so astonishingly in America—indeed, in all capitalist nations—as material life. To imagine the work, the products, the tools, and techniques of the Pilgrims requires an effort of the imagination sufficient to bring wax figures in museums to life. It is difficult to reconstruct the material life of the Lowell mill, the Homestead steel plant, even the Ford River Rouge plant. All that seems hopelessly distanced from modern material life.

In what ways distanced? First it is clear that we do different kinds of work than in the past. In 1620 everyone in America was in immediate touch with nature. In 1820 70 percent of all working persons were still farmers or farm employees. By 1900 fewer than 40 percent were engaged in agriculture. Today less than 3 percent of the labor force works in farming—and even that group does not till the soil so much as steer tractors and combines, work complicated farm machinery, fly crop duster planes, tend automatic milking machines, and worry about the cost of chemical fertilizers. Contact with the soil, in the close and intimate relationship of the Pilgrims and the sturdy homesteaders of the past, is now almost vanished.*

What, instead, do Americans do? The great exodus from agriculture has resulted in the swelling of two other major branches of endeavor—services, which employ about three-quarters of our employed labor force,** and manufacturing, which gives work to about 16 percent.

Only thirty years ago we employed 30 percent of the labor force in manufacturing. Does that mean that we are therefore in danger of losing our industrial strength? Here it is useful to reflect that the fall in manufacturing employment is dwarfed by the drop in agricultural employment which, half a century ago, was ten times as large a work force as it is today. Yet we never hear that we have too few agricultural workers to enable us to feed ourselves. This is because it is not

---

*With the exception, all too easily passed over in a bird's-eye view such as this, of the migrant (and immigrant) labor that plays a vital part in harvesting many crops. This ragged work force, often grossly abused and exploited, is still only a small percentage of the total American labor force, but it is growing rapidly and should not be lost from sight.

**The breakdown of the service sector warrants a footnote because it always surprises people. About eighty-five million men and women work in "services." The largest group, twenty-eight million, are in miscellaneous personal occupations that range from health care to restaurants, from ministers to scientists. The next group consists of nineteen million in retail trade. Then come the fifteen million in government—state and local, not federal. They are followed by almost seven million in finance, insurance, and real estate, and just over six million in wholesale trade. Next are not quite six million in transportation. Last we find about three million in the federal government.

the volume of employment that establishes our capacity to produce, but the productivity of that labor force; that productivity in turn is established by the quantity and quality of the machinery that labor uses.

Thus a small manufacturing labor force may be perfectly capable of making a vast volume of output, provided—and this is a very important proviso—it is well educated and trained, and surrounded with "intelligent" and fast-working mechanical aids. In fact, a considerable portion of our labor force in "services" adds productivity to manufacturing labor by supplying it with information, communication, research, and other such output-generating inputs.

High Technology

Two new capabilities have altered modern technology beyond its traditional limits. One of these is the ability to pry apart matter to release the volcanic forces within the atomic nucleus—an ability whose consequences for humanity are of overwhelming, perhaps suicidal, and possibly of life-giving importance. The djinn of nuclear capability has been let out of the bottle and it is very doubtful that it will ever again be induced to retreat within a safe container. Breaching the nuclear threshold is in itself enough to mark off the modern age from all that has gone before, even though, to date, nuclear power has not made a significant difference to the actual texture of material life.

Less awesome, but more freighted with significance, is a second technical advance—the development of the power to harness microcircuits in vast numbers, capable of processing and storing information in a manner that greatly narrows the gulf between brain and machine. The computer is a technical advance every bit as revolutionary as access to nuclear power, and much more immediately apparent in the fabric of daily existence.

Here is where the productivity-generating capacity of the manufacturing sector may collide with the job-creating capacity of the service sector. For the possibility inherent in the human like "skills" possessed by computers raises the possibility that work in the service and the manufacturing sectors may be increasingly performed by computerized machinery, just as work in the agricultural sector has been virtually taken over by machines. If the "robotization" of work becomes in fact a profitable avenue for development, the needs for unskilled or

Computer semiconductors

semi-skilled labor in both manufacturing and service occupations may be severely reduced.* Correspondingly, the need for highly trained, "knowledge-intensive" labor is likely to rise, although not necessarily by enough to make up for the reduced need for relatively less educated workers.

This raises important and disquieting possibilities. Can we equip most men and women for the kinds of work that will be in demand? Will there be enough positions for all who will seek them? If not, will "work" take on the form of a two-tier spectrum—an upper tier with something of the standing and expertise that we now associate with professionals, and a lower tier doing little more than oiling the great self-directing machinery of society? Such a picture has overtones of the anti-utopian fiction of Aldous Huxley's *Brave New World*. Huxley's scenario is certainly not a destination toward which we are inexorably pushed, but it is one that the changing character of material life may force us to confront unless we act to prevent it. Probably the most effective way to do so is to increase our expenditures on education in general, and on producing a highly trained labor force in particular.

ECONOMIC LIFE

The prospective possibility of a far-reaching transformation in the material life of America raises the question of what has happened to its economic life.

Economic life, we recall, is the manner in which we are integrated as individuals into a working social whole. Mainly this takes place through our engagement with the marketplace which we enter to sell our skills and work energies and to buy the products made by the skills and energies of others. Today our entanglement in the market is so complete that it is useful to recall that it was not always so. Only a hundred years ago, our farmer and artisan forebears were by no means as inextricably tied into market relationships as we. As recently as 1900, at least a third of the nation—its agricultural population—was still self-supporting to some degree, capable of sustaining its existence with only minimal recourse to the outside world through exchange. To be sure, even in 1900 everyone bought and sold in stores, and no one

*At this writing there are estimated to be some 37,500 mechanical robots "working" in U.S. industry. Japan, the world leader in robotics, claims to use seven or eight times as many.

lived in hermit-like isolation. But the agricultural fraction still represented a substantial group that could have produced its own subsistence, like the Pilgrims, even if all market relations had vanished.

No such stratum of near independence exists today. The market has
become the ubiquitous and universal solvent of daily life, the mechanism on which the overwhelming majority depends for the provision
of the most essential as well as the most trivial of its daily needs, and
to which it turns for access to that essential means of gratifying those
needs—money income.

The Supranational Economy

The economic transformation of America has thus constantly widened
the screen on which was projected the drama of market activity. But
the widening has not merely been in terms of the numbers of Americans who have come to depend on the market as buyers and sellers.
The screen has also widened beyond the boundaries of the national
economy until the forces of supply and demand that affect our well-
being now come from all quarters of the globe, not merely from activities within our national borders. We have already caught a glimpse of
this supranational economy in our last chapter. Now it is time for a
more careful look.

Modern-day global enterprise is not merely an enlargement of the
far-reaching trading enterprises of the past. It is a wholly new internationalization of production itself. Thus the "American" Chrysler Corporation builds its most successful car in Canada; the "Japanese" Honda
is produced in the United States; and the Pepsi-Cola company makes
its products in 500 plants located in 100 countries. The Phillips, Asea-
Boveri, and Electrolux companies, all members of the so-called "Club
of the 350" largest multinational companies, are in many ways too
large to be contained in their "home" economies of the Netherlands,
Switzerland, and Sweden.

Modern-day transnational business operates on a scale, and at a
level that lifts it above the nation-states in which it locates its operating
units. The magnitude of this flow has become enormous. According to
a recent study of the United Nations Center on Transnational Corporations, the combined sales of the "Club of the 350" in 1985 amounted to
one-third of the combined gross national products of all industrial
countries, and exceeded the aggregate GNPs of all the developing
nations, including China.[1]

The internationalization of the market is also compounded by the extraordinary transnational reach of banking and finance. By the 1990s, most of the world's big banks had opened branches in other nations—branches that were not subject to the credit controls that applied to their home offices, because no central bank (such as the Federal Reserve) had the authority to impose regulations or restrictions on an enterprise that lay within the sovereign territory of another nation.

As a result, the very meaning of a nation's "own" money began to blur. In 1990, for instance, the value of all commercial bank deposits within the United States—the bulk of what is called our "money supply"—came to about $826 billion. But the value of the dollars deposited in foreign branches of U.S. banks, or in banks of other nations, came to over $3,000 billion. There had thus grown up a vast pool of dollars, called Eurodollars, located abroad. This makes it very difficult for the Federal Reserve to control effectively the volume of bank credit, insofar as big corporations can easily borrow dollars abroad. Yet another indicator of the vast expansion of the reach of international finance is that the estimated global value of *daily* trading in foreign exchange is $1 trillion.

THE IMPACT OF TRADE

These astonishing figures testify to the degree to which economic linkages and relationships have leaped over national boundaries. No less sobering is the extent to which ordinary trade—the imports and exports of goods that are conveyed by boat or plane rather than being produced abroad—have also broken down the compartmentalization of the world. In 1950 the total values of exports from and imports into the United States, compared with the total value of goods—not services—produced in the U.S., was about 12 percent. This is a good measure of our exposure to the forces of the international market in the production of manufactures or raw materials. For all intents and purposes it meant that the U.S. economy was a "closed system," reliant to a modest extent on exports, more or less indifferent to the volume of imports.

Within forty years this had changed out of all recognition. By 1990, the ratio of exports and imports to GNP was 40 percent. Nowhere was the power and penetration of the international market more evident

Worker protests plant closing in Flint, Michigan

than in the collapse of America's place in steel and autos, traditionally the twin pillars of its industrial might. In 1950, U.S. steelmakers were the undisputed leaders of the world, accounting for 50 percent of all world steel output. By the 1990s, U.S. steelmakers had been reduced to one of the least efficient world producers and accounted for only 12 percent of world output. Despite the high cost of transporting steel, 19 percent of the U.S. market had been won by foreign makers, and American steel mills had been forced to ask for protective trade barriers to save themselves from still further losses.

Even more shocking was the debacle in automobiles. After the war the United States imported a mere $50 million worth of automotive vehicles and parts. America was virtually the only efficient auto maker in the world. By 1960, however, imports had grown ten times; by 1970 the value of 1960s' imports had again increased tenfold; and by 1990, imports had once more increased their value tenfold. This was a thousandfold increase over the 1950 level—enough to raise imports of Japanese, German, English, Swedish, and other cars to some $44 billion a year. Shortly thereafter, Japan became the world's largest auto producer and GM's no. 2 competitor in the United States became Toyota.

It was not in steel and automobiles alone that the international market breached the formerly impregnable dikes of American industrial strength. The computer industry, an American invention, was for all intents and purposes a Japanese-dominated field. In machine tools and electrical equipment, cameras and color TVs, tires and motorcycles, all erstwhile American-led fields, the United States market was being increasingly served by foreign makers.

Economic life in America had thus not only exposed its work force to the flux of the market, but had subjected the greatest of its corporations, like the weakest of its citizens, to the power of the market's forces. By 1982, Chrysler Corporation, a mighty U.S. giant, had escaped bankruptcy only by congressional bailout. U.S. Steel, J.P. Morgan's giant, had essentially quit the steel business and renamed itself USX Corporation, to indicate its new, rather vague, "field." IBM, long a world-renowned company, posted a loss of $5.46 billion for the last quarter of 1992, the biggest single loss in corporate history. Perhaps most significant of all, a considerable portion of American business and financial opinion, long wedded to the ideas of free trade, was beginning to think along protectionist lines, asking whether America's place in the international economy could be made secure without some form of legislative protection against the onslaughts of the world market.

A Two-Level System?

The trend toward worldwide economic activity makes it patently clear that the United States, like all advanced countries, must prepare itself to meet the challenge of global competition. What gives this question a new degree of urgency is the fear that competition will take place not merely by exporting goods but by exporting capital and that the export of capital will take the form of high-tech machinery worked by low-skilled (and very low-paid) workers.

This is by no means a merely alarmist possibility. The average factory wage in the boom city of Shenzhen in China is one-thirtieth or one-fortieth of the average Japanese wage, and the average Japanese wage is not yet as high as our own.[2] It is little wonder, then, that some foresee a day when high-productivity machinery will be uncrated in Shenzhen to create a factory capable of matching the quality, and of vastly beating the price, of anything that America has to offer. On a less dramatic scale, something like this has already been the bitter experience of American workers who have lost millions of jobs— 500,000 in automobile production alone—as American firms found themselves unable to meet competition from low-wage areas such as Mexico, and have moved part of their manufacturing operations across the border in order to forestall low-wage competition.

This prospect adds yet another dimension to the world of the supranational corporation. The new dimension is that international competition will now endanger the economies of all high-wage countries—not merely of laggard ones—because the prospect of a two-level economy with Shenzhens around the world would seriously lessen the purchasing power of labor in all high-wage capitalisms. In this prospective world, we are not so much at loggerheads with Europe and Japan as in the same boat with them.

Three Strategies for the Future

What could be the outcome of such a two-level world economy? Three possibilities seem open. The first is to continue the commitment to free and unhindered trade, a central tenet of American (although not so much of European) international economic policy since the end of the Second World War. The theory behind this policy recalls the views of the English economist David Ricardo, first set forth in his *Principles of Political Economy and Taxation,* published in 1817. Ricardo explained how two countries could profitably trade, even if one of them were more efficient in the production of "everything" than its counterpart. Differences in climate, resources, and the like would always make it profitable for each country to concentrate its efforts on the commodities in which its *comparative* advantage was greater, thereafter selling those products to the other.

The idea of specialization in international production remains a valid and important one. Imaginably, America might be better off if its industrial machinery were produced in, say, Mexico, while we concentrated in the output of something like highly skilled services. The difficulties arise when we face the problem of retraining the millions of workers who would be affected. Many years would lapse before the work force of our industrial sector had become the technicians, educators, scientists and high-skilled professionals in which our national comparative advantage lay. In the meanwhile, we could easily face serious problems of economic dislocation and social and political unrest. Hence, a policy of complete laissez faire, allowing the market to determine the employment levels and directions of the work forces of the advanced countries, seems unlikely.

Protectionism

A second response is even older than free trade. It is to exclude certain goods, or classes of goods, from domestic markets because of the economic disruption they might cause. The most common means of carrying out such a protectionist policy is the tariff, whose place in our history we have already observed.

Tariffs are by no means the only, or the most effective means of protecting domestic markets today. Quotas on allowable imports, or direct negotiations with foreign nations that result in their "voluntary" curtailment of exports, play a large part in the foreign economic policies of all industrial nations. For instance, the tonnages of steel or Japanese cars allowed into the United States are established by agreement, not by competitive price. At present, roughly 25 percent of all U.S. imports, double the amount of two decades ago, are subject to nontariff restrictions.

GATT, EC, OPEC

Efforts to regulate international trade, in one form or another, have been a well-nigh ubiquitous feature of the postwar world economy. As early as 1947, the United States and twenty-two other nations attempted to ensure an open trading system by entering into a General Agreement on Tariffs and Trade (GATT). Among other things, the agreement sought to implement a so-called most-favored-nation principle—that is, each nation had to treat all other nations in exactly the same way: the lowest tariff, the fewest restrictions, the easiest access awarded to anyone had to be given to everyone. In subsequent years GATT served as a forum for U.S.–sponsored "rounds" of trade talks among its members, now numbering 108. During the Kennedy Round (1963–67), for example, tariffs were reduced an average of 36–39 percent. The outcome of the most recent round of negotiations, the Uruguay Round, is still unclear.

GATT, it must be noted, was established in the same year as the Marshall Plan, and like that program it had a political aspect to it. GATT was an effort not only to revitalize the European economy but effectively to prohibit the establishment of trading blocks which could, in turn, develop into political or military alliances. As a result, GATT prohibited bilateral agreements among its members. But these are precisely the types of negotiations that appear now to be taking place among nations. As a result, the future role of GATT is, at this point, very uncertain.

More promising have been the efforts of nations with common geographical boundaries to open their borders to their neighbors and integrate their economies. The outstanding example of this development was the economic unification, on January 1, 1993, of the twelve nations comprising the European Community (EC), thereby creating the world's largest economic market, 337 million people. Yet at the same time that many nations have worked to establish closer economic ties, others have entered into cartels to protect their comparative advantages. Cartels are international pooling agreements that allocate world markets, establish minimum prices, and restrict output. Since the 1970s, the word cartel has become synonomous with OPEC, the Organization of Petroleum Exporting Countries. From its founding in 1960 until the Arab–Israeli War of 1973, OPEC was little more than a paper organization. Thereafter, it became the first commodity cartel to use its raw material assets as an effective economic and political weapon. What power OPEC will be able to wield in the future brings us not only into the subject of energy but also into the area of foreign policy, each a topic beyond the scope of this discussion.

No economist likes protectionism, because it has a tendency to spread like a virus. Steel is protected today, machine tools tomorrow, television sets the day after. In the end, jobs are protected, but the nation's overall productivity suffers, and with it, its real purchasing power. Nonetheless, if the two-level global economy acquires the importance that is imaginable during the coming decades, a resurgence of protectionist sentiment is very likely.

Managed Trade

A third policy is a kind of compromise between the two. Called "managed" trade, it seeks to combine the productivity gains of at least a limited free exchange with the safeguards of protectionism. It does so by tempering the bargaining process so that the Shenzhens can only enjoy a share of a developed country's market to the degree that they abide by standards of environmental protection, workers' safety, and similar policies. Observance of these standards adds considerably to the cost of production in the underdeveloped nations, and thereby narrows their cost advantages.

The Challenge to Sovereignty?

One last aspect of managed trade merits a word. The real challenge of a two-level world is that the multinational corporations are often the supplier of the high-tech equipment that combines with low-wage labor. What we then find is that transnational production presents problems that escape the regulatory reach of the nation-state. Too large to reach into the wage settlements of Shenzhen, too small to serve as a regulator of transnational flows of production or human migration, the nation-state is losing its effectiveness in regulating and guiding international exchange and supranational production. What new forms of regulation and guidance the twenty-first century may bring we do not know, but this issue is likely to become a key challenge in the years ahead.

AMERICA IN THE TWENTY-FIRST CENTURY

This now brings us back for a last look into the half-visible, half-invisible American future. For it is clear that to a greater extent than ever before, this future will be inextricably entangled in the changing structure of world economic affairs.

Why America Was a World Leader

It is useful to begin to look forward by looking back. Economic historians Richard Nelson and Gavin Wright have argued persuasively that the American technological leadership of the Western world from the middle to the late nineteenth century was based on several factors.[3] One was the sheer extent and riches of the continental market of the United States. In a day in which modern-day possibilities of transportation were unknown, these conveyed tremendous competitive advantages to American industrial leadership.

A second advantage lay in the characteristics of American leadership itself. We have seen the gradual replacement of the swashbuckling robber barons of American industry by organized management. The American variant of this movement, with its emphasis on "scientific management," became a symbol of organizational skills and techniques that were another source of American leadership.*

A third reason was a growing recognition of the role of education in promoting productivity and technology. Before World War II, Americans enjoyed roughly twice as much secondary education as did their European competitors. In addition, as late as 1969, total U.S. expenditure on R&D (research and development) was still double that of England, Germany, France, and Japan *combined.*

These general sources of America's uncontested economic superiority had disappeared by the 1960s. To begin with, extraordinary developments in the technology of international transportation greatly diminished the importance of the American market. Belgian lettuce flew overnight on jumbo jets to markets in New York and San Francisco; gigantic tankers made possible a world oil market; automatic machinery opened the manufacture of components to unskilled work forces in Mexico City, Bangkok, or Turkey. Thus, the world's work

---

*U.S. managerial technique was even admired by Lenin!

became globalized in a manner that militated against the advantages that American labor had once personified.

Second, the American advantage in managerial skills and technical know-how also became ever less visible. Because of its continuing emphasis on military-connected R&D, American preeminence in peace-related innovations began to fall behind. This was not a sign of diminishing creativity, but of a diminishingly effective application of that creativity. By 1980, a number of countries were outspending the U.S. on peacetime R&D as a percentage of GNP.* Although American scientists continued to lead the world in the capture of Nobel Prizes, American industry lost its lead in capturing the markets for automotive and jet plane and bullet-train transportation. Not least, the education needed to match the new levels of advanced technology was clearly better supplied abroad than at home, judging by international comparisons of mathematical grade scores, in which Americans regularly finished last.

As a result, each year America has been producing too few scientifically and technically trained people. By way of example, only 6 percent of U.S. college degrees are taken in engineering, as compared with 20 percent in Japan and 37 percent in Germany.

Falling Behind or Convergence?

Thus, from many perspectives it seems that America has been losing the unquestioned primacy in economic strength that it has enjoyed for a century. There is, however, another way of assessing the present and prospective state of affairs. What we are witnessing is not so much an American decline as a foreign catch-up; this catch-up is the consequence of an increasingly shared culture of technology and management throughout the industrial world.

"We believe," write Nelson and Wright, who propose this "convergence" thesis, "that the internationalization of trade, business, and technology is here to stay. This means that national borders mean much less than they used to regarding the flow of technology, at least among nations that have made the now needed social investments in

---

*All through the 1980s, we have lagged behind our competitors, spending 1.8 percent of GNP on nondefense R&D, compared with 2.6 percent for Germany and 2.8 percent for Japan.

education and research facilities. . . . It is increasingly difficult to create new technologies that will stay contained within national boundaries for very long in a world where technological sophistication is widespread and firms of many nationalities are ready to make the investments needed to exploit new generic technologies."[4]

This does not mean that individual countries may not forge ahead or fall behind. Indeed, as Nelson and Wright hasten to add, there is another interpretation of convergence—namely, that America is indeed slipping backwards, precisely because it is failing to provide the educational and infrastructural investments needed to stay abreast of its European and Japanese competition. "While we argue," say Nelson and Wright, "that the principal factor driving convergence over the last quarter century has been internationalization, we do not dismiss the possibility that the United States may be in the process of slipping into second, third, or fifth rank in productivity and per capita income. . . ."[5]

Labor–Management Relations

What could be the cause of such a relative decline in American economic capability? One possibility that has attracted the attention of many commentators is the American failure to establish a satisfactory framework for labor–management relations, a framework within which the full cooperation and participation of labor could be achieved. In part this helps explain the decline in productivity in the United States. Between 1982 and 1989, the average annual increase in productivity per worker hour in the U.S. was 1 percent, as compared with 2.7 percent in West Germany and 3.1 percent in Japan. These figures, coupled with earlier statistics, have led Paul Krugman to conclude that "the two decades since 1970 have seen the worst U.S. productivity performance of the century."[6]

Certainly there is no lack of evidence that American labor fell far short of the performance offered abroad. Here the testimony is offered by the litany of complaints, growing all through the 1960s, 1970s, and 1980s, about the poor quality of American workmanship. Indeed, in its World Competitiveness Report for 1990, the Swiss-based World Economic Forum, which evaluates business policies and standards, ranked the U.S. twelfth in product quality. Japan was ranked first. It was this poor quality, not cheaper prices, that drove American buyers to Japanese Sonys and Hondas, German Volkswagens, Swedish machinery, and similar foreign wares. Americans were willing to pay more for Sony TVs because their image was noticeably sharper and their color reproduction more lifelike and vivid. Similarly, they were willing to pay more for Hondas than for Chevrolets because their performance was better, their fuel efficiency superior, and their frequency of repair lower. Already by 1979, imports claimed 94 percent of television domestic sales. By 1980, 50 percent of all consumer electronics products, 90 percent of the cutlery, and one of every four autos bought in the U.S. was foreign made.

What was the cause of this widely noticed difference in labor attitudes? Many observers singled out as the central difficulty the antagonisms and suspicions held by labor, resulting in a tight control over factory floor operations, and the counterpart attitudes of management that reinforced these stiff and generally obstructive union postures. American managers tended to treat their workers as an expensive nuisance to be decently paid, hard worked, and otherwise ignored. German managers, in contrast, had become accustomed to union representatives on their boards of directors; Swedish managers experimented with work flows that allowed workers to determine their own pace of production; Japanese companies went to great length to secure lifetime employment for their workers and to make all employees feel that their company was part of their community. As a result of this last-mentioned policy, Japan's worker turnover rate is just 3.5 percent per annum, as compared with America's turnover rate of 4 percent per month. In other words, Japan has fewer job switches or firings in a year than the U.S. has in one month.

These managerial attitudes were not simply the expression of kindlier attitudes abroad. Most of them were concessions that had been won from management by strongly unionized and politically unified labor movements. In America, a weaker labor movement was unable to win such concessions. Paradoxically, then, the inefficiency that has characterized American labor–management practices may be the consequence of the failure of American management to accord labor its due respect.

A Social Contract

A second attempt to discover a broad explanation for the American slippage turns our attention away from the relation between management and labor to that between management and government. It is the nature of capitalism that this relationship is inherently tense and difficult. Yet in many foreign capitalisms a degree of mutual understanding, cooperation, and support has been attained between the public and the private spheres that far exceeds anything that we have achieved in the United States.

American business attitudes toward government are typically as narrow and antagonistic as American labor attitudes toward management: Many businessmen speak of "the government" as if it were an enemy that occupied the capitol. And government attitudes toward business are also unsatisfactory—chaotic and constrained, insecure and unfocused. As a result, government in America has lagged far behind governments in other capitalisms in formulating a coherent *social contract*—a policy in which government, with business and labor cooperation, determines targets for economic encouragement or retrenchment, and then uses its broad powers to realize these specific objectives.[7]

Such a social contract can serve two purposes. First, it can lessen the inflationary pressure that builds up in all modern capitalisms as soon as a boom gets under way. This pressure makes it exceedingly difficult for an economy to pick itself up by its own bootstraps through a program of sustained public investment, because inflation starts to rear its ugly head as soon as employment picks up. But the very same inflationary pressure prevents a sustained boom, even if it is propelled entirely by private investment. In both cases, the onset of rising employment is quickly followed by rising prices; these in turn call for anti-inflationary policies of tight money or fiscal retrenchment that lessen the inflationary threat—and also the prospects of economic progress.

A Three-Way Bargain

We do not know by what means this inflationary threat can ultimately be tamed, but at this writing Germany and Japan have made promising gains in establishing a kind of anti-inflationary arrangement among labor, management, and government.

Under this arrangement each side gives, and each side gets something it needs. Labor gives up the drive for wage settlements in excess of those compatible with productivity increases, and labor gets both political legitimacy and economic security. Legitimacy comes with a seat on corporate boards for participation in matters of corporate labor policy; security is gained through apprenticeship training and unemployment insurance. These government programs facilitate job changeovers as management modernizes or alters production processes.

Management also gains and gives. It gains the right to deploy labor as it wishes on the factory floor, without encountering the usual suspicions or resistance from labor unions. In turn, management gains assurances of government financial assistance for modernization programs that exceed the normal bounds of corporate finance, as well as cooperation from both labor and government in any inter-firm arrangements required to maintain global market shares.

Finally, government is able to plan a long-term program of public investment with a much higher degree of protection from inflationary pressures. In turn it must provide a new kind of economic leadership—so-called *industrial policy*—that saddles it with a high degree of economic responsibility and a corresponding risk of political failure.

Thus, a social contract can set the stage for a greater control over inflation and a more coherent direction of national economic energies in a new setting where inflation and globalism pose new and difficult challenges. This is not a blueprint for "planning" that in any way resembles the disastrous centralized system of the former USSR and its satellites, but it is certainly different from the relatively unguided capitalism of the twentieth century. The world of twenty-first century capitalism seems likely to require a more organized and socially responsive form of capitalism than in the past, and some form of social contract appears to be the most promising response it may make.

A Spectrum of Capitalisms

One realization emerges clearly from this overview. Capitalism is capable of many institutional and organizational forms—not only from one country to the next, but from one period to the next. As material life changes, so does economic life. As ideas and ideologies change, so does the relation between politics and business. As capitalism changes in its complex structure, new dynamics emerge, giving another impetus to the process of economic evolution.

This very property of changefulness leads to the first general pronouncement for the coming century. It is that capitalism is likely to present a spectrum of social variants, all of them clearly members of the same basic social formation, but not all of them equally successful. By members of the same "formation" we mean that all will be motivated by the quest for capital; all of them marked by the presence of two realms, one economic, one political; and all of them essentially coordinated by a market mechanism. When we say that not all will be equally successful, we mean that among the many permutations of these three identifying elements, not all will function with equal success in securing the social morale, the political peace, and the economic vitality needed to carry on.

This is not a prognosis peculiar to our time in history. At any time in the past 200 years one might have said that so dynamic a system as ours was likely to evolve into a spectrum of forms, some of which would prosper as societies, polities, and economies more than others. That is not to say that one could have foreseen the specific characteristics of the Dickensian capitalism of England, the Balzacian capitalism of France, the Bismarckian capitalism of Germany, or even the exuberant capitalism of America. But certainly the future would have pointed to a fan-shaped trajectory of evolution, with some of these national variants carrying on tasks of accumulation, managing the delicate interplay of polity and economy, and mastering the use of and the control over the market with a greater degree of concord, unity, and vigor than others.

The Crucial Variable

That seems a plausible way to describe those attributes that will most likely determine the success of capitalisms in the coming century. But we shall add a more specific prognosis. The crucial variable for businesses in the twenty-first century is not their relative success in finding technologies and techniques to generate capital. The internationalization of the system seems certain to bring about a greater degree of conformity than in the past. Neither is it the form of the market mechanism. Once again, the spread of common technologies and modes of management seems likely to lead in the direction of more uniformity of national market mechanisms than in the past. The crucial variable, to our eyes, seems to lie in the relationship between the worlds of business and politics, the realms of economics and government.

Put differently, the decisive element appears to reside in the appropriate combination of laissez faire and planning—on the one hand, allowing capitalism to express its self-generated energies; on the other, guiding and supplementing those energies with various means of public encouragement and discouragement. Having said that, we do not presume to know what combination will prove the most fruitful. All we say—and that is already risk enough for any historian—is that we believe *this* is where the decisive determinations will lie.

Limits of Adaptability

One further prognostication seems necessary. We appear to be moving toward one challenge for which there is no visible remedy. It is the ecological dangers to which the modern industrial processes give rise, of which by far the most awesome is the possibility of climatic change. Global warming, as it is called, is a large-scale ecological process whose causes and consequences lie outside the scope of this book.[8] While still uncertain with respect to its speed of advent, there

Heavy smog over Denver, December 1983

seems to be a growing scientific consensus that industrialization itself is a major source of carbon emissions which, once in the atmosphere, form a kind of greenhouse whose invisible panes entrap solar energy, causing a rise in the ambient temperature of the earth.

The arresting feature of this process is not just its glacier-like encroachment. It is that the control over global warming lies outside any form of social control. This is because carbon emissions do not recognize national boundaries. They also do not arise from any single form of socioeconomic organization. Capitalism produces ecological dangers and so do all known kinds of socialism. Once carbon is released into the atmosphere it can no longer be charged to any geographic source or national origin, and its effects will be distributed with complete indifference as to the origins of the problem.

How is this challenge to be curtailed and controlled? How can global warming rights be granted—or denied—to poorer nations, or more ecologically concerned nations, or more deserving nations? The problem calls for remedies that surpass the political and economic limits and capabilities of our time. It is a problem that is likely to loom ever larger in the twenty-first century and to have moved to the foreground by the advent of the twenty-second.

Beyond Capitalism?

Ecology is the most fearsome challenge, but not the only one that dwarfs capitalism, as such. Anyone who looks out over the disarray of the post–Cold War world, with its seething racial and ethnic hatreds, its horrendous extremes of poverty and wealth, its population explosions and risks of local population extinctions, must recognize that humanity in its perhaps ten thousandth year of what we call civilization is still a very insecurely anchored achievement of the human species.

Against that perspective, capitalism diminishes in importance but also takes on a special significance. Capitalism is the name for the social arrangements with which we will have to come to grips with vast problems of unprecedented consequences. We do not know how adequately these arrangements can cope with these challenges, nor do we know what other social arrangements might prove to be necessary.

What we *do* know is that in this period great decisions will be made that will powerfully affect our capability to deal with the problems ahead. We can certainly vanquish the remediable evils of poverty and ignorance. We can marshal our scientific resources to minimize and perhaps hold at bay the destruction of the ecosphere. We can begin to construct the first transnational agreements that will be needed to coordinate a unified global economy and a patchwork global sovereignty. We can become aware of our responsibilities to the future, and of the contribution we can make to it by becoming the most adaptive, the most forward-looking capitalism—not of the twentieth century, but of the twenty-first.

Notes

[1] *Report on Transnational Corporations,* cited in *The Nation,* May 18, 1992, p. 652.

[2] Paul Kennedy, *Preparing for the Twenty-first Century* (1993), p. 178.

[3] Richard R. Nelson and Gavin Wright, "The Rise and Fall of American Technological Leadership," *Journal of Economic Literature* (December 1992), 1931–64.

[4] *Ibid.,* 1961.

[5] *Ibid.*

[6] *The Age of Diminished Expectations* (1992 pb. ed.), p. 12.

[7] See Ira Magaziner and Robert Reich, *Minding America's Business* (1982).

[8] For an up-to-date review see Kennedy, *Preparing for the Twenty-First Century.*

Suggestions for Further Reading

Chapter 1 ────────────────────────────────────
ECONOMIC TRANSFORMATION AS A THEME OF HISTORY
The organizing principle for this work as a whole is based on Fernand Braudel's magisterial *Civilization & Capitalism, 15th–18th Century* (3 vols., 1979–1984). For the rise, development, and meaning of capitalism, see Max Weber, *The Protestant Ethic and the Spirit of Capitalism* (1930); R.H. Tawney, *Religion and the Rise of Capitalism* (1937); Henri Sée, *Modern Capitalism: Its Origin and Evolution* (1928); Maurice Dobb, *Studies in the Development of Capitalism* (1947); R. Hilton (ed.), *The Transformation from Feudalism to Capitalism* (1976); Karl Polanyi, *The Great Transformation* (1973); and Robert Heilbroner, *The Making of Economic Society* (9th ed., 1993).

Chapter 2 ────────────────────────────────────
THE AGE OF THE BUSINESSMAN
Two well-written introductions to the period are John A. Garraty, *The New Commonwealth, 1877–1890* (1968), and Robert H. Weibe, *The Search for Order* (1967).

Important general studies of industrialization include Samuel P Hays, *The Response to Industrialism* (1957); H.G. Vatter, *The Drive to Industrial Maturity: The U.S. Economy, 1860–1914* (1975); E.C. Kirkland, *Industry Comes of Age* (1961); Allan Nevins, *The Emergence of Modern America: 1865–1878* (1927); T.C. Cochran and William Miller, *The Age of Enterprise* (1968); Robert Higgs, *The Transformation of the American Economy* (1971); and Glenn Porter, *The Rise of Big Business* (1973). *American Business Cycles, 1865–1897* (1959), by Rendigs Fels, is an important specialized study.

There are several excellent studies on the growth of particular industries. See, for example, R.W. and M.E. Hidy, *Pioneering in Big Business, 1882–1911: History of the Standard Oil Company* (1955); H.F. Williamson and A.R. Daum, *The American Petroleum Industry* (1981); and H.C. Passer, *The Electrical Manufacturers* (1972).

On businessmen, see Matthew Josephson, *The Robber Barons*

(1934); Edward C. Kirkland, *Dream and Thought in the Business Community, 1860–1900 (1956);* Irwin G. Wyllie, *The Self-Made Man in America* (1954); and Louis Galambos and Barbara Barron Spence, *The Public Image of Big Business in America* (1975).

Social Darwinism is covered in Richard Hofstadter, *Social Darwinism in American Thought* (1955), and Cynthia Eagle Russett, *Darwin in America* (1976).

There are two excellent biographies of Andrew Carnegie: J.E. Wall, *Andrew Carnegie* (1970), and Harold Livesay, *Andrew Carnegie and the Rise of Big Business* (1975). On Jay Gould, see Maury Klein, *The Life and Legend of Jay Gould* (1986).

Chapter 3 ————————————————————————————————
THE TECHNOLOGY OF INDUSTRIALIZATION

For the technology of steel production, see Peter Temin, *Iron and Steel in the Nineteenth Century* (1964). See also W.P. Strassman, *Risk and Technological Innovation* (1981), and two works by E.E. Morison, *From Know How to Nowhere* (1974), and *Men, Machines, and Modern Times* (1966).

The best introduction to business organization in these years are the studies by Alfred Chandler, Jr.: *Strategy and Structure* (1962); *The Visible Hand: The Managerial Revolution in American Business* (1977); and *Scale and Scope: The Dynamics of Industrial Capitalism* (1990).

On the corporation, see G.H. Evans, *Business Incorporations in the United States.*

Chapter 4 ————————————————————————————————
FROM TRUST TO ANTITRUST

In addition to many of the works cited in the previous two chapters, see Ralph Nelson, *Merger Movements in American Industry* (1959), and Naomi Lamoreaux, *The Great Merger Movement in American Business, 1895–1904* (1985).

On Rockefeller, see the outstanding biography by Allan Nevins, *Study in Power* (1953). For Morgan, see Ron Chernow, *The House of Morgan* (1990).

Two important studies on antitrust are Hans P. Thorelli, *The Federal Antitrust Policy* (1955), and William Letwin, *Law and Economic Policy in America: The Evolution of the Sherman Antitrust Act* (1981). The Interstate Commerce Commission is discussed in Ari and Olive Hoogenboom, *A History of the ICC* (1976).

The careers of three important critics of monopoly are discussed in John L. Thomas, *Alternative America: Henry George, Edward Bellamy, Henry Demarest Lloyd and the Adversary Tradition* (1983). For an overview of Roosevelt's and Wilson's response to big business, see John W. Chambers, *The Tyranny of Change: America in the Progressive Era* (1980); George E. Mowry, *The Era of Theodore Roosevelt, 1900–1912* (1958); and Arthur S. Link, *Woodrow Wilson and the Progressive Era, 1900–1917* (1954).

Chapter 5 ———————————————————————————————
WORKERS AND WORK

For a general statement on the role of labor, see Stanley Lebergott, *Manpower in Economic Growth* (1964). Nell I. Painter, *Standing at Armageddon: The United States, 1877–1919* (1987), is excellent on the struggles of working people in these years.

The Knights of Labor are discussed in N.J. Ware, *The Labor Movement in the United States, 1860–1895* (1929), and Leon Fink, *Workingmen's Democracy* (1982). The AFL is the subject of Philip Taft's *The AFL in the Time of Gompers* (1957). See also S.B. Kaufman, *Samuel Gompers and the Origins of the American Federation of Labor* (1973), and Harold Livesay, *Samuel Gompers and Organized Labor in America* (1978).

For a sampling of the important testimony taken by the Senate Committee on Education and Labor in 1883, see John A. Garraty (ed.), *Labor and Capital in the Gilded Age* (1968).

For women at work, consult Alice Kessler-Harris, *Out to Work* (1982), and B.M. Wertheimer, *We Were There: The Story of Working Women in America* (1977). Other valuable works for this chapter include David Montgomery, *Beyond Equality* (1967); Montgomery, *The Fall of the House of Labor* (1987); Herbert Gutman, *Work, Culture, and Society in Industrializing America* (1976); D.T. Rodgers, *The Work Ethic in Industrial America* (1980); Charlotte Erickson, *American Industry and European Immigration, 1860–1885* (1957); G.N. Grob, *Workers and Utopia* (1972); Irwin Yellowitz, *Industrialization and the American Labor Movement* (1977); David Brody, *Steelworkers in America* (1960); Melvyn Dubovsky, *Industrialism and the American Worker, 1865–1920* (1975); Daniel Nelson, *Managers and Workers: Origins of the New Factory System in the United States, 1800–1920* (1975); Nelson, *Frederick W. Taylor and the Rise of Scientific Management* (1980); and David Gordon et al., *Segmented Work, Divided*

Workers: The Historical Transformation of Labor in the United States (1982).

On the Homestead Strike, see Leon Wolff, *Lockout* (1965), and Paul Krause, *The Battle for Homestead, 1880–1892* (1992).

A brilliant, although disputed, analysis of labor from a Marxist point of view is presented in Harry Braverman's *Labor and Monopoly Capital: The Degradation of Work in the Twentieth Century* (1975).

Chapter 6 ———————————————————————
INDUSTRIALIZATION RUBS OFF ON LIFE

There are several excellent introductions to the topic of urbanization. See Howard P. Chudacoff and Judith E. Smith, *The Evolution of America Urban Society* (1988); Blake McKelvey, *The Urbanization of America* (1963); Sam Bass Warner, *The Urban Wilderness* (1972); and Raymond A. Mohl, *The New City: Urban America in the Industrial Age, 1860–1920* (1985).

For slums and tenements, see Robert Bremner, *From the Depths: The Discovery of Poverty in the United States* (1956); Roy Lubove, *The Progressives and the Slums* (1974); and Allen Davis, *Spearheads for Reform: The Social Settlements and the Progressive Movement, 1890–1914* (1967).

On Harlem, see Gilbert Osofsky, *Harlem: The Making of a Ghetto, 1890–1930* (1965). See also Allan H. Spear, *Black Chicago: The Making of a Negro Ghetto, 1890–1920* (1967), and Kenneth L. Kusmer, *A Ghetto Takes Shape: Black Cleveland, 1870–1930* (1976).

On Pullman, see Stanley Buder, *Pullman* (1967), and Almont Lindsey, *Pullman* (1942). Alfred T. White's approach to model tenements is discussed in his *Better Homes for Working People* (1885).

On machinery and material life, see Siegfried Giedion, *Mechanization Takes Command* (1948).

Chapter 7 ———————————————————————
THE GREAT DEPRESSION

Useful introductions to the period include F.L. Allen, *Only Yesterday* (1931); J.W. Prothro, *The Dollar Decade: Business Ideas in the 1920s* (1954); William Leuchtenburg, *The Perils of Prosperity* (1958); Geoffrey Perrett, *America in the Twenties* (1982); J. Potter, *The American Economy Between the World Wars* (1974); and Michael E. Parrish, *Anxious Decades: America in Prosperity and Depression* (1992).

On economic thinking during these years, see William J. Barber, *From New Era to New Deal: Herbert Hoover, The Economists, and American Economic Policy, 1921–1933* (1985).

For the stock market collapse, see John Kenneth Galbraith, *The Great Crash* (1955), and Robert Sobel, *The Great Bull Market: Wall Street in the 1920s* (1968).

On the Great Depression, consult John A. Garraty, *The Great Depression* (1986); Robert McElvaine, *The Great Depression* (1984); Michael A. Bernstein, *The Great Depression: Delayed Recovery and Economic Change in America, 1929–1939* (1988); Charles P. Kindleberger, *The World in Depression* (1970); Broadus Mitchell, *Depression Decade* (1947); Albert U. Romasco, *The Poverty of Abundance* (1968); and Caroline Bird, *The Invisible Scar* (1966).

The plight of the unemployed is covered in John A. Garraty, *Unemployment in History: Economic Thought and Public Policy* (1978), and Irving Bernstein, *The Lean Years: A History of the American Worker, 1920–1933* (1960). The activities of the Federal Reserve Board are the subject of Milton Friedman and A.J. Schwartz, *The Great Contraction, 1929–1933* (1965), and Peter Temin, *Did Monetary Forces Cause the Great Depression?* (1975).

Two useful guides to Keynesian economics are Alvin Hansen, *A Guide to Keynes* (1953), and Robert Lekachman, *The Age of Keynes* (1975).

Chapter 8
THE NEW DEAL

William Leuchtenburg's *Franklin D. Roosevelt and the New Deal* (1963) is still the best single-volume study. Other important works include Arthur Schlesinger, Jr., *The Age of Roosevelt* (1957–60); J.M. Burns, *Roosevelt: The Lion and the Fox* (1956); Paul K. Conkin, *The New Deal* (1975); Albert U. Romasco, *The Politics of Recovery: Roosevelt's New Deal* (1983); Daniel Fusfeld, *The Economic Thought of Franklin D. Roosevelt and the Origins of the New Deal* (1956); and Harvard Sitkoff (ed.), *Fifty Years Later: The New Deal Evaluated* (1985).

Chapter 9
FROM POSTWAR BOOM TO POSTWAR INFLATION

Important general overviews include H.G. Vatter, *The U.S. Economy in the 1950s* (1963); John Diggins, *The Proud Decades, 1941–1960*

(1989); Geoffrey Perrett, *A Dream of Greatness: The American People, 1945–1963* (1979); William Leuchtenburg, *A Troubled Feast: American Society Since 1945* (1979); Otis L. Graham, Jr., *Toward a Planned Society: From Roosevelt to Nixon* (1976); and James L. Sundquist, *Politics and Policy: the Eisenhower, Kennedy, and Johnson Years* (1968).

On the Truman Administration, see David McCullough, *Harry Truman* (1992), and Alonzo L. Hamby, *Beyond the New Deal* (1973). The Employment Act of 1946 is discussed in S.K. Bailey's *Congress Makes a Law* (1980). On the Eisenhower presidency, see Stephen E. Ambrose, *Eisenhower: The President* (1984), and C. Alexander, *Holding the Line* (1975). See also Mark H. Rose, *Interstate: Express Highway Politics, 1941–1956* (1979). The Kennedy years are covered in Arthur M. Schlesinger, Jr., *A Thousand Days* (1965); Irving Bernstein, *Promises Kept: John F. Kennedy's New Frontier* (1991); J.F. Heath, *Decade of Disillusionment: The Kennedy–Johnson Years* (1975); and A.D. Donald (ed.), *John F. Kennedy and the New Frontier* (1966). Johnson's Great Society is discussed in V.D. Bornet, *The Presidency of Lyndon B. Johnson* (1983); Charles Murray, *Losing Ground: American Social Policy, 1950–1980* (1983); James T. Patterson, *America's Struggle Against Poverty, 1900–1985* (1986); and M.E. Gettleman and D. Mermelstein, *The Great Society Reader* (1967). Nixon's years in office are covered in James A. Reichley, *Conservatives in an Era of Change: The Nixon and Ford Administrations* (1981), and Stephen E. Ambrose, *Nixon: The Triumph of a Politician, 1962–1972* (1989). On Ford, see John Osborne, *White House Watch: The Ford Years* (1977). Carter's administration is studied in Clark Mollenhoff, *The President Who Failed* (1980), and Ervin C. Hargrove, *Jimmy Carter as President* (1989).

Important specialized studies for these years include John Kenneth Galbraith, *American Capitalism* (1952); Galbraith, *The Affluent Society* (1978); Michael Harrington, *The Other America* (1962); John W. Kendrick, *Postwar Productivity Trends in the United States, 1948–1969* (1973); Herbert Stein, *The Fiscal Revolution in America* (1969); Stein, *Presidential Economics: The Making of Economic Policy from Roosevelt to Reagan and Beyond* (1984).

Chapter 10 —————————————————————————

THE CONSERVATIVE ERA

Useful introductions to the Reagan adminstration include Lou Cannon, *President Reagan: The Role of a Lifetime* (1991); Robert Dallek, *Ronald Reagan: The Politics of Symbolism* (1984); Gary Wills, *Reagan's Amer-*

ica (1987); and Haynes Johnson, *Sleepwalking Through History: America in the Reagan Years* (1992).

For subjects covered in the text, see Paul Craig Roberts, *The Supply-Side Revolution* (1984); Benjamin Freidman, *Day of Reckoning: The Consequences of American Economic Policy Under Reagan and After* (1988); Joseph A. Pechman, *Federal Tax Policy* (1987); Pechman, *Who Paid the Taxes, 1966–85?* (1985); Roy C. Smith, *The Money Wars: The Rise and Fall of the Great Buyout Boom of the 1980s* (1990); David Alan Aschauer, *Public Investment and Private Sector Growth* (1990); Kevin Phillips, *The Politics of Rich and Poor: Wealth and the American Electorate in the Reagan Aftermath* (1990); Paul Krugman, *The Age of Diminished Expectations: U.S. Economic Policy in the 1990s* (1992); Lawrence J. White, *The S&L Debacle* (1991); Robert Eisner, *How Real is the Federal Deficit?* (1986); Robert Heilbroner and Peter Bernstein, *The Debt and the Deficit* (1989); David Calleo, *The Bankrupting of America: How the Federal Budget Is Impoverishing the Nation* (1992); Robert Reich, *The Work of Nations* (1991); Robert Kuttner, *The End of Laissez Faire: National Purpose and the Global Economy After the Cold War* (1991); Lester Thurow, *Head to Head: The Coming Economic Battle Among Japan, Europe, and America* (1992); Edward M. Graham and Paul R. Krugman, *Foreign Direct Investment in the United States* (1989); I.M. Destler and C. Randell Henning, *Dollar Politics: Exchange Rate Policymaking in the United States* (1989); and Allen J. Lenz, *Narrowing the U.S. Current Account Deficit* (1992).

Chapter 11 ───────────────────────────────

AMERICAN CAPITALISM: RETROSPECT AND PROSPECT

In addition to many of the works cited in the previous chapter, see, for general overviews, Robert Heilbroner, *Twenty-First Century Capitalism* (1993), and Paul Kennedy, *Preparing for the Twenty-First Century* (1993).

On multinationals, see Richard Barnet and Ronald Müller, *Global Reach* (1974), and two works by Mira Wilkins: *The Emergence of Multinational Enterprise* (1970), and *The Maturing of Multinational Enterprise* (1975).

International commerce is discussed in Gary C. Hufbauer and Jeffrey J. Schott, *North American Free Trade* (1992); Walter Russell Mead, *The Low Wage Challenge to Global Growth* (1990); John H. Jackson,

Restructuring the GATT System (1990); and Thomas R. Howell (ed.), *Conflict Among Nations: Trade Policies in the 1990s* (1992).

On Labor-management relations, see Barry Bluestone and Irving Bluestone, *Negotiating The Future: A Labor Perspective on American Business* (1992). See also Michael L. Dertouzas et al., *Made in America: Regaining the Productive Edge* (1989); and William J. Baumol et al., *Productivity and American Leadership* (1989).

Industrial policy is discussed in Otis L. Graham, Jr., *Losing Time: The Industrial Policy Debate* (1992). For the environment, consult Al Gore, *Earth in the Balance: Ecology and the Human Spirit* (1992), and William R. Cline, *Global Warming: The Economic Stakes* (1992).

PICTURE CREDITS

Opposite page 1 Bettmann Archive. **3** Bettmann Archive. **5** © Grant Heilman, Lititz, Pa. **7** © Harry Wilkes/Stock, Boston. **8** United Fruit Company. **14** Culver Pictures. **23** Brown Brothers. **25** The Byron Collection, Museum of the City of New York. **28** Brown Brothers. **38** Drake Well Park, Titusville, Pa. **42** Library of Congress. **47** U.S. Steel Corp. **56** Culver Pictures. **62** Bettmann Archive. **68** HBJ Collection. **70** Culver Pictures. **82** Library of Congress. **86** From the collections of Henry Ford Museum & Greenfield Village. **89** Brown Brothers. **98** Commercial Museum Collection, Pennsylvania State Archives. **107** AFL-CIO News. **114** From the collections of Henry Ford Museum & Greenfield Village. **117** Photo by Jacob A. Riis, The Jacob A. Riis Collection, Museum of the City of New York. **119** Science and Technology Research Center, The New York Public Library, Astor, Lenox and Tilden Foundations. **125** The Huntington Library, Album 89. **126** Courtesy Chicago Historical Society, neg. ICHi-04285. **127** Courtesy Chicago Historical Society, neg. ICHi-04191. **130** Culver Pictures. **136** Dorothea Lange, FSA, Library of Congress. **142** Brown Brothers. **147** Margaret Bourke-White/LIFE Magazine © 1937, Time, Inc. **148** Culver Pictures. **162** Culver Pictures. **165** UPI/Bettmann. **169** Bettmann Archive. **182** Courtesy of Walmart, Inc. **186** George Zimbel/Monkmeyer. **193** © James R. Holland/Stock, Boston. **196** Iris Schneider, Los Angeles Times. **200** UPI/Bettmann. **205** UPI/Bettmann. **207** AP/Wide World Photos. **210** AP/Wide World Photos. **222** Ellis Herwig/Stock, Boston. **226** © Ira Wyman. **230** Reuters/Bettmann. **234** AP/Wide World Photos. **247** UPI/Bettmann.

INDEX